UNDERSTANDING SOCIAL CITIZENSHIP

Themes and perspectives for policy and practice

Second edition

Peter Dwyer

First published in 2003
Second edition published in Great Britain in 2010 by

The Policy Press
University of Bristol
Fourth Floor, Beacon House
Queen's Road
Bristol BS8 1QU
UK

Tel +44 (0)117 331 4054
Fax +44 (0)117 331 4093
e-mail tpp-info@bristol.ac.uk
www.policypress.co.uk

North American office:
The Policy Press
c/o International Specialized Books Services (ISBS)
920 NE 58th Avenue, Suite 300
Portland, OR 97213-3786, USA
Tel +1 503 287 3093
Fax +1 503 280 8832
e-mail info@isbs.com

British Library Cataloguing in Publication Data
A catalogue record for this book is available from the British Library

Library of Congress Cataloging-in-Publication Data
A catalog record for this book has been requested

ISBN 978 1 84742 328 3   paperback
ISBN 978 1 84742 329 0   hardcover

Cover design by Qube Design Associates, Bristol.
Printed and bound in Great Britain by Hobbs, Southampton

For my mother, Jean Dwyer

Contents

Detailed contents

List of boxes, figures and tables

Boxes

Figures

Tables

Preface

When I wrote the first edition of this book in 2003 my aim was to write a book that allowed undergraduate students to explore some of the many issues that debates about social citizenship encompass. Since then I have received a good few positive (and one or two critical) comments about the original text. Following much reflection on these comments, in this second edition I have decided to retain the original structure of the book and to concentrate on updating discussions in relevant chapters, particularly, but not exclusively, in Part Two of the book, so that the chapters in this latest edition reflect policy developments that have occurred since 2003. I hope students and teachers alike will continue to find it useful.

As in the first edition this new version is divided into three main parts. **Part One**, which consists of four chapters, provides a basis for the consideration of contemporary issues and policy that informs subsequent sections. *Chapter One* introduces the notion of citizenship and moves on to consider a number of welfare concepts and debates that are of relevance to social citizenship, which is, of course, the central focus of this book. *Chapter Two* provides a historical sketch of the origins and emergence of the idea of citizenship. It outlines two contrasting philosophical traditions, namely, liberalism and civic republicanism, and explores the implications that these have for citizenship. A more detailed historical consideration of the development of social citizenship within the British context is offered in *Chapter Three*. The development of social rights in Britain throughout the late 19th and 20th centuries is traced. A critical consideration of the work of the influential theorist T.H. Marshall is also included. *Chapter Four* outlines six contemporary perspectives on social citizenship. An analysis of the social democratic tradition is followed by consideration of left-wing critics. Two approaches (which I argue exhibit a latent hostility to social rights), namely, the New Right and new communitarianism, are then discussed. The chapter then takes a look at the main themes that underpin New Labour's version of social citizenship. Finally, the chapter concludes with a new section that highlights the so-called 'New' Conservatism that is being mapped out under the leadership of David Cameron. Ultimately, the electorate will decide if he is to become the next Prime Minister, but I hope readers will find the discussion of the kind of social citizenship the current Opposition envisages for us valid, whatever the outcome of the next UK general election.

The emphasis in **Part Two** shifts to consider the issue of difference and its importance in relation to welfare rights and responsibilities. The aim of this second substantive section is to highlight some of the significant implications that social divisions constructed around class/poverty, gender, disability and 'race'/ethnicity have for the social rights and citizenship status of various individuals and groups in contemporary society. In order to do this in a clear and uncomplicated manner each chapter in Part Two focuses on one specific aspect of difference. This approach is taken to enable readers to consider a range of debates, issues and policy developments that are of particular relevance to the area under consideration. While this tactic can be defended as a device to aid understanding it is, nonetheless, an artificial division that fails to reflect the complex reality of social life. It has been noted by several authors elsewhere (for example, Brah, 1992; Yuval-Davis, 1997) that the interplay between factors such as class, gender, disability and ethnicity, and their combined impact on an individual's status within any given society, is complex. The neat separation of distinct social divisions (and any derivative advantages/disadvantages) that occurs in Part Two does not happen in the real worlds of welfare and social citizenship that people inhabit. The people most marginalised from the ideal that equal citizenship status implies are often those who endure the effects of multidimensional disadvantage and social exclusion.

Each chapter in **Part Two** highlights and discusses specific issues or areas of policy that are especially relevant to social citizenship. In *Chapter Five*, which discusses class and poverty, the policy focus is on conditionality in social welfare and the allied issue of social control. The discussion of gender in *Chapter Six* centres on the issue of informal care and the implications that such care work has in relation to activity in the paid labour market, which is fast becoming *the* essential citizen responsibility. The contemporary policy focus in this chapter is, therefore, on work–life balance and family-friendly policies. *Chapter Seven* explores some issues related to disability and welfare and outlines a vision of active citizenship that differs greatly from the one popularised by the Conservative Party in the 1980s (outlined in Chapter Four). It is argued here that the disabled people's movement provides an alternative model of 'active citizenship'. A consideration of recent policy in the areas of social security benefits and community care is also offered. *Chapter Eight* considers the impact of 'race'/ethnicity on citizenship. The substantive focus here is on UK nationality, immigration and asylum policy. The exclusive character of formal British citizenship status, and the negative knock-on effect that this had on the welfare rights of those who, at the beginning of the 20th century, did not conform to a racially constructed 'British' stereotype, have already been noted (see Chapter Three). The detailed consideration of the differential welfare rights of asylum seekers and refugees, in the latter part of this chapter, illustrates the continuing relevance of differences constructed around 'race' and ethnicity to contemporary social citizenship.

One final point about Part Two. I am aware of the absence of a separate chapter that discusses age and citizenship. Pension reform, the care of the senior citizens in old age and issues concerned with the status, protection and rights of children are all-important elements of contemporary welfare debate and merit attention. A current deficiency in the personal expertise and knowledge on the part of the author, combined with a lack of available time, leads to their continued omission here.

In **Part Three** the book moves on to consider social citizenship beyond the nation state. *Chapter Nine* looks at 'Social Europe', and more particularly the establishment of European Union citizenship. The differentiated status that such 'citizenship of the Union' currently confers and its potential to enhance the welfare rights of EU migrant citizens in the future are addressed. A new section, included in this second edition for the first time, considers Nick Ellison's (2000) discussion of proactive and defensive citizenship engagement in light of Accession 8 (A8) migration into the UK. The possibility that the concept of citizenship can be extended beyond the level of the nation state to engender a system of global citizenship has exercised the minds of theorists in the last decade. *Chapter Ten* deals with this issue and considers both transnational and cosmopolitan citizenship. Finally, the conclusion (*Chapter Eleven*) draws together discussions from throughout the book to argue that a new welfare settlement that prioritises individual responsibilities rather than welfare rights is emerging, and that it is based around a simplistic notion of welfare dependency. Six years on from the first edition of this book I am even more convinced that this is the case, although I do not expect that everyone will agree with this conclusion. However, I hope that the book will stimulate readers into further thought and discussion about the changing character of social citizenship as we begin the 21st century.

Acknowledgements

I am indebted to everyone who contributed to the publication of this second edition. First, I would like to thank all at The Policy Press for their patience and support. Second, I remain very grateful to the long list of colleagues and friends who read and commented on the original draft chapters and/or offered help in various ways when I was writing the first edition. Finally, on a more personal level, I would once again like to thank Linda, James and Anna who, thankfully, keep me firmly anchored in the real world when the academic one tries to take over.

List of acronyms

A8	Accession 8 (countries of the European Union)
ASBO	Anti-social Behaviour Order
BCODP	British Council of Organisations of Disabled People
CRE	Commission for Racial Equality
DPM	Disabled People's Movement
DRC	Disability Rights Commission
ECHR	European Convention on Human Rights
ECJ	European Court of Justice
EEC	European Economic Community
EOC	Equal Opportunities Commission
ESA	Employment Support Allowance
EU	European Union
JSA	Jobseeker's Allowance
MP	Member of Parliament
NASS	National Asylum Support Service
NDDP	New Deal for Disabled People
NHS	National Health Service
NI	National Insurance
OMC	Open Method of Coordination
PLM	paid labour market
PWWS	post-war welfare settlement
RCO	Refugee Community Organisation
SSAC	Social Security Advisory Committee
TCN	third country national
TEC	Treaty of the European Communities
TEU	Treaty of the European Union
UN	United Nations
UPIAS	Union of the Physically Impaired Against Segregation
VCS	voluntary and community sector
WCA	work capability assessment
WFI	work-focused interview
WfYB	Work for Your Benefits (programme)
WRS	Worker Registration Scheme

one

Introduction

The aim of this chapter is to introduce and define the concept of *citizenship*. It then moves on to outline and consider a number of ideas and debates that are of particular relevance to the study of social citizenship. This chapter, therefore, highlights and discusses the following topics:

- defining citizenship;
- the idea of social citizenship;
- social rights;
- the principles underpinning welfare rights;
- the concepts of equality, needs and desert;
- key aspects of social citizenship: provision, conditionality and membership.

Defining citizenship

As with many ideas associated with the study of social policy, citizenship remains a much discussed and highly contentious concept and, as such, any attempt to define it carries with it the likelihood of challenge. As Lister (1998a) and Oliver and Heater (1994) point out, the language of citizenship is used in a multitude of contexts (for example, political, legal, philosophical, academic), and in so many different ways that a universally agreed definition is virtually impossible. The philosophical and political start point of any approach can certainly greatly influence the kind of citizenship that ensues. The basic notions of the *individual* and *community* and the different ways in which they are conceived have a crucial impact within such debates. For example, at a crude level of comparison, a theory of citizenship centred around an essentially *liberal stance* that stresses the primary importance of individually held rights can be seen as having different aims from a *civic republican/communitarian* approach that places greater emphasis on individuals' commitments and obligations to a wider community (see Kymlicka and Norman, 1994; Heater, 1999; Dwyer, 2000a).

Having noted that the very idea of citizenship may vary dependent on a certain philosophical disposition, it is possible to move towards a more concrete definition by initially noting three salient points made by Lewis (1998, p 104):

- the citizen is one way of imagining a link between the state and the individual;
- the concept of citizenship implies membership of some form of community, in turn the notion of community opens up questions of inclusion and exclusion;
- citizenship is a social status that allows people to make claims in relation to state-organised welfare services.

A brief consideration of the insights of certain other authors is useful at this point. In a famous, and subsequently highly influential, discussion of citizenship, written in the late 1940s, **T.H. Marshall** (1949/92) outlined a theory in which the three linked elements of *civil* (rights to liberty and equality in law), *political* (the right to vote and to participate in the political process) and *social rights* (rights to basic welfare and full participation in society) assumed a central importance. According to Marshall, every citizen, irrespective of their class position, shared a common 'equality of status' with others who were also members of a shared (national) community. The status of the citizen entailed not only rights as previously noted but also certain duties/responsibilities:

> Citizenship is a status bestowed upon those who are full members of a community. All those who possess the status are equal with respect to the rights and duties with which that status is endowed. There is no universal principle that determines what those rights and duties shall be, but societies in which citizenship is a developing institution create an image of an ideal of citizenship against which achievement can be measured and towards which aspiration can be directed. The urge forward along the path thus plotted is an urge towards a fuller measure of equality, an enrichment of the stuff of which the status is made and an increase in the number of those on whom the status is bestowed. (Marshall, 1949/92, p 18)

Lister (1997, 2003b), noting the work of Oldfield (1990), further characterises citizenship as a concept in which a key issue is the relationship between citizenship as a *status*, which brings with it enjoyment of civil, political and social rights, and citizenship as a *practice*, which requires the acceptance and performance of wider communal responsibilities and duties. This status–practice dichotomy reflects the two different traditions of thought, namely liberalism and civic republicanism/communitarianism noted above. A full consideration of these two approaches forms the basis of Chapter Two. Marshall's influential theory of citizenship is explored in detail in Chapter Three.

The broad scope that the study of citizenship may entail is captured by **Keith Faulks** (1998), who notes that citizenship is usually defined by reference to three main criteria: according to a legal definition, a philosophical definition or a socio–political definition (see ***Box 1.1***).

Box 1.1: Faulks on the definition of citizenship

In the literature concerning the meaning of citizenship three main types of definition can be identified. These definitions are *legal* definitions, which define the rights and duties of citizens in relation to the nation-state; *philosophical* definitions, which are concerned with normative questions such as which model of citizenship can best deliver a just society; and *socio-political* definitions, which emphasise citizenship as a status denoting membership of a society that involves a set of social practices....

Legal definitions

As a legal term, citizenship is often used interchangeably with nationality.... The core right of citizenship in this legal sense is that of abode. If a person is a legal citizen of a country in international law that person cannot be expelled from that country, and can expect to be able to ... freely return. Citizenship of a particular nation-state also carries with it duties *to* that state and rights, beyond the right of abode, which the individual can claim *from* the state....

Philosophical definitions

... of citizenship tend to be concerned with such questions as: the correct role of the state in providing for citizens' needs, what the state can reasonably expect from the individual citizen in terms of duties, how the individual should relate to other members of the nation, and whether rights should be absolute or dependent upon duties rendered. In these senses citizenship is a deeply normative question....

Socio-political definitions

Citizenship in any society has to be understood in the context of power relationships that exist in that society and the political, economic and cultural changes that affect that society.

Source: Faulks (1998, pp 2-4)

In everyday life, aspects of the three elements highlighted in ***Box 1.1*** often overlap. This tripartite definition is important, however, because the issues and questions noted by Faulks are central to any text that is primarily focused on citizenship and welfare issues.

The idea of social citizenship

This book's particular focus is on *social citizenship*. As Twine (1994) notes, citizenship is a 'three-legged stool'. Civil (legal) rights (for example, right to residence, own property, fair trial) and political rights (for example, right to vote, to take part in the political process), while important, must be backed up with some level of entitlement to welfare (that is, social rights) in order for citizenship to have a substantive meaning for all members of a given community. According to Marshall (1949/92), the founding of the welfare state in the late 1940s brought about the establishment of social citizenship centred around the universal right of citizens to an extensive set of state-guaranteed social and economic provisions. It was Marshall's assertion that social citizenship would ensure the inclusion and full participation of even the poorest members of society (Morris, 1998). This notion of social citizenship retains a useful purpose. It has the potential to provide a benchmark against which it is possible to assess the status of certain individuals or groups in relation to access to the agreed welfare rights and resources that are generally available to all those who are regarded as citizens within a specific community. Social citizenship, therefore, offers the capacity for an exploration of the dynamics of social divisions/exclusion to take in a number of important dimensions (for example, class, gender, 'race', disability, age) when assessing both the levels and causes of inequality within a society.

Social citizenship is a centrally important aspect of any wider notion of citizenship, and rights to welfare continue to be regarded by many as a centrally important aspect of 'effective citizenship':

> Citizenship is very much about relationships between individuals, groups, rights, duties and state institutions; it is also about relative degrees of incorporation and empowerment.... In any event amongst its possible attributes effective citizenship certainly means being included in the systems of rights and welfare provisions that are mediated or managed by state agencies, and having one's needs met through mainstream political intermediation. (Harrison, 1995, pp 20-1)

Social rights

Rights, and in particular social or welfare rights as they are often referred to, are central to the idea of citizenship. They help to define the extent and quality of a citizen's substantive welfare entitlements and are also often the focus of wider welfare debates and struggles (Dean, 2002a). There is an extensive introductory literature on the nature and origin of rights (for example, Freeden, 1990; Jones, 1994), but given this book's remit subsequent discussions focus primarily on social/welfare rights.

Hartley Dean's work (2001, 2002a) offers some useful insights. First, he argues that welfare rights, indeed all rights, are socially constructed. Second, he defines the essential character of welfare rights as:

> … 'distributional' in the sense that they relate to the social redistribution of resources. They are concerned either to prevent poverty by limiting the extent of social inequality, or to relieve poverty after it has struck. (2001, p 1)

A key question then becomes: how might such rights redistribute resources? Here Dean argues that for 75% of the time the package of rights that British citizens currently enjoy act according to an individual 'savings bank principle', where money and resources are redistributed over a person's lifetime. A citizen contributes via paid work and gets back certain benefits/resources at various stages in their lifetime when they are outside paid employment, for example, when retired or unemployed. The 'Robin Hood' principle of taking resources from richer citizens and redistributing them to poorer ones is not as prevalent as is often imagined.

Third, Dean outlines two different conceptual frameworks for considering the origin and development of welfare rights. He states that welfare rights may be seen by some as being based on a 'doctrinal concept' that emerges from classic liberal thinking which is concerned to enunciate a theoretical position built around the equal worth of each individual. Rights here are viewed as an inherent part of the human condition and bestowed on individual human beings from birth. This approach centres around a concern to ensure equal opportunity through the redistribution of opportunities, rather than outcomes. By contrast, a more radical 'claims-based' concept of rights can be linked to the 'social democratic' tradition. Here social rights are seen as originating and developing from the political struggles of various marginalised groups who demand to have their needs satisfied or their claims met. "Claims based rights lay down a challenge to social inequality, demanding not merely formal equality of status, but the actual redistribution of resources" (Dean, 2001, p 1). This concept of welfare rights informs the work of what is sometimes called the *welfare rights movement*, welfare rights professionals and activists involved in casework or legal challenges to the social welfare system via tribunals or the courts.

Both approaches have certain drawbacks as well as attractions. Although Marshall's theory arguably makes a case for social rights to be part of the 'doctrinal' package of rights that each citizen should enjoy, Dean argues that social rights are still often widely regarded as subordinate to legal and political rights. The claims-based understanding of rights is also not without its pitfalls. On a general level a lack of political muscle may mean that the needs of certain citizens remain unmet. Competition over scarce resources also exists. In some circumstances the successful action of one group in claiming their rights to welfare may be won at the expense of others. More specifically, the work of welfare rights professionals individualises the rights-claiming process. The way in which welfare rights work progresses through legal challenges carried out by experts on behalf of a client can isolate and disempower poor people. Ultimately, victory in the courts can also be overturned by the introduction of new legislation in the courts (Dean, 2001).

It has previously been noted that contemporary ideas about citizenship entail three basic rights elements: civil, political and social rights. Within this triumvirate a distinction is sometimes made between negative and positive rights. In simple terms *negative rights*, that is, civil and political, are generally favoured by the political Right and are characterised as individual 'freedoms from' coercion or interference. *Positive social rights*, on the other hand, are held to be of a different order. They are seen as entitlements to certain state-provided/guaranteed benefits and services usually associated with, and asserted by, those on the Left of the political spectrum. The Left–Right divide is a crude representation of a more complex reality; nonetheless, this distinction is important because it signifies a latent hostility by many of those on the Right towards social rights. Indeed, some commentators continue to argue that the welfare rights element should not be seen as a legitimate part of the citizenship package. Such debates are explored more fully in Chapter Three.

Social rights are perhaps the most contentious part of citizenship. As Marshall (1949/92) pointed out, there is no fixed consensus about which welfare benefits and services should be available to citizens or the levels and quality of provision deemed to be necessary. A consideration of the 1980s and 1990s indicates that social rights can be diminished as well as expanded. In light of the trend towards retrenchment that characterised this period, supporters of social rights have been keen to explore ways in which social rights might be protected in future. One way forward may be to build a number of *basic social entitlements* into a constitutional framework and make the right to certain specified benefits and services legally enforceable (Lister, 1998a). Citizens would then enjoy a number of substantive rights to welfare, that is, legally enforceable entitlements to particular benefits and services. An alternative, and perhaps complementary, approach may be to favour procedural rights (Coote, 1992; Kellner, 1999), which are entitlements to specified forms of service delivery and redress. The focus is on guaranteeing individuals equal access to services and subsequent fair treatment by welfare institutions. The argument is that citizens should be given advice and assistance about the rights they can expect, and, if they are unfairly treated (for example, because of gender, age or ethnicity) by a public welfare provider, they are then able to seek redress via specialist tribunals or the courts.

Regardless of how debates concerning the origin and protection of welfare rights are resolved, the social element is, as Jones (1994) reminds us, central to contemporary notions of citizenship for three main reasons. First, because at the very least a minimum right to material resources is essential for citizens to survive and function within any society. Second, because the provision of welfare has a collective benefit that reaches beyond the individual and benefits wider society. Third, the idea of entitlement to welfare is of a different order to the charitable provision of the past and this may help to reduce the stigma felt by welfare recipients. Having restated that social/welfare rights are of fundamental importance to contemporary notions of citizenship, it is now necessary to discuss the various principles that underpin such rights as these have a significant effect in governing an individual's welfare entitlements.

The principles underpinning welfare rights

Welfare is subject to a number of political and economic restraints. The provision of a service or benefit may depend on a range of factors such as the wider state of the economy, levels of taxation or popular support for certain policies. Given that limits exist, a critical question for social policy and also for citizens is how resources are going to be allocated in order to best meet the various needs that occur (Lister, 2003a). One useful way to see how this question of rationing is resolved is to look at the key competing principles that govern public welfare provision, that is, the rules that control a citizen's access to benefits and services. Questions of who gets what, how they get it and why they are seen as being entitled to it are very much part and parcel of social citizenship debates (Dwyer, 2000a).

As Titmuss (1958) and Mann (2001) show, the state intervenes to provide welfare in a range of different and often overlapping ways. In the current mixed economy of welfare various combinations of direct state provision, and public subsidy and regulation of welfare, combine in complex ways with private, voluntary and familial provision to deliver welfare. How, then, is it possible to make sense of what is going on? Within the sphere of public welfare there are a number of differing principles that underpin the variety of benefits and services that may be regarded as social rights. In effect, individuals have to meet various criteria laid down by the state in order to exercise their right to a particular benefit or service.

A basic distinction can be drawn between two differing principles – *universalism* and *selectivism* – that seek to resolve issues about access to public welfare in two distinct ways. Indeed, the differing universal and selective approaches mirror a wider debate concerned with ideas about the 'good society' and the part that social rights may or may not play in establishing it. A *universal principle* holds that welfare services and benefits should be provided to all citizens on an equal basis. Every citizen should enjoy access to the same set of social rights. The intention is that welfare state services should be equally available to every citizen and used by all who need to benefit from them. Some critics (for example, Barbalet, 1988) have argued that there is no such thing as a universal right to social provision. After all, an individual can only claim the so-called 'universal' benefits when they meet a stated criteria or contingency. For example, Child Benefit, which is often seen as an exemplar of universal benefit, is only available to those who are the primary carer of a dependant child. Such critics are, however, confusing issues of universal availability with universal enjoyment. Nobody is suggesting that Child Benefit be paid to people without children, but universalists would argue that once you have primary responsibility for a child, the benefit should be available to you as a right. In contrast, benefits and welfare services based on *selectivism* (sometimes referred to as a social assistance principle) are limited to certain specified individuals or groups usually by the application of a means test. This is a mechanism widely used to limit access to benefits/social security systems to individuals or groups whose income and/or assets fall below a specified level. As Deacon and Bradshaw (1983) note, this promotes a residual public welfare system that is reserved for poor people.

Complicating things still further, certain kinds of welfare benefits are dependent on individuals making some form of contribution to society that is generally recognised as being of value to wider society (a contributory/social insurance principle). This usually entails employees having National Insurance (NI) contributions deducted from their earnings in the paid labour market (PLM), although on occasions the state tacitly recognises other forms of contribution by paying basic NI contributions for some of those citizens involved in providing informal familial care. Because such contributions are paid by the state at a minimal level many carers, most of whom are women, are disadvantaged in relation to the benefits and pensions that they may subsequently claim. (See Chapter Six for a fuller discussion of gender issues.) In recent years a fourth principle also appears to be assuming more significance. A principle of *conditionality* (Deacon, 1994), which holds that eligibility to certain basic, publicly provided, welfare entitlements should be dependent on an individual first agreeing to meet particular compulsory duties or patterns of behaviour, is increasingly a feature in the United Kingdom (Dwyer, 1998, 2000a, 2002, 2004b) and many welfare states across the world (Lødemel and Trickey, 2000; Goodin, 2000, 2002; Deacon, 2002). The key point to note is that very few rights to welfare are totally unconditional. With the possible exception of much National Health Service (NHS) treatment which remains largely unconditional,[1] access to a whole range of what are commonly referred to as social rights are routinely governed by differing principles that define and limit access to the benefits and services that we associate with the welfare state. The advantages and disadvantages and the implications that these various principles have in relation to citizenship are outlined in *Table 1.1*.

In drawing this discussion of principles to a close it is useful to reiterate a number of important points. First, the welfare interventions of the state are complex. Second, the differing principles that underpin welfare rights reflect wider views about the role of public welfare in promoting the 'good' society. Third, there are very few universal, unconditional rights to welfare. The various principles outlined are ways of resolving questions about who gets what welfare, and how and why they receive it. Such questions often revolve around the contentious concepts of equality, needs and desert. These are briefly considered below.

Equality, needs and desert

Equality?

The concept of citizenship implies a notion of equality in that citizens are said to share a common status in respect of the rights and duties that they hold. However, it is important to be aware of the different types of equality that may be pursued and the implications that this may have for welfare policies. Policies that attempt to achieve an equality of outcome between citizens are essentially about trying to secure a type of equality that ensures uniform end results or outcomes. Traditionally this approach has been linked to policies that attempt to redistribute income and wealth across classes. In the most extreme case, the successful pursuit of policies designed to achieve equality of outcome would see the eradication of inequality within a society and each citizen's share of the collective material wealth

Table 1.1: Principles of welfare

Principle aspect	Universal principle	Social assistance/ selectivist principle	Social insurance principle	Conditionality principle
Prioritises	Extensive welfare rights	Selective/residual welfare rights	Welfare rights based on contributions via PLM	Duties and individual responsibility
Example(s)	Child Benefit (contingent) NHS hospital/GP services (unconditional)	Income Support	State pension JSA (non-means tested)	The 'New Deals' Probationary tenancy periods
Advantages	Low administration costs Promotes social integration Promotes egalitarianism, ie, everyone gets treated the same Reduced stigma so high take-up rates Avoids poverty trap	Targets resources at needy individuals Reduces pressure on public expenditure Promotes self-relaince	Links individual rights to previous contributions promotes work ethic Links welfare claim to contribution	Prevents welfare dependency Promotes personal responsibility Expressly links enjoyment of welfare rights to individual responsibilities/ specified duties
Disadvantages	Relatively expensive so seen by some as drain on the economy Benefits go to those who do not need them Not used equally by all – better-off make much greater use of health and educational services	High administration costs Promotes a residual public welfare system Stigmatises recipients Low levels of take-up Socially divisive	Accepts and builds on existing hierarchies in PLM Disadvantages informal carers (mainly female)	Ignores issues of need Excludes 'irresponsible' individuals Disproportionately affects rights of poor citizens

would be of equal value. The endorsement of an equality of opportunity approach is very different. Policies introduced under this remit aim to give each individual an equal starting point in an unequal society. The focus here is very much on the redistribution of life chances. A central belief is that society is a meritocracy. The idea is that each citizen should be guaranteed the opportunities to prosper, for example, the right to access appropriate education and training. This will ensure that everybody has a fair chance to achieve success and prosper to different levels that reflect individual talents and endeavours. The final outcome of this type of equality may well be a degree of inequality but this would be seen as reasonable and acceptable. It is important that all citizens are equally able to access relevant social institutions to nurture and develop their talents without prejudice. Having developed those talents this approach to equality remains meaningful only if social mobility is possible and people have the equal opportunity to take up positions of influence if they so wish.

Wants, preferences and needs

The meeting of social needs is a central concern of social welfare institutions. A vast literature exists that offers competing definitions, constructions and discussions of need and how it relates to welfare (for example, Croft and Beresford, 1989; Taylor, 1989; Doyal and Gough, 1991; Wetherly, 1996; Hewitt, 1998; Langan, 1998). It is important to note that the ways in which *need* is defined and determined have a crucial effect on the type and extent of social rights enjoyed by different individuals and groups of citizens (Clarke and Langan, 1998). Claims to welfare rights are often underpinned by differing views as to what constitutes a legitimate need and the role that the state or other agencies should then play in meeting that need.

An initial way forward in defining the concept of need is to distinguish it from two closely related concepts, *wants* and *preferences*. Blakemore (2003) defines wants as an *individual declaration for some goods or services irrespective of need*. As Manning (1998) states, want is a more inclusive concept than need; we may want things that we do not necessarily need. Conversely, we may need something that we may not want due to either ignorance or desire. For example, a person may need surgery but may not be aware of the need to be hospitalised. Alternatively, they may well be aware of the need for treatment but actively choose to avoid it. The closely related notion of preference is different from both needs and wants in that preferences are only revealed when people are able to actually make choices. In debates about access to public welfare the lack of choice that individual citizens face has been heavily criticised in some quarters. This has led to a critique that favours the development of a more consumer-orientated approach to social rights; the pros and cons of this are discussed in Chapter Three.

Need is an elastic concept that can be defined in a number of ways. Manning (1998) makes three basic distinctions. *Felt needs* are needs that we are aware of ourselves, for example, when we are ill we realise that we need medical help. *Expertly defined needs* are those needs that are defined by professionals or others who may be able to take some sort of objective view based on specialised knowledge. *Comparative needs* are revealed when the situation of one individual or group is assessed in relation to others. All three dimensions are important for decisions about the allocation of welfare. For example, some citizens may feel that they are living in poverty, and certain experts may agree/disagree depending on how poverty is defined and measured. The decision about whether or not the particular citizens are in poverty may well be decided according to a relative scale that compares their income, wealth and assets with other different groups within their society. Whether certain needs are acknowledged and action taken to meet those needs may depend ultimately on whether a broad or narrow definition of need is adopted by the state or other provider of welfare. Need remains an important concept because, as Lister (2003a) states, the endorsement of a broad-based definition of need has very different implications for social citizenship from a narrow definition of need. A *broad definition of needs* emphasises an expansive universal notion of citizenship that favours extensive shared rights to public welfare. In contrast, a *narrow definition of needs* leads us towards a residual welfare state in which welfare is discretionary and entitlement often subject to a means test.

A key question when discussing needs at the beginning of the 21st century is whether it is possible for citizenship to continue to place a universal conception of need at the centre of contemporary notions of social citizenship or whether it has now become necessary to acknowledge the particular needs of different groups of citizens. Doyal and Gough (1991) strongly assert that a number of universal human needs can be identified, and that it is the duty of any government to ensure that such needs are met in accordance with a society's prevailing level of development (see ***Box 1.2***):

> The notion that all people have basic human needs and that we can chart how far they are met is central to any coherent idea of social policy and social progress. (Gough, 1998, pp 50-1)

Doyal and Gough (1991) argue that all humans are essentially social beings, and that as such we all share the same universal goal – the avoidance of serious harm. Universal preconditions to meaningful social participation exists; there are certain basic needs that must be met if each and every one of us is to have the ability to engage in the social activities that are central to the human condition. While it is asserted that human beings have two basic universal needs (physical health and autonomy), Doyal and Gough (1991) accept that the ways in which these basic needs may be met vary according to a specific society or time; but that does not stop them from being 'universal' needs. On its own, this assertion could, of course, lead to a minimalist definition of social citizenship that guarantees only residual welfare rights. In outlining an additional set of 'intermediate' needs that are necessary to ensure that the basic needs of health and autonomy are met, Doyal and Gough make clear that they are in favour of extensive social rights.

Box 1.2: Doyal and Gough on universal human needs

Basic human needs: physical health and autonomy
Are the universal prerequisites for the successful and, if necessary, critical participation in a social form of life. We identify these universal prerequisites as physical health and autonomy, ie, the ability to think and act.

Source: Gough (1998, p 53)

Intermediate needs

Nutritional food and clean water	Protective housing
A non-hazardous work environment	A non-hazardous physical environment
Appropriate healthcare	Security in childhood
Significant primary relationships	Physical security
Economic security	Appropriate education
Safe birth control and child rearing	

The only criterion for inclusion in this list is whether or not any set of satisfier characteristics universally and positively contributes to physical health and autonomy.

Universal satisfier characteristics are (thus) those properties of goods, services activities and relationships which enhance physical health and human autonomy in all cultures.

Source: Doyal and Gough (1991, pp 157, 158)

Questions about the definition of need and debates about the extent to which citizenship, which is a notion built around the universal rights and responsibilities of all citizens, may or may not be compatible to more particular claims to welfare remain a focus of much debate. The value of

Doyal and Gough's (1991) analysis is that it provides a forceful argument that it is the duty of every state to meet to the best of their ability the diverse range of needs of all its citizens.

Desert

Need continues to be important when discussing welfare rights and social citizenship but it is not the only significant issue. Deliberations about who deserves access to public welfare and, importantly, who is seen as undeserving, have long been part of welfare debates (Mann, 1992). Desert-based claims to rights are often based on a sort of social contract argument where certain types of activity are seen as important and positive to the function of society, and if people meet their wider responsibilities then society itself has obligations to provide certain services in return. Certain types of activity are generally seen as more deserving than others. Many feminists have long argued that informal care work in a family setting is not valued as highly as paid employment, and that this is reflected in the inferior rights to benefit of many carers, most of whom are women. Also, as previously noted, a principle of conditionality is based around the view that those who do not contribute (do not meet their wider responsibilities) are undeserving and should expect to have their social rights reduced or removed (Dwyer, 1998). It is important to note that ideas about desert can relegate issues of need to secondary importance. Once communities enter into such debates the central question is not whether an individual *needs* welfare but whether they are seen to have a *deserving* claim to welfare.

Key aspects of social citizenship: provision, conditionality and membership

The concept of social citizenship opens up the possibility of numerous avenues for further exploration. The three key themes of provision, conditionality and membership are certainly of major importance (Dwyer, 2000a). As previously noted, the idea of social citizenship implies that citizens have certain rights to welfare. The question of provision, of who/which institutions should provide the welfare services and benefits to which citizens are entitled, is central. Citizens are entitled to certain rights but the principles and concepts that underpin them are open to debate, challenge and change. Social rights can contract as well as expand. It has also been noted that citizenship entails responsibilities as well as rights. Again, these responsibilities are subject to often intense argument and debate. The relationship between welfare rights and responsibilities is central to any notion of social citizenship. *Conditionality*, the extent to which welfare rights should (if at all) be dependent on citizens agreeing to meet communal responsibilities, defined in the modern context – primarily but not exclusively – by the nation state, is crucial to individual citizenship status. The concept of citizenship also implies membership of some form of community; in turn the notion of community opens up questions about inclusion and exclusion. Rules about who has a legitimate claim to welfare rights and who does not, and the reasons why certain claims are viewed as valid while others are dismissed, are of more than theoretical interest. The notions of distributive justice that social citizenship entails presuppose a bounded world in which distribution takes place (Walzer, 1995). To enjoy social rights individuals need to have their right to membership recognised by others within a community. As Drake (2001) points out, simple membership is not enough; participation within society is also a requirement of full citizenship. If certain individuals or groups lack substantive rights to welfare, and they are unable to participate in society in meaningful ways, then the very idea of citizenship, of a shared common status, begins to unravel.

Note

[1] Some aspects of British public health provision have long been subject to various means tests, for example, dentistry, pharmaceutical prescriptions, spectacles and so on. Postcode rationing may also effectively deny people in certain localities access to a variety of treatments. It currently remains the case, however, that if you are ill, legally resident and you present yourself for NHS treatment no one (at the moment) is going to turn you away because of a lack of past contributions or because you have the financial means to pay for private treatment.

Summary

This chapter has raised a number of important points:

* Citizenship is a contested concept.
* Citizenship can be loosely defined as being concerned with a number of important interlocking relationships. It is fundamentally concerned with the relationship between individuals and the communities in which they reside, particularly, but not exclusively, the relationship between the individual citizen and the state.
* Citizenship includes at least three connected rights elements: civil, political and social rights.
* Citizenship also involves certain responsibilities; this in turn opens up important questions about the ways in which citizenship rights may be linked to those responsibilities.

- Wider debates about the principles that underpin welfare rights and concepts such as equality, need and desert may at times appear both dry and abstract but they are of considerable importance to the definition of social citizenship and social rights.
- The issues of provision, conditionality and membership, or, more precisely, formal and *effective* (or substantive) membership, that is, the ability to fully participate in a society, are key aspects of social citizenship.

Further reading

Lister (2008) provides an excellent accessible discussion of citizenship and the principles underpinning welfare provisions. The chapter by **Lewis (1998)** on citizenship is an excellent introduction to many of the issues discussed above. The chapters entitled 'Citizenship' in both **Drake (2001)** and **Fitzpatrick (2001)** are also good basic introductory chapters, as is **Dean (1999)**. Readers interested in debates about meeting needs will find **Doyal and Gough (1991)** a stimulating place to start.

Two traditions of thought: civic republicanism and liberalism

This chapter considers two different traditions of thought that each have important theoretical and practical implications for citizenship, that is, *civic republicanism* and *liberalism*. To begin, the origins of each approach are briefly outlined. While it is not the intention of this book to provide a detailed historical review of the development of citizenship (such debates are covered more effectively elsewhere), the aim is to contextualise each position discussed. The second half of the chapter then moves on to explore how differing philosophical positions impact on ideas about the character and relative importance of the individual and the communities that they inhabit and how these lead to the development of two contrasting notions of citizenship. One final note of caution before proceeding further – the civic republican–liberal divide is in many ways a crude dichotomy, as a range of standpoints exists within each category. When considering the two traditions it is best to consider each as an ideal type that helps to clarify important differences and aid understanding. Indeed, the latter half of the chapter seeks to differentiate between two types of liberalism: libertarian liberalism and egalitarian liberalism; both share some common features but are also different in their attitude towards social rights. These two positions are then contrasted with communitarianism, a vision of society that draws on civic republicanism for its philosophical justifications. It is also noted here that communitarianism can itself be divided between its more radical and conservative wings. The chapter therefore provides:

- a brief outline of civic republicanism in the city states of ancient Greece;
- a historical sketch of the emergence of the liberal tradition;
- a consideration of the key theoretical differences between libertarian liberalism and egalitarian liberalism;
- an outline of the communitarian critique of liberalism;

- a consideration of the differences between the liberal and communitarian traditions of thought;
- a discussion of the implications of these two traditions when theorising about citizenship and particularly social citizenship.

The origins of citizenship: a brief overview of civic republicanism

The concept of citizenship can be traced back to the ancient Greek city states of Athens and Sparta and the period between the 6th and 4th centuries BC. A citizen was characterised by *his* (citizenship was exclusively a male domain) willingness to actively engage with public duties within the polis (that is, the city). The ancient Greek notion of citizenship centred round citizens recognising a common commitment to their civic duties in matters of government and the defence of the state (Heater, 1999; Faulks, 2000). This classic 'civic republican' vision of citizenship demands loyalty and engagement from citizens who are expected to live according to shared values and rules. The key aspects of this approach are outlined in **Box 2.1**, where Heater (1999) discusses the views of the philosopher Aristotle, the thinker most associated with defining Athenian citizenship.

Under this system citizens are charged with both making and obeying the laws by which they live. The wider public interest takes precedence over any personal considerations; such public-spirited virtue becomes the guarantee of good government. This is also the world of the male citizen-warrior. A willingness when called on to defend the state through active military service was an essential duty. This exclusive, patriarchal citizenship relegated women to the private sphere that was seen as being of secondary importance. As Ignatieff notes, classic civic republican citizenship "inheres only in those capable of material, social and intellectual dependence" (1995, p 57). The ideal was very much the citizen landowner, connected directly to the territory of the city state, and by very definition a patriot who would react positively to the call to arms if required. That is, this citizen had a vested interest in defending the 'motherland' because he and his comrades actually owned it! The ultimate goal was to achieve "an anti-bureaucratic or anti-imperial ideal of self-rule by adult, male property owners, equal among themselves, sustained by an economy of non-citizens" (Ignatieff, 1995, p 59). Women, slaves and outsiders could not be trusted with the affairs of the state but they were, nonetheless, essential to its maintenance.

The civic republican tradition did not end with the demise of the Greek city states. Citizenship in the Roman Empire was influenced by the Athenian tradition through philosophers such as Cicero, who looked to remind Rome's ruling elite of the necessity of virtue and civic duty

Box 2.1: Heater on Aristotle and citizenship in the ancient Greek city states

What then is particularly characteristic about Aristotle's conception of citizenship? Size of population is important for him. The body of citizens should be sufficiently compact as to enable them to 'know one another's characters' (Aristotle, 1948, p 1326b). Only by means of this intimacy could the necessary communal bonds of true fraternal citizenship – 'concord' – be tied.... Another of his ideal characteristics of citizenship, for which in fact Athens did provide an apposite model, was that citizens should 'share in the civic life of ruling and being ruled in turn' (Aristotle, 1948, p 1283b). There is no room for apathy: citizens are expected to be publicly active.

But the crucial requirement was that citizens must be possessed of and display *arete* (goodness or virtue). By this Aristotle meant fitting in, in social and political behaviour, to the style of the particular constitution of the *polis*. In a sense, therefore, civic virtue was for Aristotle a relative quality. Even so, a basic moral calibre was essential in whatever *polis*: the good citizens were those wholly and efficiently committed through thought and action to the common weal. Moreover, by living such a life the citizen benefited himself as well as the state: he became a morally mature person. There was, indeed, no other way of becoming a fulfilled human being because, Aristotle asserted, 'man is by nature an animal intended to live in a polis' (Aristotle, 1948, p 1253a).

Source: Aristotle (1948), cited in Heater (1999, p 45)

when conducting public affairs (Heater, 1999). As the Roman Empire expanded, the ethic of brotherly participation was stretched to breaking point and the idea of citizenship being based on common origin and kinship rendered redundant. In its place a citizenship status centred on a set of (limited) legally defined rights and duties emerged. Citizenship was gradually extended to a range of conquered peoples and an edict in 212 AD granted citizen status to virtually all people living in the Empire. In some ways this can be seen as the first steps towards a universalistic citizenship status associated with certain common rights. It should not be forgotten, however, that Rome was using citizenship as a pragmatic instrument of social control, looking to bestow it as a way of incorporating conquered people. This was certainly a more inclusive vision than that of the Greek city states but it was not a democratic one. Power remained concentrated in the hands of wealthy Roman magistrates and senators (Heater, 1999; Castles and Davidson, 2000a; Faulks, 2000).

The imperial ambitions of the Romans highlight a limit of Athenian citizenship that emphasised the central importance of a close-knit community. Although civic republicanism continued to exert a strong influence in Machiavelli's vision of citizenship for the city states of 18th-century Italy, and also impressed certain other significant thinkers such as Rousseau, ultimately, its importance began to wane as a more modern liberal tradition began to emerge in the late 17th and early 18th centuries. Civic republicanism should not, however, be dismissed as invalid for more modern conceptions of citizenship. Its ideas and tone have heavily influenced the thinking of a range of contemporary communitarian scholars who promote a very different understanding of citizenship from many liberal thinkers. The emergence of the liberal tradition is now briefly considered.

The emergence of liberalism

The liberal tradition of citizenship is linked to the development of capitalism and the nation state. It emerged out of wider social changes that represented a challenge to the old feudal order of states governed by absolute monarchs who claimed a direct link to God as the basis of their sovereign right to rule. Against this backdrop early liberal theories of citizenship began to evolve as a direct challenge to the arbitrary and tyrannical power of the state and its then embodiment, the monarch. For example, Locke (1960), writing in around 1680, outlined a theory of natural freedom and equality based on just treatment by law and individual rights to liberty and, importantly, property (for further discussion, see Heater, 1999). Such declarations found their expression in the English (1688), American (1776) and ultimately French (1789) revolutions, as certain groups of citizens looked to declare their political rights and assert themselves (Castles and Davidson, 2000a). The rise of liberalism is thus characterised by Heater as a shift from a "monarch–subject relationship to a state–citizenship relationship" (1999, p 4), which was cemented throughout the 19th and 20th centuries as calls for the extension of civil and political (Oliver and Heater, 1994) and then social rights (see Chapter Three) unfolded. The notion of individual freedom, the right for each person to choose and to be at liberty to pursue their own preferences in life, is central to early liberal doctrine. This is highlighted in the famous extract from John Stuart Mill (1859), presented in *Box 2.2*.

Central to the early liberal ideal is the ability for individuals to lead their lives free from any interference of an overbearing state. This is largely achieved through the promotion and protection of civil and political rights. Mill held that citizens' participation in political affairs was crucial as this would enable them to guard against bad forms of government that interfered with individual freedoms. He was also keen that men and women should share the same rights. In other ways Mill was less inclusive in his approach. He was, for example, against extending the right to vote to those people who he believed lacked the relevant education to make sound judgements (Oliver and Heater, 1994). As Roberts (2003) notes, Mill appears to believe that citizenship should be reserved for the middle classes; this view was also shared by A.H. Marshall (1873), who was himself influenced by Mill's work (see Chapter Three).

Box 2.2: John Stuart Mill on liberalism and the centrality of individual freedom

The object of this Essay is to assert one very simple principle, as entitled to govern absolutely the dealings of society with the individual in the way of compulsion and control, whether the means used be physical force in the form of legal penalties, or the moral coercion of public opinion. The principle is, that the sole end for which mankind are warranted, individually or collectively, in interfering with the liberty of action of any of their number, is self-protection. His own good, either physical or moral is not sufficient warrant. He cannot rightfully be compelled to do or forebear because it will be better for him to do so, because it will make him happier, because, in the opinions of others, to do so would be wise, or even right.... Over himself, over his own body and mind, the individual is sovereign.... (pp 13-14)

The only freedom which deserves the name, is that of pursuing our own good in our own way, so long as we do not attempt to deprive others of theirs, or impede their efforts to obtain it. Each is the proper guardian of his own health, whether bodily, or mental and spiritual. Mankind are greater gainers by suffering each other to live as seems good to themselves, than by compelling each to live as seems good to the rest. (p 17)

Source: Mill (1859) (page references refer to a 1998 reprint from Oxford University Press)

In contrast to civic republicanism, with its emphasis on communal duty, the liberal citizen is in essence the bearer of individual rights and preferences (van Gunsteren, 1994). Liberalism is less personally demanding than civic republicanism; becoming a citizen does not require that an individual has to give up the pursuit of self-interest (Heater, 1999). Liberal citizenship is also intrinsically linked to membership of the nation state, a much larger and looser community than that required by civic republicans.

The differing visions of liberalism and communitarianism

Having previously outlined the development and central tenets of both the civic republican and liberal schools of thought, this section moves on to present a more detailed consideration of the philosophical differences between them and their potential impact on notions of citizenship. Initially, liberalism, and more particularly two strands of liberalism, libertarian liberalism and egalitarian liberalism, is discussed. Then communitarianism is considered. The communitarian tradition can in many ways be seen to draw heavily on classic civic republican thinking.

The liberal position

Liberal political theory covers a broad spectrum of ideas and authors (Avineri and de Shalit, 1995); however, all share one important common theme, that is, the primacy of the individual actor when framing an understanding of social reality. Lukes (1973) identifies the importance of this individualism to the liberalism that developed in England in the latter half of the 19th century. Four basic ideas are central: the dignity of man [sic], and individual rights to autonomy, to privacy and to self-development. The individual is seen as the 'natural' human condition, and we each have individual wants, purposes and needs that are arrived at by personal, rational thought and choice. Society, or more specifically the communities that we inhabit at differing levels (from local neighbourhoods up to the nation state), are seen merely as sets of actual, or possible, social arrangements which respond to these individual requirements.

The political and economic implications of this liberal individual approach have a particular relevance to the citizenship debate. Citizens here are held to be independent, rational beings able to be the best judges of their own interests. Theoretically the primary purpose of a government is seen as the recognition and protection of individual rights with the legitimacy of government based on the consent of its citizens as indicated by their preferences at the ballot box. A 'neutral' and minimal state is assumed appropriate, with government seen as a referee of varying individual interests while simultaneously stressing individual rights to liberty and property.

Economic individualism, underpinned by the belief that different individuals have differing abilities that each should be allowed to develop in open competition with others, complements this view of the political world. It is the market built on the institutions of free trade and private property that provides the arena for the contest. It is taken for granted that a minimal state will provide the conditions necessary for personal liberty, while a competitive market system will meet any requirements for efficiency and equity. This view is central to one powerful strand of liberal thinking that is probably best described as libertarian liberalism.

Libertarian liberalism: a citizenship of civil and political rights

Nozick (1995), Friedman (1962) and Hayek (1944) all advance libertarian liberal arguments that envisage a limited role for the state. They believe that the function of government is to ensure basic limited civil and political rights but beyond this it should not intervene and attempt to promote or sustain any particular ideal of a just society. It is argued that beyond the random inequality of the market it is impossible to reach a consensus about a fair distribution of wealth, and any attempt to reach one would lead only to false definitions. The state action required to secure social justice merely interferes with market mechanisms, the key source of individual liberty. The rewards distributed by the market alone are held to be the only just ones as they will reflect individual ability and effort.

As King (1987) reminds us, latter-day libertarian liberals draw heavily on **Adam Smith's** (1776) laissez–faire approach in which the 'invisible hand' of the market is said to produce a kind of spontaneous social order in which self-interested individuals, as actors in the marketplace, produce a collective social prosperity. The crucial point is that individual citizens are liberated from state interference and given the freedom to engage in economic transactions of their own choice. The state's role is to ensure the continued operation of a free market system, a primary requirement being state support for a legal framework that guarantees the property rights necessary for such economic activity.

Crucially, Smith (1776) also believed that the state had a responsibility to provide some *limited* public goods for its citizens that the market alone would fail to produce. This is a crucial and contested part of debates about the scope of liberal thinking and also wider citizenship debates. The extent to which state intervention into the workings and outcomes of the market is accepted or rejected affects greatly the scope of social rights. The central issue here is whether or not a measure of material equality (that is, access to specified social rights) is to become as integral a part of citizenship as the individual freedom that libertarian liberals hold to be of paramount importance.

For 'libertarian' liberals the state recognises the extent of its responsibilities to its citizens by promoting such an economic framework while simultaneously upholding individual civil and political rights. The distribution of goods that then ensues from the efficient functioning of a market economy is regarded as just. Individuals are entitled to what they can get provided they do not cheat or violate another person's individual rights. This, however, is only one standpoint within the liberal tradition, and egalitarian liberalism takes the issue of individual rights and distributive justice a significant step further.

Egalitarian liberalism: embracing social rights

The egalitarian liberalism of **John Rawls** (1971, 1995) pushes the ideals of liberal theory beyond traditional libertarian preoccupations with civil and political rights, and argues that liberalism needs to elaborate a notion of distributive justice which attempts to take into account the equality of claims of each individual in respect of basic needs and the means by which those needs will be met. He rejects the principle that the market will distribute goods fairly, pointing to a random distribution of both the talents and assets that help to define the end rewards under such a system. In doing so Rawls tacitly acknowledges the need for the state to recognise certain social rights. It is therefore seen as legitimate for the state to intervene in the lives of its citizens to ensure a redistribution of material resources so that all individuals can become free to pursue their own definition of the good life. In any just society, Rawls argues that:

> ... all social primary goods – liberty and opportunity, income and wealth and the bases of self-respect are to be equally distributed unless an unequal distribution of any or all of these goods is to the advantaged of the least favoured. (1971, p 303)

The dilemma for liberal theories of citizenship centres on whether or not, and the extent to which, individuals should be able to make claims against the state for social rights. The most famous assertion of an egalitarian liberal theory of citizenship that counters limited libertarian approaches remains that of T.H. Marshall (circa 1950). This influential approach built on a triumvirate of civil, political and social rights is discussed in detail in Chapter Three.

As Delanty (2000) notes, within the liberal tradition there are then two dominant models of citizenship: one centred round an individual's relationship to the market, and the other with the individual's relationship to the state. These can be seen as: (a) a right-wing libertarian strand of thinking, which stresses rights to own property and to conclude contracts, and (b) a left-wing egalitarianism which promotes a state-based model of liberal citizenship aimed at reducing certain market-based inequalities via the recognition and protection of certain rights to state welfare provision.

Communitarianism

Communitarianism can be seen as the lasting legacy of civic republicanism. In drawing from the classical thinking of the past, it strongly refutes the atomistic individualism at the heart of liberalism and emphasises instead loyalty to community and conformity to shared values (van Gunsteren, 1994). Communitarianism holds that the liberal outlook does not take sufficient notice of the importance of community in shaping individual identity and wider moral or political thinking. The overtly individualistic liberal view of the 'unencumbered self' is held to be ontologically false. Communitarians believe that the individual central to liberalism is an impossibility; individuality, self, identity, a notion of who we are, is said to be socially embedded. Self-determination is exercised within a social and communal setting. The only way to understand human behaviour is to refer to individuals in their social, cultural and historical contexts, as we are first and foremost social beings (see Kymlicka, 1992; Avineri and de Shalit, 1995; Bell, 1995; and more specifically, Sandel, 1995; Taylor, 1995). Similarly, communitarian thinking rejects the idea of liberal universalism as overarching societal principles cannot be defended; objective standards of morality or justice are said not to exist as they take little account of the importance of community or social context when developing a political approach (MacIntyre, 1995; Walzer, 1995). It is only as members of a community that we can find and sustain deep moral beliefs. A strong sense of 'community', defined here as "a body with some common values, norms and goals in which each member regards the common goal as her own" (Avineri and de Shalit, 1995, p 7), is for communitarians a basic need. Community makes individual autonomy possible by protecting and sustaining its members and in return is able to demand and justify individual loyalty to communally defined obligations and practices that are particular and specific to a designated community.

Although some communitarian scholars do not believe that the concept of community can be stretched to encompass debate at a national level, Walzer (1995) sees the possibilities for modern nation states to embrace a communitarian approach. Miller's (1995) discussion also centres on the viability of a national community bound together by a common citizenship; importantly, one that stresses obligations as the direct corollary of rights and also a communally shared notion of the 'common good'. A benchmark against which other people's preferences are viewed, this 'common good' "takes precedence over the claims of individuals to the resources and liberties needed to pursue their own conception of good" (Kymlicka, 1992, p 207). The way in which communal life is lived will determine the relevant concept of the good life. An important attendant consequence of this idea is that if a national community is so radically divided that a single set of rules (as the basis for a common citizenship) cannot be agreed, then the nation must divide into smaller territories (Walzer, 1995).

The importance of obligation

The primacy of the rights thesis that liberalism presupposes is further challenged by Taylor (1995). He argues that by asserting individual rights before all other considerations liberals stand in danger of destroying the societies which they inhabit; not only are others deprived of their ability to exercise their rights but the capacity to exercise rights in a social (communal) setting is undermined. He believes that it is important to recognise obligations beyond individual preferences and that people have to conform to certain shared rules and values for a society to function. The capacity for autonomy is developed in a social setting and this in turn creates significant obligations to reaffirm the value of this definition of freedom. Identity, a notion of who or what we are, according to Taylor, is centrally based on interactions with other members of 'our' society.

Communitarians hold that an individual cannot become detached, theoretically or otherwise, from the communities that they inhabit. Community is said to be constitutive of the individual and any notion of justice must emanate from the individual's particular social location and the traditions into which they are born. Communitarianism is a direct challenge to the central tenets of liberalism (individual autonomy, the possibility of universally held values, the neutrality of the state) and draws on the civic republican tradition for its defining principles. The communitarian goal is to encourage participatory politics in which people recognise their social obligations as well as their individual rights. This they actively achieve within specific communities.

The communitarian ideal has several important implications in relation to any social element that citizenship may imply. Walzer (1995) maintains that membership of various forms of community is one of the primary goods that human beings distribute to each other. Any notion of distributive justice presupposes a bounded world in which distribution takes place. Membership of a community is of great individual relevance as it determines many other important factors such as who is included and who is excluded when it comes to making collective choices, who members require obedience and taxes from and who then services and goods are allocated to. Crucially it is members who are in charge of how they distribute the goods that the community generates; therefore, they are the ones who dictate their relationship with strangers excluded from the community. It is only as members that individuals can hope to share the security and social goods of the community. An appeal to 'community' presupposes a bounded world advantageous to its members but often problematic to those unable or unwilling to join or abide by the communal rules. In the communitarian world claims to any collective welfare provisions routinely imply a willingness to contribute to the common good in communally specified ways. Rights and responsibilities are intrinsically linked.

Radical and conservative communitarianism

As with liberalism, it would again be far too simplistic to assume that communitarianism is not the subject of much internal philosophical disagreement and debate. At one extreme of communitarian thinking there is a vision of a wider society ordered by complementary and functional hierarchical inequalities bound together by an inherently conservative ethic. At the other, as Gutmann (1995) and Plant (1978) make clear, communitarianism can become a rallying call for radical action. An important strand of Marx's work was a powerful criticism of the individual isolation that capitalism can promote. For Marx, the liberal notion of the state as a universal community that attempts to reconcile differences in civil society is an illusion; the state merely represents the interests of the ruling capitalist class. 'Community' would only be achieved once the proletarian revolution had secured common ownership of the means of production. This Marxist view seeks to pursue a non–hierarchical vision of the common good that will ensure the autonomy of those neglected by capitalism. Plant (1978) suggests that despite the radical differences between socialist and conservative approaches, both see the re-establishment of a strong sense of community as imperative. Today a communitarianism influenced by conservative considerations is evidently ascendant (see further discussions in Chapter Four).

Two traditions, two types of citizenship?

Leaving aside the internal disputes previously noted, it is reasonable to argue more generally that the liberals and communitarians aspire to create two very different visions of citizenship. These two contrasting notions of what citizenship entails are neatly summarised by Plant and Walzer in *Box 2.3*.

As noted by Lister (1997), liberalism sees citizenship primarily in terms of a status that emphasises that citizens are first and foremost bearers of rights. Civic republican/communitarian notions of citizenship prioritise duty and obligation and stress that it is only by recognising and practising our wider communal responsibilities that we can truly become citizens.

> ## Box 2.3: Liberalism and civic republicanism/ communitarianism: contrasting visions of citizenship
>
> The first [liberalism] sees citizenship as a status that is not fundamentally altered by the virtue (or lack of it) of the individual: it does not ask whether the citizen is making a recognised contribution to society.... You should thus be able, as a citizen, to claim benefits even if you are not discharging what others may regard as your proper obligations to society.... The second [civic republicanism/ communitarianism] and alternative view, places much less emphasis on rights, and focuses instead on obligation, virtue and contribution. In this view citizenship is not a kind of pre-existing status, but rather something that is achieved by contributing to the life of a society. The ideas of reciprocity and contribution are at the heart of this concept of citizenship: individuals do not and cannot have a right to the resources of society unless they contribute to the development of that society through work or other socially valued activities, if they are in a position to do so.
>
> *Source:* Plant (1998, p 30)
>
> The first [communitarianism] describes citizenship as an office, a responsibility, a burden proudly assumed: the second [liberalism] describes citizenship as a status, an entitlement, a right or set of rights passively enjoyed. The first makes citizenship the core of our life, the second its outer frame. The first assumes a closely knit body of citizens, its members committed to one another; the second assumes a diverse body and loosely connected body, its members (mostly) committed elsewhere.
>
> *Source:* Walzer (1989, p 216)

Summary

This chapter has:

- provided a historical sketch of the origins and emergence of the idea of citizenship;
- outlined two contrasting traditions of thought, liberalism and communitarianism, each with a differing vision of what a properly constituted notion of citizenship should entail;
- highlighted that significant differences exist both within and between the liberal and civic republican/communitarian traditions;
- noted that the legitimacy, extent and conditions attached to social rights are a prominent site of disagreement.

Policies in the real world do not often follow the neat philosophical divide that has been used to explore differing approaches to citizenship. Certain aspects of the communitarian critiques may well be taken up by liberals to inform their approach. It is possible for thinkers from both camps to utilise aspects of the other. Liberal communitarians and communitarian liberals would probably have much in common and would occupy the centre point on a linear representation of ideas that had libertarian liberalism and conservative communitarianism at either extreme. The two opposed sets of ideas discussed in this chapter remain important because, as subsequent discussions will indicate (see Chapter Four), they continue to exert an influence in more contemporary settings, particularly in relation to welfare. Prior to considering such issues the next chapter looks at the development of social citizenship in the 20th century.

Further reading

Those who wish to pursue further enquiries into the historical development of liberalism and civic communitarianism should refer first to **Heater (1999, chs 1 and 2)** and **Castles and Davidson (2000a, ch 2)**; both provide accessible overviews. **Chapter Two** of **Dwyer (2000a)** covers the differences between liberal and communitarian visions, particularly in relation to welfare issues, in more depth. **Part One** of **Delanty (2000)** provides a more general sociological overview.

The development of social citizenship in Britain

The aim of this chapter is to outline and discuss the emergence of social rights in Britain from the late 19th to the mid-20th century. Initially, the work of Alfred Marshall is considered. His paper 'The future of the working classes', first published in 1873, is notable because it implies that a right to some form of basic state-provided education may be central to the development of citizenship in Victorian England.

The chapter then moves on to look at the involvement of the state in the provision of welfare in the first two decades of the 20th century. This early development of British social citizenship can be seen in part as emerging out of popular pressure from certain social movements (for example, organised sections of the labour movement, first-wave feminists) for the state to fulfil a role in providing welfare. However, as Barbalet (1988) notes, the evolution of social citizenship is also often linked to the security requirements of the state. Using the work of Williams (1989, 2003), Vincent (1991) and Mann (1992), it is noted that the state and other well-placed actors often used their power and influence to support certain claims to welfare while simultaneously excluding other less powerful groups and individuals from access to publicly provided welfare provisions. The chapter then discusses T.H. Marshall's seminal account of citizenship written in the late 1940s, and discusses some of his many subsequent critics. In brief, this chapter considers:

- the Victorian economist Alfred Marshall and his arguments in favour of a basic right to education;
- the development of social rights in early 20th-century Britain;
- T.H. Marshall's famous theory of citizenship as outlined in 'Citizenship and social class' (1949/92);
- critics of T.H. Marshall's account;

- issues of inclusion and exclusion, discussed throughout in relation to two themes – first, the deserving–undeserving distinction; second, social divisions (constructed around class, gender and 'race') and their effects on citizenship status.

Alfred Marshall: 'roughs', 'respectables' and the future of the working classes

In certain respects, the economist **Alfred Marshall** can be considered one of the more progressive thinkers of the Victorian era. Marshall believed that in the late 19th century the British state had the financial capacity and the technological ability to improve the situation of the working classes. His view was that the quality of individual lives and the wider collective social and economic prosperity of the nation could be enhanced if the state were to engage in such a task. His approach, however, should not be misconstrued as some radical plan to fundamentally reduce the great material inequalities that existed in Victorian England. Marshall was arguing that it was possible, and, indeed, desirable, for the state to try to 'civilise' working men by the diminution of heavy work and the extension of a right to basic education. Central to Alfred Marshall's crude analysis of the Victorian manual workforce was a distinction between 'respectable' sections of the working class (that is, skilled artisans) and its 'rough' unskilled elements. When discussing the 'respectables', he concluded that many were already developing the capacities and adopting the sort of lifestyle that was indicative of 'gentlemen citizens' (see **Box 3.1**).

In contrast to 'gentlemen citizens', he believed that 'rougher' sections of the working class remained burdened by long hours of heavy unskilled manual labour. This was seen as having a debilitating effect on the character of those engaged in it. Such men are described as preferring the 'coarse pleasures of the public house' to their own homes and generally being unable, or unwilling, to engage with wider 'civilised' intellectual pleasures. Alfred Marshall's aim was to encourage the 'roughs' to take up the more virtuous behaviour of 'respectable' sections of the working class. This, he argued, would benefit individuals and the wider community in equal measure. To achieve this he asserted that the right to an education should be extended to every working man in his youth, and that working hours should be limited in order to allow time for the "intellectual and artistic enjoyment in the evening" (1873, p 10). Society, he believed, had a responsibility to ensure that children did not grow up in ignorance. In return every man had to accept an individual responsibility to ensure that before marrying and subsequently fathering children, he could meet the expense of educating them. He even goes so far as to state that a failure on the part of an individual to accept this responsibility should be seen as an act of treason against the state. Anticipating criticism about the damaging effects on the national economy of this strategy, he pointed out that it was both possible and affordable because new technology and more efficient machinery meant that people would be able to work less hours without loss of profit or national output.

> ## Box 3.1: Alfred Marshall's Victorian vision of gentlemen citizens
>
> The question is not whether all men will ultimately be equal – that they certainly will not – but whether progress may go on steadily if slowly, till the official distinction between working man and gentleman has passed away; till, by occupation at least every man is a gentleman. I hold that it may and that it will.... (p 102)
>
> They [gentlemen citizens] are steadily aiming at a higher and more liberal preparation in youth; steadily learning to value time and leisure for themselves, learning to care more for this than a mere increase of wages and material comforts; steadily developing independence and a manly respect for themselves, and, therefore, a courteous respect for others; they are steadily accepting the private and public duties of a citizen; steadily increasing their grasp of the truth that they are men and not producing machines. (p 105)
>
> *Source:* Marshall (1873) (page numbers refer to a reprint in Pigou, 1925)

Alfred Marshall's early account is significant for three reasons. First, because it outlines a strong case for the state to recognise, guarantee and enforce a basic social right, the *right to an education*. Second, because T.H. Marshall's (who is not related to Alfred Marshall) highly influential account of citizenship refers to Alfred Marshall's insights. Third, 'The future of the working classes' highlights the exclusive nature of early theorising on citizenship and social rights. The status of 'citizen' is clearly associated with what Alfred Marshall considers to be the respectable behaviour and pursuits of gentlemen. Citizenship here is about the promotion of Victorian middle-class values of self-improvement and respectability rather than a concern to address material socio–economic inequalities through the promotion of basic social rights. Those who refuse to be civilised are not considered to be citizens. On a first reading, Alfred Marshall's account can also be considered as gendered. Certainly the language used implies that it is boys who are to be educated in order to assume their future responsibilities as civilised citizens. Women, however, are not entirely absent from his mind. He cites a poem at length that highlights the daily drudgery of a 'sad old needle woman'. Taking his lead from John Stuart Mill (see *Box 2.2*), Marshall is also concerned on the first page of his essay to lament the absence of women from the public sphere of citizenship. The exclusion of certain individuals and groups, including women, from full citizenship status and any emerging collective rights to social welfare that ensued was an essential part of the development of social provision in Britain. Such issues are discussed more fully in the next section.

Work, family and nation: issues of inclusion and exclusion

Fiona Williams (1989, 2003) sets out a framework for understanding the development of early welfare citizenship in Britain. She argues that social divisions constructed around class, 'race' and gender were woven into much British welfare legislation of the late 19th and early 20th centuries. Williams' central point is that issues of work, family and nation (that is, class, gender, 'race') had a defining impact on the citizenship status of individuals and consequently their access to social rights throughout the last century.

Work mattered for two reasons. First, whether or not an individual was employed or unemployed had a crucial impact on their ability to access early forms of collective welfare. The only option for many unemployed people who fell into destitution was the much feared workhouse introduced under the New Poor Law (1834). Second, an employed person's position within a highly stratified paid labour market was also vitally important (Mann, 1992). The period between 1870 and 1920 was an era in which the state, in Britain and many other Western European nations, became increasingly involved in welfare provision. These early forms of state collective welfare were linked to the development of industrial capitalism and the emergence of a newly enfranchised labour movement, sections of which were becoming highly organised.

The spectre of poverty, caused either by unemployment and/or inadequate wages, was never far away for the working classes. A number of studies, most notably Rowntree's (1901) famous study (which claimed that approximately 28% of the inhabitants of York lived in poverty), forced the plight of poor people into the public domain and ignited an ensuing debate about the causes of poverty. Vincent (1991) believes that the development of concepts of primary and secondary poverty by Rowntree made it easier for some critics to claim that a large proportion of poor people were in poverty as a result of their own actions. Irrespective of the causes of poverty

Vincent notes that its negative effects were real enough for many members of the working classes:

> If a particular member of a family was adequately fed, the others were not; if the fire was burning well the table was ill provided; if cultural hunger was diminished, bodily malnutrition was increased; if short-term respite was supplied by a money lender, long-term recovery was postponed; if recourse to the Poor Law prevented physical extinction, nevertheless it destroyed social standing. For the most practical reasons the schemes of the poor were always impractical. (1991, p 4)

This is not to imply that working people were simply passive victims of poverty. Many poor women engaged in low-paid, part-time work and children routinely did their bit to supplement the family income. Short-term credit from the corner shop was another possibility, as was the use of pawnbrokers. Limited help from neighbours was also available at times. Such methods of 'getting by' entailed a certain loss of status but were seen as better options than recourse to Poor Law provisions. Strategies of self-help, or limited collective help, within the confines of the local neighbourhood, were part of everyday life but often proved to be inadequate (Vincent, 1991).

Approaches to social welfare built around a combination of the workhouse, charity and self-help had failed to meet the welfare needs of a large proportion of the population (Mann, 1992). Against this backdrop, and a realisation of the extent of poverty, the state became increasingly involved in the provision of material welfare for its citizens. The Liberal governments prior to the First World War, fearful perhaps of the demands of organised sections of the working class and the growing electoral threat of the Labour Party, introduced a series of Acts that extended certain welfare rights to a growing proportion of the population. Vincent (1991) points out, however, that this was not merely the case of a benevolent state concerned to bestow rights on the poor and downtrodden. Rights to welfare were to be reserved for those who were deemed to be 'deserving' of assistance:

> The issue for the new century was not whether but how the principle of interfering in the conduct of the poor could be best attained ... classifying and deterring the poor by the single device of the workhouse test was no longer feasible, but there was little doubt that these remained among the proper objectives of welfare legislation. The figure of the loafer and the wastrel haunted bodies as diverse as the COS, the ILP, the Fabians and the trade unions. The more the poor were helped according

to their diverse needs, the greater the risk that the state would loose its capacity to reform or punish the ever-present residuum. (Vincent, 1991, p 24)

The state looked to define acceptable behaviour and limit welfare to 'deserving' cases. For example, the 1908 Pensions Act removed older citizens from the punitive grip of the Poor Law by recognising the right of those aged 70 and over to a small state pension. Initially, certain clauses within the Act disqualified anyone who had previously failed to maintain themselves or their families and/or who had acquired a criminal record from the right to a pension. Although these stipulations were later withdrawn, the 1908 Act is a good example of the state trying to limit early social citizenship rights according to deserving–undeserving distinctions. As Vincent indicates, the state was not alone in its exclusionary vision. Organised sections of the skilled working class were not opposed to the exclusion of the low skilled, those viewed as being voluntarily idle, or non-unionised workers from access to collective state social provisions (rf Mann, 1992).

It can be argued that work and issues of class were of great significance in defining access to collective welfare. Gender similarly had an important impact. Within families roles were gendered. Men were generally viewed as the main wage earner and head of household and women were charged with the domestic role. If working men's responsibilities were defined by their role as wage earners who supplied the housekeeping, working-class women's responsibilities often centred round making it last until the next pay day. This regularly involved personal sacrifice: "The first priority of a poor man's wife was to put herself last" (Vincent, 1991, p 6). Furthermore, Williams (1989) argued that much of the social legislation introduced at the beginning of the 20th century (for example, 1906 Education [Provision of School Meals] Act; 1908 Children Act; 1918 Maternity and Child Welfare Act), while providing services to meet women's needs, was also about the state defining and regulating the lives of women in accordance with a specific concept of motherhood. This served the purpose of confining women to the domestic sphere while simultaneously meeting the wider needs of the British nation and empire by physically and culturally reproducing the population:

> While these services met women's needs they also served to consolidate women's place in the home and to tie women's role in the family to the development of 'race' and nation.... Women as bearers of children and reproducers of culture, forearmed a real and symbolic link between racialized ideals of nationhood

and nation building by unifying the nation, populating it and servicing it. (Williams, 2003, p 150)

Issues of family, nation and empire entwined with each other in early welfare legislation; nation and motherhood became interlinked. It was taken for granted that the 'British Race' was superior, but many held that it would only remain supreme if a fit and healthy workforce and army could be reproduced. Williams argues that British social policy of the time was as concerned with maintaining national economic efficiency and colonial supremacy throughout the empire as with meeting the needs of women and children.

The dignified, key duty of women was seen, both literally and metaphorically, as being the mothers of the nation. The belief was that state welfare could, and should, play a part in facilitating such a role. It is also worth noting that although the mothering role was actively supported by the state, many women (especially married women) were not expected to enter the paid labour market and were therefore excluded from coverage for sickness insurance under the 1911 Social Insurance Act. A government official of the time stated: "it is the husband's and not the wife's health which it is important to insure. So long as the husband is in good health adequate provision will be made for the family" (cited in Fraser, 2003, p 182). The 1911 Social Insurance Act did nothing for those often most in need. Rights to healthcare and unemployment benefits were limited to those in specified industries who contributed to schemes; wives, children and the casually employed were not covered and were thus unable to access provision.

Williams (1989) also points out that legislation at the beginning of the 20th century that introduced rights to social welfare took place within a context in which the boundaries of citizenship were becoming more restricted by issues of nationality. The idea of the nation state had become increasingly important. Greater emphasis was being placed on the notions of national identity and national unity. The notion of a national society within specified geographical boundaries with an imagined homogeneous cultural, linguistic, racial and ethnic community was increasingly the backdrop against which the social element of citizenship developed. The welfare rights of citizenship were to be reserved for British citizens, that is, those seen as meeting nationality criteria both in terms of physical location and/or common cultural and racial characteristics.

A clear example of this is provided by the 1905 Aliens Act, which introduced UK immigration controls for the first time. The Act stated that immigrants could only land at recognised British ports and included strong powers to return 'undesirables' to their country of origin. Aliens entering Britain had no recourse to public funds or welfare provisions and anyone who became homeless within 12 months of arrival was liable to be deported. These measures, which attracted widespread support from all the mainstream political parties and most labour organisations, were initiated to deal with what was perceived as the problem of Jewish immigration into Britain. Panics about foreigners swamping Britain helped to racialise definitions of 'Britishness', and these definitions were subsequently institutionalised in immigration and welfare legislation that attempted to formally exclude outsiders, that is, those who did not fit the 'British' stereotype of white, English-speaking and Christian, from access to social rights. Indeed, the Alien Acts of 1905 and 1914 set the pattern for much later legislation (see Chapter Eight).

Those who were not British subjects were not eligible for certain benefits. Williams (1989, 2003) provides several other relevant examples. Anyone who had not been both resident and a British subject for 20 years did not have the right to a public pension as made available in the 1908 Pensions Act. Similarly, under the terms of the 1911 National Insurance Act non-British residents who had been in Britain for less than five years were entitled to receive only a reduced amount in benefits. They were, nonetheless, expected to make full contributions. Williams provides a further example of the racist eligibility criteria that underpinned early social rights. In 1919, following the First World War, mass unemployment and the fear of widespread unrest saw the government introduce a form of unemployment benefit commonly known as 'Addison's out of work donation'. Initially, returning soldiers who were unemployed were eligible to receive the benefit, but its scope was gradually extended to include civilian workers. This was a non-means-tested, non-contributory benefit, with an allowance for dependants built in, and its purpose was to meet the basic needs of those who were not eligible to claim unemployment benefits under the 1911 National Insurance Act. However, the Ministry of Labour refused to allow aliens access to the donation and secret instructions were sent to the staff at labour exchanges stating that black seamen should not be told about their right to access benefit under the scheme. Such evidence indicates that access to social provisions delivered by the state has been linked to racialised notions of British nationality since the beginning of the 20th century (cf Cohen et al, 2002).

Issues of class, gender and 'race', both separately and in interaction, served to exclude certain individuals and groups from access to social welfare provisions in this period. Although the British state began to play an increasingly important role in the provision of social welfare, it is highly debatable as to whether such benefits and services could be properly considered as citizenship rights in any meaningful sense. According to

T.H. Marshall (1949/92), the incorporation of an extensive set of social rights as an integral part of citizenship status only came about with the establishment of the post-war welfare state in the late 1940s. This highly influential account is considered next.

T.H. Marshall: civilising capitalism

Originally published over 60 years ago, 'Citizenship and social class' (1949/92) has been the focus of much subsequent discussion. In this section the key aspects of **T.H. Marshall's** highly influential account of citizenship are first examined and the important element of social rights is then explored in detail. The views of some of Marshall's many critics are also outlined. When considering Marshall's theory it is also important to remember that he was writing in the period immediately following the Second World War, when the classic welfare state of the late 1940s had recently been established as part of the post-war welfare settlement (PWWS). Circumstances were certainly very different from today.

Key aspects of T.H. Marshall's citizenship theory

In defining citizenship, Marshall was clear that the status of citizen involved membership of a national community. This status implied that each citizen could expect specific rights from a (nation) state and that in return it was expected that individual citizens would be willing to take on certain duties. He is clear that there is no overarching universal principle that emphatically defines what citizenship grants or requires. The extent of the rights and duties that citizenship entails is open to ongoing debate and challenge over time. Nonetheless, he is positive about the development and enrichment of citizenship at the time of writing. The key elements of Marshall's discussion of citizenship are presented in *Box 3.2*.

Essentially Marshall outlines a theory in which three linked universal rights elements, that is, civil, political and social rights, assume a central significance. For Marshall such rights are embedded in developing social institutions and material conditions; consequently, he argues that individual freedoms and the evolution of citizenship are linked to the ongoing development of British society. He therefore asserts that the demise of the feudal order and the onset of capitalism (which required the freeing up of labour and capital) ensured that the legal (civil) rights necessary for individual freedom within a marketplace were developed through the courts and the establishment of a legal system. Following this, political rights emerged as systems of parliamentary and local representation were established. According to Marshall it is the founding of the welfare state in the late 1940s and the establishment of the universal right of citizens to an extensive set of state-guaranteed, social and economic provisions (the culmination of a long struggle) that gives rise to citizenship in which civil, political and social rights become parts of an integrated whole.

Box 3.2: Key aspects of citizenship according to T.H. Marshall

A definition

Citizenship is a status bestowed upon those who are full members of a community. All those who possess the status are equal with respect to the rights and duties with which that status is endowed. There is no universal principle that determines what those rights and duties shall be, but societies in which citizenship is a developing institution create an image of an ideal of citizenship against which achievement can be measured and towards which aspiration can be directed. The urge forward along the path thus plotted is an urge towards a fuller measure of equality, an enrichment of the stuff of which the status is made and an increase in the number of those on whom the status is bestowed. (p 18)

Three rights elements: civil (legal), political and social

The civil element is composed of the rights necessary for individual freedom – liberty of the person, freedom of speech, thought and faith, the right to own property and to conclude valid contracts, and the right to justice. The last is of a different order from the others, because it is the right to defend and assert all one's rights on terms of equality with others and by due process of law.... By the political element I mean the right to participate in the exercise of political power, as a member of a body invested with political authority or as an elector of the members of such a body.... By the social element I mean the whole range from the right to a modicum of economic welfare and security, to the right to share to the full in the social heritage and to live the civilised life according to the standards prevailing in society. (p 8)

Equality of status

What matters is that there is a general enrichment of the concrete substance of civilised life, a general reduction of risk and insecurity, an equalisation between the more and less fortunate at all levels – between the healthy and the sick, the employed and the unemployed, the old and the active, the bachelor and the father of a large family. Equalisation is not so much between classes as between individuals within a population which is now treated for this purpose as though it were one class. Equality of status is more important than equality of income. (p 33)

Rights and responsibilities

If citizenship is invoked in defence of rights, the corresponding duties of citizenship cannot be ignored.... (p 41)

The duty whose discharge is most obviously and immediately necessary for the fulfilment of the right is the duty to pay taxes and insurance contributions. Since these are compulsory, no act of will is involved, and no keen sentiment of loyalty. Education and military service are also compulsory. The other duties are vague, and are included in the general obligation to live the life of a good citizen, giving such service as can promote the welfare of the community.... Of paramount importance is the duty to work.... (p 45)

The essential duty is not to have a job and hold it, since that is relatively simple in conditions of full employment, but to put one's heart and soul into one's job and work hard. (p 46)

Source: Marshall (1949/92) (all page numbers refer to the 1992 reprint of the 1949 lecture; an abridged version of the original lecture is widely available in Pierson and Castles, 2006, pp 30-40)

A fundamental focus of Marshall's work was centred on how, by developing the notion of citizenship, on both a theoretical and practical level, to include rights to welfare (the social element), it may be possible to remove some of the inequalities generated by the continuing operation of an essentially capitalist market system. The intention was to check the worst excesses of capitalism by the promotion of citizenship, to modify rather than destroy: "The inequality of the social class system may be acceptable provided the equality of citizenship is recognised" (Marshall, 1949/92, p 70). The equal rights that citizenship status implied could not, and should not therefore, ensure equality of condition; the thorough reduction of merit-based inequalities was deemed undesirable. It is, as Marshall asserts, the addition of a comprehensive package of social rights that generates the conflict between citizenship and the market. Described by Marshall in the boldest terms, as a 20th-century 'war' between citizenship and the capitalist class system, this conflict is inevitable given his expansive description of the social element. A paradox exists in that, while the economic system that is the basis of modern British society continues to generate inequality, citizenship is organised around a struggle for greater equality (Turner, 1986; Barbalet, 1988). When writing 'Citizenship and social class', he was clearly aware of the limits of his theory, noting in a later work that the "hyphenated society" (Marshall, 1985, p 123) of modern democratic–welfare–capitalism combined an expansion of the progressive egalitarian rights of citizenship with the continuation of an economic system that generates inequality. It would be wrong to attribute to Marshall a more radical agenda; Marshall's citizenship theory fits comfortably within the liberal democratic tradition which seeks to emphasise equality of opportunity and simultaneously make tolerable continuing inequality of outcome by the promotion of universally held rights.

According to Marshall, the 'equality of status' that existed between each individual citizen in terms of common rights and duties would ensure that citizenship as an institution reduced some of the inequalities of individual conditions generated by the continuing operation of a class system within a capitalist market economy. The principle of a guaranteed minimum (which the establishment of social rights brings about) does not necessarily affect income differentials but does provide a 'real' income for all in the form of state-subsidised and funded essential goods and services, or even actual income in cases such as pensions and Child Benefit.

So the egalitarian real income of social citizenship lies side by side with an inegalitarian money income system. Marshall believed, however, that circa 1950 there was an ongoing 'double movement' to remove non-legitimate inequalities within both the economic system and the citizenship arena, but that the measure of legitimacy in each of the spheres differed. In the latter, notions of social justice prevail; in the former this is combined with the logic and needs of the market. The two may be in opposition but, as Marshall makes clear, "we are not aiming for absolute equality" (Marshall, 1949/92, p 45). Marshall's citizenship is clearly a vision of society in which the enrichment of the universal status of citizenship is combined with the recognition and stabilisation of certain status differentials, largely through educational training and achievement, which are then consolidated by awarding different levels of monetary income tied to a stratified occupational hierarchy. In short, market-generated class-based inequalities are held in check by the promotion of citizenship. He believed that individuals would tolerate certain social inequalities provided that such inequalities were generally accepted as legitimate. This approach assumes that a universal system of values exists for all members of society, and that these values will continue to exist, and a certain level of inequality is generally regarded as fair provided rapid and open social mobility exists, or is at least seen to exist. As Turner (1986) reminds us, if open access to positions of importance, and the increased incomes that they often entail, is no longer generally perceived to be universally available to all with the correct technical training and qualifications, inequality may become a dynamic for resentment and the value of Marshall's citizenship theory undermined. Citizenship could no longer then be seen as a universal system of rights and resources that allowed all individuals to pursue their individual self-interests (Plant, 1988).

Marshall saw citizenship as a status that entailed both rights and duties. His consideration of the duty component is, nonetheless, particularly brief. Compulsory duties, the duty to pay tax and NI contributions, to accept compulsory education and the now defunct military service, are seen as relatively unproblematic, and it is taken for granted that if the citizen wishes to claim their rights then they must accept such attendant duties (Rees, 1995b). Paramount importance is attached to the duty to work. Marshall's emphasis on this 'essential duty' and more importantly "to put one's heart into one's job" (1949/92, p 46) clearly indicates that the individual citizen has a duty whenever possible to recognise a responsibility for themselves and the wider communities that they inhabit. This is a stance further emphasised when Marshall points to a general obligation to live the life of a good citizen (a call for people to uphold the law), and appeals to individuals to give such voluntary service as they can to the wider community.

The duties that Marshall outlines are not as unproblematic as they may at first appear. A potential clash between citizenship duty and individual autonomy soon becomes apparent if we consider two examples offered by Oliver and Heater (1994). A legally imposed duty exists that demands we pay tax; however, many people would like to pay as little as possible. There is a fine line between avoidance and evasion, but both are opposed to the tone of Marshall's argument. Second, Marshall implies a duty to obey and uphold the law. This is in essence an ethical obligation that we, as individuals, can choose to ignore by failing to assist the police or even actively engaging in a life of crime. What appear in the first instance to be two of the most straightforward of citizenship duties are not without their dilemmas. Although it has been argued that in his later works Marshall exhibited a "growing ambivalence about the proliferation and assertion of rights" (Rees, 1995b, p 357), it is clear that the extension of rights rather than responsibilities is his primary concern in outlining a citizenship theory.

T.H. Marshall wrong about social rights?

Rights, especially social rights, are central to Marshall's account of citizenship. In particular it is the addition of a substantive set of social rights, and the importance that Marshall attributes to these welfare rights, that makes Marshall's contribution to the citizenship debate distinctive. The inclusion of a social element within Marshall's approach has been challenged and a number of subsequent authors have questioned whether or not social rights can be properly considered as a valid part of citizenship in any meaningful sense. Several commentators (Roche, 1987; Barbalet,

1988; Oliver and Heater, 1994) have pointed to a conflict of principles between civil and political rights as opposed to social rights, the former having their basis in individual freedoms while social rights are centred around notions of collective equality. Oliver and Heater (1994) view social rights as distinct and separate from civil and political rights, stating that social rights, with their emphasis on a redistribution of goods and services, stand in opposition to a market-based economy, while civil and political rights are viewed as necessary for the continued functioning of such a system. Civil and political rights are seen as 'first generation rights': they are residual in nature, have their basis in formal legal equality and law and are central to the liberal tradition. They are held to not conflict with the values that underpin the capitalist system to the same degree as social rights. Civil rights are seen as necessary to ensure the freedoms that are required for the successful operation of a market economy. The ensuing extension of political rights is important in legitimating the continuation of a market approach by linking it to notions of democratic choice. Social rights and the economic commitments that they usually entail are viewed as 'second generation rights'. Often an entitlement to services, they are to be found in positive legislation that establishes such rights and gives the legal authority for governments to raise, via taxation, the funds necessary to finance public welfare provision. Consequently the level of funding required to guarantee social rights is apparently substantially greater than that required for either civil or political rights. Ensuring that the financial resources to meet the costs of social rights are available is largely a matter of political will. Social and economic rights cannot, therefore, be regarded as 'residual'. They are not rights or freedoms that remain once all legally established limitations on individual actions or freedoms are taken into account, but result from affirmative action by the state (Oliver and Heater, 1994).

Rees (1995a) and Barbalet (1988) further question whether social rights can be regarded as citizenship rights at all. Although they accept that social rights may facilitate the participation of some individuals as 'full members of the community', Barbalet believes that Marshall is wrong to make them an integral part of his citizenship theory, as they are at best only conditional opportunities. Barbalet argues that social rights are dependent on professional and bureaucratic infrastructures (and ultimately fiscal policy) and as such cannot be regarded intrinsically as rights. Such claims can be countered by pointing out that both the legal system and modern politics share the same essential financial features (Plant, 1992; Rees, 1995b). Barbalet also notes that social rights do not meet one of Marshall's main criteria for inclusion as citizenship rights per se, namely, universality. Social policy is often directed at specific targets, which means that benefits and provisions can only be enjoyed by particular individuals. Barbalet appears here to confuse the issues of universal availability and universal enjoyment of rights. Social rights are universal rights in the sense that once certain criteria of individual need, contingency or past contribution are met, access to the entitlements specific to that provision becomes available as a right. A person may then enjoy the benefits (and it might be useful to add, any potential drawbacks), associated with that provision. As Marshall states, there is no "universal principle" (1949/92, p 18) that determines rights; if there were, social policy and its associated costs would not be a central focus for political debate or disagreement. The criteria and conditions for provision are defined as a society develops and various groups and classes lay claim initially to 'their' rights, crucially often in conflict with one another. Social and economic rights and the struggle that surrounds them are, therefore, central to citizenship.

Attempts to distinguish between civil/political and social rights have been further challenged. Twine (1994) and Turner (1986) point to a false dichotomy in such debates, arguing that individuals and society coexist in an interdependent relationship, with the human actor (very much a social being) achieving and maintaining personal satisfaction and fulfilment only within a cooperative social environment:

> Citizenship [which includes here a substantial social element] is the institutional framework by which individual agents can be developed and cultivated in a modern capitalist environment. (Turner, 1986, p 93)

By including social rights alongside civil and political rights, Marshall's conceptualisation of citizenship makes some measure of autonomy possible for a large number of individuals in modern society. For many, particularly marginalised groups, social rights ensure that citizenship becomes a substantive status.

Marshall's many critics

Marshall's theory of citizenship has attracted criticism from many quarters. A number of the most important critiques are set out in **Box 3.3**.

It should be noted that certain of these criticisms have subsequently been developed, and many of the contemporary approaches to social citizenship outlined in Chapter Four draw on them when outlining alternatives to what has been characterised as Marshall's "essentially social democratic ... left wing liberalism" (Delanty, 2000, p 21). Given the prominence that Marshall attributes to welfare rights, and the focus of this book, it is appropriate to begin by considering those issues that relate directly to the social element.

Marshall clearly sees an extensive set of state-guaranteed social rights as a legitimate part of the citizenship package. He is, however, rather vague in defining the content and scope of such rights (Powell, 2002). Marshall's definition of social rights (outlined previously in ***Box 3.2***) is essentially contradictory in that it contains a minimalist definition ("the right to a modicum of economic welfare and security", 1949/92, p 8) which is immediately followed by an expansive vision of social citizenship that entails "the right to share to the full in the social heritage and to live the civilised life according to the standards prevailing in society" (1949/92, p 8). This catch-all approach remains contentious. At one extreme it can be argued that Marshall was outlining a status that merely implied access to basic welfare rights with the state as provider of last resort for those of limited means. Alternatively, it can be argued that the universalism at the heart of Marshall's theorising and the tone of the second part of his definition of social rights suggest much more. The problems that ensue from fully adopting either position are soon apparent. If the more residual definition is taken, does this mean that social rights are effectively reserved only for poor citizens? If so, what of the universality that citizenship apparently promises? If the more expansive definition, which implies full participation in society, is adopted, central questions about the meaning of 'civilised' and the setting of 'prevailing standards' need to be resolved. Should the state subsidise the performing arts industry so that everybody has the opportunity to enjoy opera and ballet? If so, what then of other people's preferences for watching professional football?

> ### Box 3.3: Some criticisms of T.H. Marshall's theory of citizenship
>
> * Vague on the definition of social rights (Powell, 2002).
> * Cost implications of social rights not considered (Dwyer, 2000a).
> * Limited universality (Alcock, 1989; Williams, 1992).
> * Exclusive in language and outlook, for example, in relation to gender, disability, 'race' (various authors, see Chapters Six to Eight of this book).
> * Theory on the sequential development of citizenship flawed (Walby, 1994; Delanty, 2000).
> * Anglocentric (Mann, 1987).
> * Not radical enough (Ferge, 1979; Bottomore, 1992).
> * Misplaced optimism (Roche, 1987; Heater, 1999).
> * Rights are privileged over responsibilities and this promotes passivity (Roche, 1992; Giddens, 1994; Selbourne, 1994; Etzioni, 1995, 1997).
> * An outdated theory (Delanty, 2000).

It has recently been suggested that Marshall's intention may well have been to encompass both approaches in his conceptualisation of social citizenship. Such arguments are persuasive given that Marshall was in many ways attempting to combine liberal and social democratic thinking in his theory. Powell (2002) argues that it is important not to see the social element as "an undifferentiated mass" but rather one that can be:

> ... disaggregated into the minimalist conditional citizenship of cash [social security benefits] with the maximilist unconditional citizenship of kind [health services] reflecting the [Marshall's] minimum and optimum. (p 241)

Marshall has also been criticised for failing to fully consider the important question of funding extensive social rights (Dwyer, 2000a). Given that social rights are a priority within Marshall's approach, the omission of a proper consideration of this may seem odd to contemporary readers, but Marshall's optimistic statement that the 'war' between citizenship and capitalism was being decided very much in citizenship's favour may have clouded his judgement. Marshall apparently believed that the public and politicians alike had come to some sort of consensus view that it was right and proper for the state to finance and provide extensive social provisions for its citizens and that this situation would always prevail. An element of contradiction in his later work seems to suggest that Marshall never managed to quite resolve his own feelings on this important issue. After initially stating that "social policy must be conceived as a part of a general economic policy and not a separate area of political action governed by principles peculiar to itself" (Marshall, 1965, p 71), a possible indication that all social policy is closely tied to (if not governed by) economic policy, he later notes that "nobody seriously proposes that the rate of expenditure should be fixed first and the standard of service adjusted accordingly" (Marshall, 1965, p 134). This would seem to imply that Marshall viewed social rights as important enough to be subject to funding principles that would at least ensure a reasonable level of service. Hindsight allows us the dubious luxury of pointing out that what is deemed reasonable by some is condemned as inappropriate or inadequate by others, depending on the political stance taken.

A range of critics have pointed to deficiencies in Marshall's thinking on a more general level. 'Citizenship and social class' is somewhat exclusive in its language and outlook, and a large number of authors (for example, Alcock, 1989; Williams, 1992; Heater, 1999; Dwyer, 2000a) have pointed to the limited universality of his vision. In reality the universal status that Marshall proclaimed appears to have reflected the world of the white, able-bodied, upper-middle class, male citizen that Marshall himself knew best. Furthermore, through a historical, comparative analysis of the development of citizenship in several nations, Mann (1987) has highlighted the Anglocentric character of Marshall's thinking. His theory on the development of citizenship may have some relevance to the English experience but it is seen to be flawed when applied to other nations. Marshall's teleological account is also shown to be suspect in relation to some British citizens. Walby (1994) notes that in certain instances political or social rights for British women preceded civil rights. Married women, for example, only gained the right to a tax status independent of their husbands in 1990. The sequential development of first civil, then political and finally social rights as outlined by T.H. Marshall can thus be challenged. Others (Ferge, 1979; Bottomore, 1992) note that, while a theory of citizenship that includes rights to social welfare is an improvement on those that do not, social citizenship as envisaged by Marshall is not enough. Such left-thinking critics argue that citizenship will only deliver substantive rights to poor people when a more fundamental reordering of the predominant capitalist economic order is undertaken.

It is also possible to counter Marshall for his inherent optimism (Roche, 1987; Heater, 1999). He seemed to assume that individual citizens would willingly accept the duties that citizenship implies. Such naivety may be understandable given that he delivered his lecture in the period immediately following the Second World War. After all, many citizens had recently paid the ultimate sacrifice and laid down their lives for their country, and a future of full employment also appeared to be a real possibility. The 'golden era' of the welfare state, the crisis years of the 1970s and the retrenchment of the 1980s and 1990s, with its attendant fears of a welfare-dependent 'underclass', had yet to be played out. Many (Roche, 1992; Giddens, 1994; Selbourne, 1994; Etzioni, 1995, 1997), however, have since criticised his account for privileging largely unconditional social rights to the neglect of the important duty/responsibility element. The claim here is that his rights-based vision of citizenship promotes passivity at the expense of participation that is necessary for meaningful citizenship to ensue. Furthermore, Marshall's misplaced belief that his account of citizenship, with its additional extensive set of (largely unconditional) state-guaranteed social rights, would be widely accepted as an essentially apolitical concept of uncontested universal worth (Roche, 1987) is probably his greatest error.

In the light of these extensive deficiencies it needs to be asked if Marshall's theory has any relevance to contemporary debates about welfare and citizenship. Two points are noteworthy here. First, Marshall's account with its emphasis on the "fundamental importance" (1949/92, p 49) of social rights helped to force welfare firmly onto the citizenship agenda where it remains the subject of much contentious debate. Second, as Williams (1996) notes, his approach continues to be of use when asserting welfare rights as part of a combined package of civil, political and social rights. It remains a potential benchmark against which exclusion from full citizenship status can be measured and the dynamics of social divisions constructed around several dimensions explored. More negative appraisals are of course possible. Powell (2002) questioned whether a 50-year-old benchmark was entirely appropriate for evaluating welfare states at the beginning of the 21st century. Delanty (2000) believes that Marshall's theory, centred as it is around a notion of a universal equality of rights and responsibilities, lacks the subtlety to effectively deal with difference. Delanty further argues that with the onset of the global age theories like Marshall's that link citizenship directly to the nation state are now outdated. (See Chapter Ten for further discussions around this theme.)

Summary

This chapter has considered aspects of the development of social citizenship in Britain from the late 19th to the mid-20th century. As well as providing some historical context for the contemporary theories of citizenship to be discussed in Chapter Four, the following areas/issues have been covered:

- Alfred Marshall's (1873) early proclamation of a social right to education presented in the language of citizenship.
- The development of early social rights in Britain, particularly the Liberal reforms of the first two decades of the 20th century.
- The importance of a deserving–undeserving distinction in governing access to early forms of collective social welfare provision.
- The significance of class, gender and 'race' in relation to citizenship status and enjoyment of early social rights.
- That (in response to particular pressures) the state may grant or extend welfare rights to certain groups but simultaneously seek to exclude others, both within and/or beyond the nation state, from enjoyment of such rights.
- T.H. Marshall's highly influential theory of citizenship.
- The many and varied critiques of T.H. Marshall's approach.

As a final conclusion to this chapter, and as a precursor to the more contemporary approaches explored in Chapter Four, a summary of T.H. Marshall's approach is useful. According to Marshall:

- Citizenship implies an equality of status universally enjoyed by all who are full citizens.
- Citizenship is fundamentally ordered around three rights elements: civil (legal), political and especially social rights.
- Citizenship is about rights and responsibilities.
- Rights are embedded in social institutions.
- Social citizenship is in conflict with capitalism. It provides a guaranteed minimum of welfare and also a limited measure of equality for all citizens.

Further reading

The fourth edition **(2009)** of **Fraser's** *The evolution of the British welfare state* contains a wealth of information on the development of British welfare provisions in the 19th and 20th centuries. Readers who are interested in more critical appraisals of debates about social inclusion/exclusion around issues of class, 'race' and gender and the development of social welfare in 19th/20th-century Britain should read **Williams (1989)** and/or **Mann (1992)**. **Vincent's (1991)** book is also an excellent critical historical analysis of the British state's policy interventions and its effects on the lives of poor people.

Contemporary approaches to social citizenship

This chapter focuses more directly on debates about *citizenship and welfare*. In many respects the two are closely connected. Citizenship implies membership of a community, most usually in the contemporary context, membership of a nation state. Formal citizenship is often (although not always) a precondition for the receipt of welfare benefits and services. It is important to note, however, that systems of welfare are not only concerned to make welfare services available to citizens or other individuals, but that welfare policy can also be used in an instrumental way to advance particular outcomes or to promote certain attitudes or types of behaviour (Fullinwider, 1988; Deacon, 2002). Each of the approaches to social citizenship considered below also looks to policy to prioritise certain types of social provision as a way of engendering a wider notion of the social order or common good that fits with their specific normative vision of a good society. As noted in Chapter One, such issues are essentially philosophical in nature, but the ways in which they are resolved have a profound practical impact on the kinds of welfare rights that citizens are able to access.

Chapter Three concluded with a consideration of T.H. Marshall's theory of citizenship, built around civil, political and, importantly, social rights; this is a vision that is closely associated with the PWWS of the late 1940s. As the many ensuing criticisms of Marshall's theory indicate, his influential notion of social citizenship has provoked a range of differing responses from thinkers and groups associated with a wide range of ideological standpoints. New approaches to citizenship, in particular its welfare element, have subsequently developed. Many thinkers from both the Left and the Right of the political spectrum have been highly critical of the egalitarian liberal/social democratic compromise that Marshall's theory represents. This chapter explores the basis of such critiques and examines their implications in relation to social citizenship. Initially, the chapter locates T.H. Marshall's theory within the social democratic tradition of the Centre–Left and then moves on to consider some more critical and/or contemporary approaches to social citizenship. A range of perspectives and issues are covered in the following sections:

• T.H. Marshall and the social democratic tradition;
• social citizenship and challenges from the Left;
• the challenge from the New Right;
• new communitarianism: a latent hostility to social rights?;
• New Labour: a 'third way' for social citizenship;
• after New Labour: a 'New Conservatism'?

T.H. Marshall and the social democratic tradition

A number of positions can be located under the banner of Social Democracy; they all, however, share some common ground. According to George and Wilding (1994), democratic socialists (their preferred label) believe that although the process of industrialisation has made possible unprecedented levels of general wealth, it has also generated a range of attendant social problems. Democratic socialists look to harness the positive potential of industrial economies by a gradual reform of capitalism, which ultimately leads to new forms of social organisation based on the principles of parliamentary socialism. The working class is seen as an important motor driving this process and many democratic socialists would argue that the struggles of the labour movement played a central role in the development of many social rights. The welfare state is, therefore, seen largely as a positive outcome of class struggle. At an individual level social rights are seen as positive because they eliminate suffering and want, reduce inequalities and enable all citizens to fulfil their individual potential. At a more collective level the welfare state helps to promote altruism and social integration and also stimulates (through investment in the training, support and care of citizens) the wider economy, leading to the generation of greater collective national wealth.

Titmuss and the welfare society

As Alcock and Oakley (2001) note, **Richard Titmuss** was, and has remained, a particularly influential thinker on welfare within the social democratic tradition. His belief was that the state should take the leading role in establishing and maintaining a universal system of welfare. Members of the national community would then be bound together through a common citizenship status that included shared rights to a full range of publicly provided welfare benefits and provisions. An extensive welfare state was, he believed, not only the best way of ensuring that citizens' needs could be met, but also a viable way of promoting social integration and common purpose within a modern national industrialised society (Deacon, 2002).

Universal rights to welfare that underpinned a common status of shared social citizenship are central to Titmuss's approach. In terms of provision he was clear that the state should primarily be concerned to use welfare rights to redistribute resources in order to reduce inequalities between citizens. This universalism would, he believed, help promote the altruistic concern for others that the welfare state should (quite properly according to his own views) seek to engender among citizens. Titmuss was opposed in principle to means testing and residual systems of welfare which he held would lead to the stigmatisation of those in receipt of visible social welfare benefit, and undermine any sense of shared community of common citizenship status (Deacon, 2002).

Titmuss's essentially optimistic view of human nature is reflected in his non-judgementalism and his rejection of a principle of conditionality. Dismissive of explanations of poverty based on individual failings or inappropriate individual behaviour, he believed that welfare rights should be largely unconditional (Deacon, 2002). Welfare should not be about ensuring claimants meet various personal responsibilities or prescribed patterns of behaviour, but rather concerned with the meeting of needs and the elimination of want. As Deacon (1993, p 237) notes:

> The problem of poverty was not one of individual character and its waywardness but one of economic and industrial organisation. As such it could not be relieved by measures focused upon the character.

Titmuss saw unconditional universal rights as the best way of simultaneously promoting equality and a sense of common membership and community. In his later work, Titmuss argues that such rights are of particular importance to those who bear the social costs of the continuing operation and progress of industrial capitalism, and that welfare rights should be organised according to a principle of 'selective positive discrimination'. He is clear that it is right and proper that those who suffer the 'diswelfares' inherent in modern British society should be compensated by access to the most comprehensive package of social provisions (Titmuss, 1958). An essential part of any social democratic vision of citizenship must be to tackle any existing illegitimate inequalities through the promotion of a common citizenship status that places welfare rights at its centre (see ***Box 4.1***). In this way welfare rights ensure effective membership of, and participation in, society for many marginalised citizens.

Box 4.1: A social democratic vision of social citizenship

The importance of universal welfare rights

One fundamental historical reason for the adoption of this principle [universalism circa 1948] was the aim of making services available and accessible to the whole population in such ways as would not involve users in any humiliating loss of status, dignity or self-respect. There should be no sense of inferiority, pauperism, shame or stigma in the use of publicly provided service; no attribution that one was being or becoming a 'public burden'. Hence the emphasis on the social rights of all citizens to use or not to use as responsible people the services made available by the community in respect of certain needs which the private market and the family were unable or unwilling to provide universally.... (p 117)

Using universalistic values to confront particular inequalities

The challenge that faces us is not the choice between universalist and selective social services. The real challenge resides in the question: what particular infrastructure of universalist services is needed in order to provide a framework of values and opportunity bases within and around which can be developed socially acceptable selective services aiming to discriminate positively, with the minimum risk of stigma in favour of those whose needs are greatest? This is the fundamental challenge.... In all the main spheres of need, some structure of universalism is an essential prerequisite to selective positive discrimination; it provides a general system of values and a sense of community, socially approved agencies for clients, patients and consumers, and also for the recruitment, training and deployment of staff at all levels; it sees welfare not as a burden, but as complementary and as an instrument of change, and, finally it allows positive discriminatory services to be provided as rights for categories of people and for classes of need in terms of priority social areas and other impersonal classifications. Without this infrastructure of welfare resources and framework of values, we should not be able to identify and discuss the next steps in progress towards a welfare society. (pp 122-3)

Source: Titmuss (1968) (page numbers refer to a reprint in Alcock et al, 2001)

Although the vision outlined in ***Box 4.1*** can be seen to be consistent with the dominant views about the state and welfare in the years immediately following the Second World War, Titmuss's views retain a contemporary relevance. Deacon (2002) argues that his influence subsequently led to the establishment of a 'quasi–Titmuss paradigm' within academic social policy. These scholars (for example, Townsend, 1979) advocate unconditional welfare and the redistribution of material wealth, but are less concerned to engage with the altruistic aspects of Titmuss's work and wider questions of using welfare to promote specific moral values.

T.H. Marshall: a democratic socialist vision of social citizenship?

The question remains, however, where does **T.H. Marshall's** theory of citizenship sit in relation to social democracy? It has previously been noted that Marshall's egalitarian liberalism had much in common with social democracy (Delanty, 2000). Marshall (1949/92) himself believed that the PWWS put in place by the Labour government (with an extensive welfare state at its heart) was, indeed, democratic socialism in action. Several similarities can be traced between Titmuss's approach and Marshall's. First, both attached significant importance to universal and largely unconditional welfare rights. Second, although the class struggle is often seen by many democratic socialists as an important factor in the development of social citizenship, both Titmuss and Marshall suggest that the evolutionary development of British industrial capitalism is of greater significance for the emergence of social rights. Third, the two writers share the same optimism about the motivations that underpin human nature. Marshall and Titmuss both assumed that citizens would generally behave in a responsible manner and look to enhance their own lives, and the lives of fellow members of their national community, rather than exploit any advantages that social rights bring for individual self-interest.

Ultimately, the decision about whether or not T.H. Marshall's vision for citizenship can be seen as social democratic depends on personal interpretation of his works and whether or not his minimalist or maximalist definition of social rights is prioritised (see Chapter Three, this volume). Both Powell (2002) and Rees (1995b) outline persuasive arguments against T.H. Marshall's inclusion in democratic socialism's hall of fame. Rees (1995b) believes that it is possible to trace two theories of citizenship in T.H. Marshall's work, with the essentially social democratic tone of 'Citizenship and social class' giving way to a growing ambivalence or even hostility to proliferation of social rights in his later works (for example, Marshall, 1985). Rees (1995b) argues that Marshall's language shifts from a discussion of rights to one of legitimate expectations, and that he comes to view the discretion of welfare officials as being acceptable in certain decisions about accessing public welfare. In the late 1970s Marshall became increasingly critical of strike action in the public sector and also voiced concerns about fraud involving both benefit claimants and business people. A growing anxiety about the development of a self-interested citizenry abusing their rights perplexed Marshall and this has led to the assertion that:

> If the more familiar Marshall is social democratic, or in Janowitz's phrase, 'reflects the outlook of a sociologist orientated towards British socialism', then the less familiar one is indeed the 'perfect liberal', or at heart the perfect New liberal, complete with a degree of nervousness about the moral hazard which might ensue from the relatively easy availability of welfare benefits. (Rees, 1995b, p 359)

Key themes that are central to Social Democracy have been identified as: the promotion of equality, freedom (including freedom from material deprivation), social integration and universal rights to welfare (George and Wilding, 1994). Arguably Marshall's (1949/92) endorsement of these beliefs mark him out as a social democrat of sorts, even if he perhaps moved away from this position in later life.

Social citizenship and challenges from the Left

Although many social democrats are generally supportive of the idea of social citizenship as envisaged by Titmuss and Marshall, a number of critiques of their approach, and of the welfare state that emerged post-Second World War, have developed. Some Centre-Left commentators have been critical of aspects of T.H. Marshall's theory. Their reservations are discussed in the second part of this section. Many Marxists, however, have more serious misgivings and are hostile to the very notion of social citizenship, and remain cynical of an essentially capitalist state delivering social rights.

Marxism and the critique of social rights

Marxism is centrally concerned with issues of class inequality and conflict. In very simple terms, according to Marx, society is divided into two main classes: the dominant capitalist class (the bourgeoisie) who own the means of production, and the exploited working class (the proletariats), who have to sell their labour in order to survive. Marx held that the economic structure of society determined the constitution of all other institutions in society including welfare organisations. Indeed, many subsequent neo-Marxist writers who draw on Marx's original analysis refer not to the 'welfare state' but to 'welfare capitalism' because they argue that state-guaranteed social rights, which social citizenship promises, do not fundamentally alter the class relationships central to a functioning capitalist economy (George and Wilding, 1994).

The rights to social welfare that are so fervently favoured by social democrats/egalitarian liberals provoke a range of reactions from ambivalence to disdain among Marxists. As the quote from Offe (1982) in *Box 4.2* indicates, the welfare state presents many on the far Left with a dilemma. Social citizenship and the provision of welfare rights may relieve the suffering of workers to some extent, but they also benefit capitalists and thus assist in the continued exploitation of the working class. Much of Bottomore's (1992) criticism of Marshall is based around the view that the addition of a set of universally guaranteed social rights to the previously acknowledged civil and political elements of citizenship cannot successfully challenge inequality while they remain tied to an essentially capitalistic market system which perpetuates inequality. Social rights are seen as purely ameliorative measures that do not tackle the root cause of economic divisions and existing material inequalities within society. Administrative and structural considerations often mean that welfare institutions mirror the inequalities that are already present within a society. Ferge (1979), like Bottomore (1992), believes that a more radical reconstruction of the economic and social structures on which capitalism is based is necessary to reduce class-based inequalities. They argue that only the development of more fundamental 'societal policies' will curb the excesses of capitalism and ensure substantive citizenship for all.

Three fundamental and interlinked neo-Marxist criticisms of social citizenship are highlighted by Offe (1982) in *Box 4.2*. First, he argues that the welfare state is ineffective and inefficient. This is because it merely acts to compensate certain people for some of the negative consequences of capitalism but fails, in spite of substantial and increasing welfare expenditure, to address the causes of their problems and/or adequately meet the needs of many citizens. Second, social rights are repressive because in order to access them, citizens are subject to the social control of state bureaucracies. Individuals have to meet state-defined categories of need, be seen to be 'deserving' of collective support and must also routinely fulfil certain behavioural conditions in order to access the various welfare benefits and services available (see Chapter Five in this volume for a fuller discussion of this issue). Third, Offe argues that social rights serve to obscure the real causes of inequality inherent in capitalism. People lose sight of the fact that the social ills that welfare rights seek to remedy are actually caused by the economic system that underpins them. In treating the symptoms with social welfare, the state deflects the working-class gaze away from the causes of its own oppression. By developing this false understanding (or consciousness, as Marxists prefer to call it), the state undermines any radical potential of the working class to transform economic and, therefore, wider social relations. Dean succinctly sums up the bases of Marxist critiques of social citizenship, noting:

> The essence of the neo–Marxists' case against social rights is, first that in ameliorating the exploitative impact of capitalism they help to ensure its survival; second, that social rights provide a powerful mechanism for state/ideological control. (2002a, p 65)

Box 4.2: A Marxist critique of social citizenship

The welfare state has served as the major peace formula of advanced capitalist democracies for the period following the Second World War. This peace formula consists, first, in the explicit obligation of the state apparatus to provide assistance and support (either in money or in kind) to those citizens who suffer from specific needs and risks, which are characteristic of market society; such assistance is provided as legal claims granted to citizens. Second, the welfare state is based on the recognition of the formal role of the labour unions both in collective bargaining and the formation of public policy. Both of these structural components of the welfare state are considered to limit and mitigate class conflict, to balance the asymmetrical power relation of labour to capital, and thus to overcome the condition of disruptive struggle and contradiction that was the most prominent feature of pre-welfare state, or liberal capitalism. In sum, the welfare state has been celebrated throughout the post-war period as the political solution to societal contradictions.... (p 66)

Although it would be nonsensical to deny that the struggle for labour protection legislation, expanded social services, social security and union recognition which has been led by the working class movement for over a century now, and which has brought substantial improvements to the living conditions of most wage earners, the socialist critique of the welfare state is nevertheless a fundamental one. It can be summarised in three points ... the welfare state is said to be (1) ineffective and inefficient, (2) repressive and (3) conditioning a false ideological understanding of the social and political reality within the working class. In sum, it is a device to stabilise rather than a step in the transformation of society. (p 72)

Source: Offe (1982) (page numbers refer to an abridged version published in Pierson and Castles, 2006)

The Left and the positive potential for a reformulated notion of social citizenship

A combination of Marxist scepticism and democratic socialist optimism has been influential in mapping out the Left's position on social citizenship in recent decades. In critical mode **Pete Alcock** (1989) outlines the lack of real universality at the heart of the social citizenship of the PWWS. He notes that the welfare needs of certain groups (for example, black people, unemployed people, many women) were excluded or marginalised and that full citizenship rights were only afforded to white working men. Alcock then goes on to argue that rather than meeting the needs of poor people, state welfare has generally been more successful in serving the requirements of wealthier citizens. Having noted these limitations, however, Alcock remains positive about the potential of social citizenship. He argues that a citizenship that really promotes and extends universal rights to welfare can benefit everybody and also help to empower previously excluded groups.

Other commentators of the contemporary Left see a reformulated notion of citizenship as having value in challenging the paternalistic assumptions and lack of accountability that they believe characterised state welfare in the past. Some of the marginalised subjects of the PWWS (for example, ethnic groups, women, disabled people, gay rights activists) have collectively responded to their exclusion and sought to redefine social citizenship from below by engagement in campaigns and direct action to secure welfare rights. Lewis (1998) notes that while there is no denying that real differences exist between these groups on occasions, it is also possible to sketch out some common ambitions between them and to talk of new social movements that share three common positions. First, all such new social movements argue for equal rights on the basis of common group membership rather than on an individual basis. Second, they all seek a greater redistribution of wealth and power between social groups rather than just increased individual opportunity. Third, they all look for an expanded version of the welfare state in the future.

There is also a growing body of work on the contemporary Left that seeks to explore how citizens themselves understand and make sense of the idea of social citizenship (Dean and Melrose, 1996, 1998, 1999; Beresford and Turner, 1997; Dwyer, 1998, 2000a, 2002; Lister et al, 2003). One aim of this work has been to allow some 'bottom-up' views of citizenship to influence the debates and processes of ongoing welfare reforms. As Iredale (1999) notes, since the late 1960s citizen involvement and public consultation have become features of policy making across Europe. In order to remedy what has been identified as a democratic deficit in conventional processes of public policy decision making, many governments have been increasingly keen to consult with citizens using a range of methods (for example, surveys, focus groups, citizens' juries). Although regarded as generally positive, this kind of user involvement raises a number of important questions, the most significant one being the overall objective of user involvement. Is it merely to consult with their views, or is it about encouraging participation and/ or empowering citizens to be actively involved in decisions about welfare services?

> The crucial difference between public consultation and public participation is that the latter entails a real shift in authority and control over the decision making to the citizens involved. (Iredale, 1999, p 179)

Other problems may occur. First, successful user groups may become incorporated into existing power structures and lose touch with the grass-roots concerns and radicalism previously central to their agenda. Second, as resources are finite, the needs and concerns of the most organised user groups may prevail over others who have equally valid claims but who lack the level of power, voice or resources to set welfare agendas. For example, breast cancer and senile dementia are both pressing welfare issues but arguably the former attracts more public support and resources than the latter. Third, users may be primarily concerned with quality of service and not particularly interested in wider issues of management and policy process. Fourth, the use of a catch-all 'user' category that attempts to bring together a number of disparate groups may be problematic. Fifth, the exclusion of the most marginalised may be exacerbated by the continuing process of consultation/participation of well-placed user groups. Finally, some policy makers may be reluctant to actively involve users in welfare policy in any meaningful sense (Iredale, 1999).

Beresford's work (2000, 2001, 2002) is useful in answering some of the above questions and highlighting the positive potential of the user approach. He argues that a democratic rather than consumerist approach to participation which prioritises autonomy, rights and inclusion, and which recognises the validity of the experiences of those whose citizenship has been denied or curtailed by the welfare state in the past, offers real potential for enhanced social citizenship in the future. In response to the particular criticism that everybody is a welfare service user in some respect and that the 'user' approach actually involves prioritising specific needs and voices, Beresford counters that such critics are missing the point. He argues that while we are all welfare service users, routinely going to the doctors or attending a state school is not the same as being a disabled person who is unable to control their personal care package, or living a hand-to-mouth existence on benefits. Such "long term regulatory intimate and segregating contact with welfare services is different and is associated with stigma, discrimination poverty and exclusion" (Beresford, 2001, p 507). It is not about certain service users and their organisations pushing out other perspectives; rather it is about those who were previously excluded claiming a voice and exercising control over their own welfare. Beresford argues that the populist and limited version of social citizenship that dominates at present can only be properly challenged by fully engaging with welfare service users and allowing their full involvement in policy formulation and implementation.

Echoing Beresford above, Carr (2005) argues that the involvement of welfare service users in the policy process should challenge the status quo. She notes that user involvement implies a participatory notion of citizenship that emphasises marginalised groups asserting their rights to be meaningfully involved in the formulation of policy and practice. It is not simply about being a 'consumer' of welfare services organised and delivered according to dominant professional discourses. Although service user choice and control have become central tenets of health and social care policies over the past 15 years, and the participation of users is now a legal requirement in certain instances, many argue that power differentials continue to exist between service users and the professionals who manage and deliver welfare. User involvement is an established part of New Labour's rhetoric, but as Cowden and Singh argue, the government's is a:

> ... Supermarketized vision of user involvement ... [in which] the language of progressive social movements have been appropriated and become a passenger on the vehicle of welfare retrenchment. (2005, pp 6, 18)

Some user involvement can be little more than window dressing that does nothing to challenge the inequalities that exist between service users and professional providers (Hodge, 2005). Evidence suggests that a 'hierarchy of expertise' continues to exist and that many policy makers and professionals remain resistant to sharing power with service users (Heenan, 2009).

In the past some on the political Left were ready to dismiss citizenship. Today many can see the positive potential of a reformulated concept of social citizenship. Previous discussions have noted the contradiction between the universalist claims made for the citizenship of the PWWS and its exclusive reality for certain individuals within and beyond the borders of the nation state. Contemporary thinkers on the Left have tended to focus on how the universalistic claims of citizenship can be reconciled with the demands of difference so that a more inclusive notion of citizenship can be built. Lister (1998a) outlines two linked ways forward. The first involves developing an idea of 'global citizenship' that draws on human rights discourses and moves beyond traditional concerns that linked enjoyment of full citizenship rights to formal membership of a nation state. Arguably, increased migration across national borders, ecological issues and heightened awareness of the poverty between, and not just within, nations make such national approaches redundant (see Chapter Ten, this volume). The second necessitates the development of a 'differentiated universalism' to underpin citizenship (Lister, 1998a, 2003c) (see Chapter Eleven, this volume, for a fuller consideration).

The preferences of the contemporary social democratic Left in relation to citizenship can be briefly summarised as follows. They prioritise the state provision of welfare rights over individual responsibilities. They have a predisposition in favour of unconditional rights to welfare and look to recognise diverse forms of contribution outside the paid labour market (for example, informal care work), as a valid basis on which to claim full social citizenship rights (Lister, 2003c). They are also inclined to argue that, whenever possible, access to social citizenship should be based on agreed universal definitions of need (Doyal and Gough, 1991) and shared common membership of the human race rather than on issues related to past contribution or desert (Dwyer, 2004a).

The challenge from the New Right

The **New Right's** vision of social citizenship differs greatly from the social democratic approach. Emerging in the late 1960s and early 1970s, the New Right mounted a systematic, and to a certain extent successful, challenge to the collectivist assumptions that underpinned both the PWWS and Marshall's conceptualisation of citizenship, which emphasised universal, state-guaranteed social rights. It is important to stress from the outset that a variety of disparate thinkers are often labelled under a New Right banner, and that the term is convenient shorthand for a range of allied opinions (Faulks, 1998). Drawing on the traditions of both libertarian liberalism (with its emphasis on individual freedom, a 'free' market, limited government and the basic right to property), and social conservatism, which stresses the government's central role in establishing and maintaining a particular moral order, New Right thinkers believe that a reduction of the state's welfare role is both positive and progressive. They argue that the welfare of citizens will be best served by a system that encourages greater individual responsibility in meeting welfare needs, with only a limited, often highly conditional, residual role reserved for the state (Dwyer, 2000a). Antagonistic towards the very idea of social rights, only civil and political rights are regarded as essential to citizenship status (Plant, 1992; Bellamy and Greenaway, 1995; Pratt, 1997). The New Right believe that there is a need to reassert individual/familial responsibility when meeting welfare needs; indeed, an emphasis on such responsibilities overrides any concern to promote or protect social rights as part of a common citizenship status.

The New Right see inequality as an acceptable and inevitable part of the human condition, and any attempt to try to promote common purpose and/or reduce inequality via a comprehensive system of social rights is seen as an impossible and flawed dream. In line with the libertarian liberal thinking discussed in Chapter Two, individual citizens are believed to hold competing and differing welfare preferences and wants. Supporters of the welfare state fail to understand human nature, that is, that people are essentially individualistic, self-interested, rational actors. The only fair social order is created spontaneously by the 'invisible hand' of the market. Markets provide just outcomes and each individual reaps the rewards that their talents and efforts deserve.

As George and Wilding (1994) note, the New Right become hostile, suspicious and anxious when the state attempts to deliver a particular brand of social justice through the collective provision of welfare. The resultant welfare state is seen as a threat to the freedom of individual citizens who, as actors within a market economy, should decide on how to meet their welfare needs. This ideological critique of state welfare from the New Right is combined with a belief that extensive social rights undermine rather than enhance the proper functioning of society. They regard the welfare state to be: inefficient and ineffective (in that it serves the interests of bureaucrats and professionals rather than meeting the needs of its clients); economically damaging (because it reduces the ability of the free market to deliver wealth and demands high levels of taxation); socially damaging (in creating and encouraging an 'underclass' characterised by 'feckless' behaviour and long-term passive dependency on the state); and also politically damaging (in that a government's role is reduced to the management of the self-interested rights claims of competing interest groups, rather than the pursuit of its primary purpose of promoting the common good) (George and Wilding, 1994). The welfare state is thus viewed as a major cause of, rather than a solution to, contemporary Western society's social and economic problems. Social democratic attempts to advance a measure of equality through the promotion and protection of social rights is viewed as encouraging welfare dependency rather than alleviating poverty. The work of two influential US scholars highlight the New Right solutions to this problem of dependency.

Murray, Mead and the 'underclass': one problem, two solutions

In outlining the development of an 'underclass' in Western societies the accounts of **Charles Murray** (1984, 1994, 1996a, 1996b, 1999) and **Lawrence M. Mead** (1982, 1986, 1997a, 1997b, 1997c) are built on similar assumptions (Hill, 1992, 1994; Deacon, 1994, 1997a). First, that the right to extensive, state-funded welfare entitlements creates and reproduces an 'underclass' of welfare dependants. Second, that it is dysfunctional behaviour rather than economic inequality that distinguishes the 'underclass' from mainstream society. Murray and Mead take an explicitly moral stance by highlighting and condemning aspects of that behaviour and, likewise, both commentators see its solution in the fundamental reform of social welfare (Hill, 1992). Although their assumptions about the causes and effects of the 'underclass' phenomenon are similar, they offer differing solutions.

Murray is keen to state that, "the underclass does not refer to a degree of poverty, but to a type of poverty" (1996a, p 23). The 'underclass' is not defined by reference to a disadvantaged financial condition but in terms of common patterns of behaviour that violate respectable norms. Parallelling Victorian distinctions between the deserving and undeserving poor (see the discussion of A.H. Marshall in Chapter Three), Murray outlines the emergence of a British 'underclass' (that shares similar characteristics to its US counterpart), a distinct population characterised by three important dimensions: a disproportionate number of illegitimate children, a high incidence of (violent) criminal activity and a lack of employment in able-bodied males. This group is vividly portrayed as a real threat to civilised society whose standards it refuses to accept (see *Box 4.3*).

Arguing that the right to benefit on the simple demonstration of need has led to welfare dependency and, therefore, is in itself constitutive of much ensuing poverty, Murray's solution (*Box 4.3*) is simple: end all cash benefits except for short-term unemployment insurance payments. State welfare could then be replaced with locally administered relief subject to the terms and conditions of the local community. The lack of an adequate state-guaranteed minimum to fall back on would force individuals to be self-reliant once again and simultaneously "reinforce the work norms, family authority and individual responsibility" (Hill, 1992, p 117) necessary to counter the subculture of the 'underclass'.

Whereas Murray would do away with state welfare to remove dependency, Mead attempts to use it to reform the character of the poor by establishing a principle of conditionality. In contrast with some of the New Right, Mead (1982, 1997a, 1997b, 1997c) consistently expresses the view that his primary concern is not with the economic cost of state welfare, but with the behaviour that it engenders in the separate 'underclass' that is either unwilling or unable to work. For Mead, however, it is not simply the existence of social rights in the form of state benefits that is the problem, but the fact that they are unconditional, that is, that the state offers support but expects little in return. Mead's solution is to enforce responsible behaviour. In short, state welfare rights should be dependent on recipients accepting attendant state-defined work responsibilities (see *Box 4.3*).

Mead (1997b) argues that not only is conditionality both generally popular and functional but also that the imposition of compulsory work conditions for the recipients of state benefit effectively re-establishes their right to be regarded as citizens. He believes that previously permissive welfare regimes and the unconditional nature of their benefits marked out the poor as recipients of state charity rather than as citizens entitled to state support in return for their acceptance of specified responsibilities. Conditionality thus restores their right to equal citizenship status because, as Mead has previously stated, "only those who bear obligations can truly appropriate their rights" (Mead, 1986, p 257). A case for recipients of social welfare to voluntarily accept their obligations could of course be made, but Mead has rejected this as unlikely to succeed. Those most in need of employment are, as Deacon (1997b) reminds us, regarded by Mead as "dutiful but defeated" (Mead, 1982, p 133); in such circumstances Mead sees it as necessary for the state to use paternalistic authority to compel individuals to return to the labour market.

UK Conservatism and welfare policy 1979–97

The importance of Murray and Mead's common emphasis on the value of individuals largely assuming responsibility for their own welfare via paid employment should not be overlooked. This reaffirmation by New Right thinkers of the desirability of self-help and the view that the state should have a greatly reduced welfare role have been influential in challenging, both in principle and in practice, the existence of an extensive social rights element within citizenship. In Britain, to a certain extent, such views found a political expression in the legislative programmes of the Thatcher and Major governments.

Successive Conservative administrations of the 1980s and the 1990s sought to redefine social citizenship by drawing on New Right agendas. The Thatcherite vision for welfare was very different from the one advocated by Marshall and Titmuss. Policies sought to diminish the state's welfare role, reduce or at least contain public welfare expenditure, challenge the power of the welfare state professions, promote a residual welfare state and introduce quasi-markets (King, 1987; Le Grand and Bartlett, 1993; Clarke, 1996; George and Miller, 1996; Le Grand, 1997; Wilding, 1997). The clear endorsement of conditionality is also apparent. The establishment of the Child Support Agency (1993), extensions to the conditions attached to unemployment benefits (for example, the 1995 Jobseekers Act) and the

---

Box 4.3: Murray and Mead: solving the problem of the 'underclass'

Defining an 'underclass'

Britain has a growing population of working-aged, healthy people who live in a different world from other Britons, who are raising their children to live in it, and whose values are now contaminating the life of entire neighbourhoods, which is one of the most insidious aspects of the phenomenon, for neighbours who don't share those values cannot isolate themselves. There are many ways to identify an underclass. I will concentrate on three phenomena that have turned out to be early warning signals in the United States: illegitimacy, violent crime and drop out from the labour force.

Source: Murray (1996a, p 25)

Murray's solution: the removal of social rights

We have available to us a program that would convert a large proportion of the younger generation of hardcore unemployed into steady workers making a living wage. The same program would drastically reduce births to single teenage girls. It would reverse the trend line in the break up of poor families. It would measurably increase the upward socio-economic mobility of poor families. These improvements would affect some millions of persons.... The proposed program, our final and most ambitious thought experiment, consists of scrapping the entire federal welfare and income structure for working-aged persons, including AFDC, Medicaid, Food Stamps, Unemployment Insurance, Worker's Compensation, subsidized housing, disability insurance and the rest. It would leave the working aged person with no recourse whatsoever except the job market, family members, friends, and locally funded services. It is the Alexandrian solution: cut the knot, for there is no way to untie it.

Source: Murray (1994, pp 227-80)

Mead's solution: enforce conditionality

The troubling behaviour and condition of disadvantage is due to social programs on which so many are dependent.... Government must now *obligate* [welfare] program recipients to work rather than just entice them. What is obligatory cannot simply be offered as choice – it has to be enforced by sanctions, in this case the loss of welfare grant.

Source: Mead (1982, pp 22, 28)

1996 Housing Act all illustrate that the Conservatives were willing to make welfare rights conditional on individuals accepting certain patterns of behaviour of additional responsibilities (Dwyer, 1998, 2000a). Two other aspects of Conservative welfare policy that fit with New Right sentiments – consumerism and 'active citizenship' – also require brief discussion.

In Chapter One (this volume) it was noted that citizenship was one way of imagining the link between the individual and the state. Given their aversion to the very notion of social citizenship, those on the Right have also been influential in pushing an alternative consumerist approach to welfare provision. As Clarke notes:

> Consumers are economic actors who get to choose and their choices are co-ordinated by the market in ways that squeeze out inefficient providers and reward efficient ones. (1998, p 17)

Citizens with rights to welfare derived from a common status are displaced. Instead, individuals become customers/clients of welfare services. The appeal to individual preferences and welfare markets fits well with the New Right vision. One outcome of this type of approach in the UK was the Conservative's 'Citizens' Charter' initiatives introduced by Margaret Thatcher's successor John Major. In spite of their name, such charters have little to do with the extension of welfare rights; they allude instead to a weaker set of largely unenforceable minimum service standards for welfare institutions (Hill, 1994; Bellamy and Greenaway, 1995). This 'consumers-of-welfare' idea certainly appeals to the New Right, but interestingly, some on the Left also see the potential benefits of such an approach (see Clarke, 1998) and, arguably, New Labour's welfare reforms are based around the notion of the 'citizen-consumer' (Needham, 2003). However, a basic problem remains for this consumerist organisation of public welfare. While it is possible to create effective welfare markets, the ability of those in poverty to exercise any real choice is constrained by their lack of material wealth.

UK Conservatives were also keen to endorse the idea of the *active citizen*. This active citizen is also one who recognises that s/he must accept, first and foremost, responsibility for his/her own (and their family's) welfare. Beyond this any philanthropic actions (the public giving of private time and money) that they engage in within the wider community are seen as enhancing that individual's right to claim their citizen status. Through involvement in charitable and voluntary work the active citizen is defined as individually and socially responsible, while also meeting the welfare needs of the less fortunate (Hurd, 1988; Thatcher, 1988; Kearns, 1992; Meikle, 1994; Oliver and Heater, 1994; Bellamy and Greenaway, 1995). Recourse to increasingly limited state provision is viewed as a last resort, as a system of welfare that was previously based on institutionally situated welfare rights is superseded by one centred around individual responsibility and charitable giving.

A principal argument of the New Right is that the state provision of welfare services and the gradual expansion of the state's role from the 1950s onwards had driven up public expenditure to a point where the costs of state welfare interfered with the successful operation of a free market economy. Allied to this is the belief that welfare rights undermine individual/familial responsibility and nurture the development of a welfare-dependent 'underclass' (Alcock, 1996). The New Right have been influential in outlining why a proliferation of welfare rights may be damaging to individuals and the wider society. A strong enmity towards state provision in general, and unconditional social rights in particular, can be detected, concerns that the new communitarian thinkers discussed next also share.

New communitarianism: a latent hostility to social rights?

New communitarian writers draw on the philosophical critique of liberalism outlined in Chapter Two. They reject the rights-based individualism central to the liberal vision as flawed, and stress instead the importance of obligation, loyalty to community and conformity to shared values and norms in which individuals are nurtured and developed. Deacon (2002) notes that four core values can be ascribed to communitarian thinking in relation to welfare. First and foremost, there is an assertion that it is both desirable and proper that access to collectively provided welfare benefits and services should be conditional on individuals accepting communally defined obligations. A reciprocal relationship between welfare rights and responsibilities is taken for granted. Second, there is a belief that it is right and proper for government to establish popular support for the communitarian reform of welfare through a politics of popular persuasion. Third, new communitarians are comfortable with the idea that social policy should seek to promote a particular moral framework and judge the actions of individual citizens. For, as Deacon states, "above all, communitarian welfare would not take people as it found them but would try to change them" (2002, p 76).

Although new communitarianism is a broad church, with a range of opinions (interested readers should refer to debates in Sacks, 1997; Etzioni, 1998; Tam, 1998; Deacon, 2002), the works of Selbourne (1994) and Etzioni (1995, 1997) illustrate some common concerns of new communitarian writers that have implications for social citizenship. Both commentators identify a crisis within Western society, a crisis caused primarily by the dominance of individualistic liberal philosophy and the expansion of unconditional rights. In turn, each outlines a solution that places great emphasis on the role of ordered communities and on individuals, recognising the importance of their obligations and duties to the communities in which they are situated. Importantly, both Selbourne and Etzioni appear to view extensive state welfare provision as undermining the establishment of a 'good' society in that it removes duties of care from, in their view, the proper realm of individuals, families, voluntary associations and local communities.

Selbourne: the primacy of duty over rights

Selbourne (1994) concludes that a proliferation of 'dutiless rights' has led to a malaise that strikes at the heart of modern citizenship and threatens social cohesion. The way to halt this demise is to assert the primacy of a 'principle of duty' over and above the idea of rights, particularly in the social sphere. Rights to public welfare are seen here as 'generally lesser order entitlements' to privileges and benefits, which do not possess, nor should be afforded, similar legal status to civil and political rights. Furthermore, he holds that "notions of egalitarian entitlement to such 'rights' *which owe nothing to the individual's desert or merits*" (Selbourne, 1994, p 60; original emphasis) undermine the moral basis of the civic order. For these reasons Selbourne argues that publicly provided welfare benefits and services should not be viewed as part of the package of rights that inform a universally held status of 'citizen' but that they should be seen as potential privileges that a society may bestow on dutiful members who meet their personal responsibilities and behave in a manner deemed appropriate by the wider community. In short, what Marshall famously referred to as social 'rights' are nothing of the sort – they are merely highly conditional entitlements (cf Dwyer, 2004b). Individual responsibility and duty are clearly identified as having primary importance over and above rights. Selbourne is clear that those who refuse to accept the demands of the prevailing civic order shall be subject to sanctions and, ultimately, that they have no right to enjoy any of the social or material benefits that membership of a particular community may bring (*Box 4.4*). It is certainly a robust version of citizenship that makes demands on citizens to participate in the formulation of, and to simultaneously uphold, the rules of their community. In many respects it is a contemporary vision of the good society that draws heavily on the civic republican ideals outlined in Chapter Two.

> ## Box 4.4: Selbourne: a modern civic republicanism?
>
> **The primacy of the 'principle of duty'**
> The principle of duty, the sovereign ethical principle of the civic order, demands both general and particular duties of the citizen – to himself [sic], to his fellows, and to the civic order as a whole – and, likewise, general and particular duties of the civic order and of its instrument the state, to its members.... Such duties ... have ethical precedence over the rights, benefits, and privileges with which the citizen is vested as a member of such civic order; and, fulfilled, signify that the individual who fulfils them is playing his part. (p 147)
>
> **The endorsement of sanctions**
> Compulsion and deprivation in defence of the civic order may take many forms, including ordering the citizen to do certain things ... and the taking away of certain things from the citizen, including his [sic] liberty, but also his privileges, benefits, licences, and rights, and even citizenship itself. (p 256)
>
> *Source:* Selbourne (1994)

Etzioni's limited vision of social citizenship

The best-known advocate of new communitarianism is **Amitai Etzioni** (1995, 1997), who claims support from across the Left–Right spectrum of mainstream British and US politics. Central to his approach is a call for the restoration of the 'correct' balance between rights and responsibilities. For Etzioni, a functional communitarian community is dependent on achieving the correct balance between the two key components of *individual autonomy* (that is, rights) and the *common good* (an agreed order that recognises the importance of shared responsibilities). In stating, "Respect and uphold society's moral order as you would have society respect and uphold your autonomy" (1997, p xviii), Etzioni's 'new golden rule' essentially asserts that neither should be privileged over the other. For Etzioni (1997), the establishment of a good society rests on a general acceptance of shared core values that reflect this principle. The formulation of a persuasive culture of "voluntary compliance" (Etzioni, 1997, p 13) that sets out a particular moral environment in which certain actions or behaviours are held to be both individually and communally acceptable or unacceptable is, according to Etzioni, the best way for a community to reach agreement about the correct balance between rights and responsibilities. The right for local communities to develop a collective moral voice and 'chastise' those who violate communally defined norms is seen as a positive response to selfish individual behaviour. While the individual autonomy of community members is recognised as important, any such autonomy is conditional on individuals first of all respecting the rules of the communities that they inhabit (Heron and Dwyer, 1999).

In stating clearly that "It follows that we must shore up our moral foundations to allow markets, governments and society to work properly again" (1995, p 25), Etzioni's priorities surface; his approach is concerned with moral regeneration rather than material redistribution. In what amounts to a hierarchy of self-help, he argues that:

> First people have a moral responsibility to help themselves the best they can. The second line of responsibility lies with those closest to the person including kin, friends, neighbours and other community members. (Etzioni, 1995, p 144)

Lip service is paid to the ethic of helping less fortunate community members, but at a national level any form of social right to state-funded welfare or entitlement is extremely restricted. In his 1995 account national unemployment insurance appeared to be the limit of any social rights that Etzioni envisaged. In his later work it is clear that he approves of the state agreeing to provide only a minimal safety net of welfare via the provision of 'social basics'. Society has a limited responsibility to provide welfare but only at a basic level. Furthermore, Etzioni's endorsement of 'community jobs' and his acceptance that these may be organised along workfare principles shows a similar comfort with sanctions that conditionality implies. In spite of his previously declared preference for persuading individuals of the virtue of this approach he is obviously not adverse to compelling compliance when required (see **Box 4.5**).

Limiting the right to publicly provided social welfare, he argues, lowers financial costs, helps to reduce welfare dependency, and simultaneously helps to restore the balance within welfare away from rights and back towards responsibility. Further investigation illustrates that cutting the tax burden of the affluent citizen is not far from Etzioni's mind. He laments that people today "have to pay the hired hand for what used to be done by the community" (Etzioni, 1995, p 125). The acceptance of progressive taxation as a means for funding social provisions seems to be deemed an inappropriate moral stance for the new communitarians to embrace.

Surprisingly, given the amount of time that they spend criticising libertarian liberalism, new communitarians share much common ground with the New Right in relation to welfare. For both, an endorsement of wider communal welfare responsibilities (to individuals beyond family and other restricted community members), other than charitable giving, appears to be lacking. There is certainly little overt support for a redistribution of social and financial wealth across smaller community or group borders. An endorsement of conditionality as a principle by which to arrange limited public welfare provision and a predilection with moral agendas and particular patterns of behaviour are also common to many New Right and new communitarian thinkers. It is somewhat ironic that two approaches that begin from two fundamentally different philosophical positions ultimately end up endorsing similar stances on public welfare.

Box 4.5: Etzioni's new communitarianism and welfare

Rights balanced with responsibilities
Communitarians call to restore civic virtues, for people to live up to their responsibilities and not merely focus on their entitlements and to shore up the moral foundations of society.

Source: Etzioni (1995, p ix)

Community jobs
Public funds might be allocated (under a workfare program to replace part of welfare, for example) to schools, hospitals, public libraries, environmental protection agencies and other institutions, to hire people to carry out work which these institutions would otherwise not be able to afford. (p 82)

Social basics
One can reduce social costs, public expenditures, and dependency by lowering the safety nets without removing them. Psychological security does not rely so much on the specific level of support available if a person is out of work, disabled or sick, as on the firm conviction that they and their children will receive some basic help; that they will not be cast into the street, without medical assistance or basic provisions. (p 83)

Source: Etzioni (1997)

Against a backdrop of perceived social crisis (blamed largely on a sense of moral decay) the appeal of new communitarianism rests on the assumption that the restoration of strong community at all levels (family, neighbourhood and nation state) will restore a crumbling social fabric. Egalitarian considerations are not a central concern of the social citizenship being mapped out by the new communitarians. There appears to be a latent hostility to the idea that citizens may possess social rights as an integral part of their citizenship status. Where limited social provisions are available they are routinely conditional, and consideration of a citizen's past contribution is often central to decisions about whether or not an individual has a legitimate claim to collective support.

New Labour: a 'third way' for social citizenship

In May 1997 a New Labour government was returned to power, ending 18 years of Conservative administration. Much of the subsequent rhetoric that emanated from the new government emphasised a break with the past. The theme presented was very much 'out with the old, in with the new', and New Labour was very keen to present its welfare reforms as new and radical initiatives that were part of a wider programme of 'third way' politics (Blair, 1998; Darling, 1998; DSS, 1998a). This new politics simultaneously rejected what it regarded as the Old Left approach to social citizenship (that is, the social democracy of Titmuss and Marshall, typified by state control, high taxation and public spending), and the New Right approach with its hostility to collective forms of welfare. Both the then Prime Minister, Tony Blair and the sociologist, Anthony Giddens, looked to replace the polarised politics of the past with a 'third way' built around certain core values (see **Box 4.6**).

In setting out its principles for welfare reform in the 1998 Green Paper, *New ambitions for our country: A new contract for welfare* (DSS, 1998a), the government's message was clear, that they had inherited an ineffectual and wasteful welfare state which had failed to maximise its own potential and the capabilities of those who used it:

> The welfare system is a proud creation. But reform is essential if we are to realise our vision of a modern nation and a decent and fair society. Through our proposals we will aim to break the cycle of dependency and insecurity and empower all citizens to lead a dignified and fulfilling life. We need a new 'contract' between citizen and state, with rights matched with responsibilities. We will rebuild the welfare state around a work ethic: work for those who can: security for those who cannot. (DSS, 1998a, p 1)

New Labour obviously saw reform as essential if welfare was to meet the needs of citizens in the future. The quotation also highlights four linked themes that Powell (1999) has identified as central to New Labour's approach to welfare reform and the kind of social citizenship that they advocated. First, the new welfare state must be an active and preventative welfare state. Successive Labour administrations have promoted an active welfare system in which people are encouraged, or, as some would argue, compelled to change their behaviour and attempt to improve themselves rather than passively sitting back and expecting state benefits to meet their needs. Second, as far as New Labour is concerned, work was the best form of welfare for any individual, and paid work was central to New Labour's welfare agenda. Reform should concentrate on 'making work pay' through a system that encouraged and cajoled people back into the PLM via a combination of carrots (for example, tax credits, the minimum wage, support with childcare costs), and sticks (that is, benefit sanctions for those who refuse to work). This brings us on to the third theme, that rights come with responsibilities. Influenced by new communitarian thinking (Driver and Martell, 1997; Heron and Dwyer, 1999; Heron, 2001; Prideaux, 2001, 2003; Deacon, 2002), a reciprocal relationship between welfare rights and

---

Box 4.6: A 'third way' for welfare

The Third Way in welfare is clear: not to dismantle it [the welfare state]; or to protect it unchanged; but to reform it radically – taking its core values and applying them to the modern world.

Source: Blair (1999, p 12) (page number refers to a reproduction of the speech in Walker, 1999)

One might suggest as a prime motto for new politics, *no rights without responsibilities*. Government has a whole cluster of responsibilities for its citizens and others, including the protection of the vulnerable. Old style social democracy, however, was inclined to treat rights as unconditional claims. With expanding individualism should come an extension of individual obligations. Unemployment benefits, for example, should carry the obligation to look actively for work, and it is up to governments to ensure that welfare systems do not discourage active search. As an ethical principle, 'no rights without responsibilities' must apply not only to welfare recipients, but to everyone. It is highly important for social democrats to stress this, because otherwise the precept can be held to apply only to the poor or to the needy – as tends to be the case with the political right.

Source: Giddens (1998, pp 65-6)

Core values of the third way

Blair: Equal worth, Opportunity for all, Responsibility, Community.
Giddens: Equality, Protection of the vulnerable, Freedom as autonomy, No rights without responsibility.

Source: Powell (1999)

attendant responsibilities was at the heart of New Labour's welfare policy. Finally, New Labour was adamant that a third way welfare state should concentrate on redistribution of opportunities rather than income (Lister, 1998b).

New Labour and social citizenship

Although the language of the third way has now largely been sidelined, a specific notion of citizenship, which builds on the four core themes noted above, has long informed New Labour's approach:

> A modern notion of citizenship gives rights but demands obligations, shows respect but wants it back, grants opportunity but insists on responsibility. So the purpose of economic and social policy should be to extend opportunity, to remove the underlying causes of social alienation. But it should also take tough measures to ensure that the chances are taken up. (quoted in Blair, 1996, p 218)

The government was also willing to accept a pragmatic role for markets in the provision of public welfare (Driver and Martell, 1998; Oppenheim, 1999), and it expected those citizens with adequate means to assume a greater level of responsibility for their own welfare, particularly with regard to pensions and care in old age (DSS, 1998a, 1998b; Powell, 1999, 2000). New Labour's 'new politics' suggested that in relation to welfare the promotion of a particular type of moral community in which citizens earned access to their social rights through a combination of hard work, responsible behaviour and personal contribution became the primary concern (Darling, 1998; Deacon, 1998; DSS, 1998a; Dwyer, 1998, 2000a; see also the 1999 Welfare Reform and Pensions Act). In short, New Labour used its welfare reform agenda in an instrumental way to persuade citizens of the superiority of a citizenship perspective that emphasised notions of individual and mutual responsibilities rather than individual rights.

The provision of state benefits, although seen as important for a minority who were unable to work, seems to have become an issue of secondary consideration, behind attempts to ensure the highest level of labour market participation. New Labour accepted that the state should assume a leading role in the provision of training and work opportunities but in return it expected citizens to take up those opportunities and contribute to both their own and society's well-being (Page, 1997); or alternatively to accept that they had little right to expect support from the national community in the form of welfare. In this way New Labour clearly endorsed social rights based on a principle of mutual responsibility rather than agreed definitions of need.

Early government rhetoric (Blair, 2000; Labour Party, 2000), the establishment and expansion of the various 'New Deals' (see Blunkett, 1998; Finn, 1998; Oppenheim, 1999) and policies, for example the necessity for all new benefit claimants to attend an advisory interview before receiving benefits and plans to impose benefit sanctions on those claimants who broke court orders (Brindle, 1999; Blair, 2000), indicate an approval in principle and practice that social security rights came with attendant responsibilities (see also **Box 5.3** in Chapter Five). While the early New Labour administrations continued to state that they would not force lone parents with young children or disabled people to accept jobs or training, it is clear that ultimately they believed that such individuals had a responsibility to enter paid employment if it was at all possible (Smith, 1999; Hyde, 2000).

All three Labour governments under the leadership of both Blair and Brown have built on the agenda of their Conservative predecessors by extending the reach of conditionality. Where previously the largely unconditional rights to benefit of lone parents and disabled people were recognised (either because, as lone parents, they were seen as making socially valid contributions as carers, or because the labour inactivity of disabled people was seen as a consequence of individual impairment or illness), New Labour have challenged their exemption from participation in the PLM (Trickey and Walker, 2001).

More recent developments further illustrate New Labour's commitment to extending the reach of conditionality to encompass groups that in the past, for various reasons, were regarded as having legitimate claims to social welfare benefits. In March 2007 the Secretary of State for Work and Pensions, John Hutton, re-endorsed the "fundamental principle of rights and responsibilities; of something for something" and denounced condition-free systems of welfare as exclusive (2007, p 9). Similarly, the Freud Report (2007), established by the government to review welfare reform and to consider further ways of reducing work inactivity, noted:

> The government has made a commitment to rights and responsibilities a central feature of policy.... The report recommends maintaining the current regime for the unemployed, introducing stronger conditionality in line with the Jobseeker's Allowance for lone parents with progressively younger children and moving to deliver conditionality for other groups (including people already on incapacity benefits).

Arguing for a 'strengthened framework' that 'rebalances the system' away from unconditional welfare, Freud believes that a clear consensus has now emerged (in the minds of public and politicians alike), whereby those who are supported to return to work must accept greater responsibility to help themselves or tolerate the possibility of benefit sanctions. Freud recommends an increase in the frequency of state interventions and the extension of the rights and responsibilities agenda to cover all economically inactive benefit recipients in future. This would include lone parents, many people with impairments, the partners of benefit claimants and those people with complex needs due to 'chaotic lifestyles'.

Within the social housing sector, the government has also used its legislative powers to build on its Conservative predecessor's attempts (1996 Housing Act) to deal with tenants and citizens who do not behave responsibly. What should not be overlooked is that those who refuse to accept the rules of membership as laid down by the government (that is, assume paid work responsibilities, behave in a reasonable manner) will be deemed 'undeserving' of full welfare rights. New Labour believed that it was reasonable to treat such individuals as third-rate welfare subjects dependent on meagre, strictly controlled and residual means-tested benefits (Hewitt, 2000).

New Labour endorsed and expanded the approach of their predecessors and looked to limit the rights of citizens engaged in irresponsible behaviour. A range of instruments is now available to social landlords and the exclusion of nuisance neighbours via the denial of a tenancy is an established part of policy. Definitions of anti-social behaviour encompass a wide range of conduct, for example children's play annoying neighbours, serious criminal activity, racial harassment, violent attack (Flint, 2002). The linking of rights to responsible behaviour is far from straightforward. Nonetheless, a series of Acts and initiatives clearly indicate New Labour's sustained enthusiasm for advancing a rights/responsibilities agenda in managing the problematic behaviour of certain citizens (for example, 2003 Anti-Social Behaviour Act; 2003 Criminal Justice Act). The 'personalisation' of rights and responsibilities has also been identified as one of the five guiding principles for those citizens who are identified as suffering multiple disadvantages (SETF, 2007). While the government promises individualised support packages to provide opportunities, and it recognises that a range of issues (for example, a lack of basic skills, mental health problems, substance misuse, debt and homelessness) may play a part in people's lives, the message is again clear:

> [Where] contact with services is instead frequently driven by problematic behaviour resulting from their chaotic lives – such as anti-social behaviour, criminality and poor parenting ... [the government is willing to apply tough] ... sanctions such as

prison, loss of tenancy and possible removal of children. (SETF, 2007, p 74)

In short, the principle of conditionality is now being applied across a wide range of UK welfare policy areas and to increasing numbers of people. See ***Box 5.3*** in the next chapter for further details and also Dwyer (2008) for fuller discussions.

After New Labour: a 'New Conservatism'?

Early opinion polls indicate that a Conservative government is the most likely outcome in the forthcoming UK general election in 2010. It is therefore important to explore the kind of social citizenship envisaged, what some have labelled the 'New Conservatism' (Cruddas and Rutherford, 2008a), which is currently being mapped out under the leadership of David Cameron. In moves that echo New Labour's in the late 1990s, the Conservative Party is keen to present itself as offering a new radical approach to welfare reform and as a viable alternative to what it considers to be a largely discredited and failing New Labour administration (Conservative Party, 2008b). Rhetorically, at least, the Conservatives are also keen to disassociate themselves from the economic individualism favoured by the New Right that was a central ideological foundation of Margaret Thatcher's governments. Indeed, with more than a nod towards Mrs Thatcher's famous quote that "there is no such thing as society" (Thatcher, 1988), Cameron has stated "there is such a thing as society, it is just not the same thing as the state" (2009, p 2).

Political rhetoric aside, such statements enable the contemporary Conservative leadership to place some distance between themselves and the governments of the 1980s and, simultaneously, create the space to draw on the New Right's long-term antagonism towards the state playing a key role in the provision of social welfare to citizens (Lawson, 2008).

Whereas Thatcherism was once bold in tackling the economic problems of British society, advocates of the New Conservatism see their key task as tackling the social breakdown that is seen as endemic in many communities. It is argued that a revolution in social policy is now required to match the economic transformation under the last Conservative administrations (Conservative Party, 2008b; Letwin, 2008).

The policy documents and political speeches emerging from the Conservative Party consistently portray British society as in the midst of a social crisis. "Poverty, crime, social disorder, deprivation and a lack of common decency blights far too many of our communities, making them grim and joyless places to live" (Conservative Party, 2008b, p 1). Drawing on an analysis that explicitly identifies a dysfunctional 'underclass' (see Duncan Smith, 2007), more recently Cameron (2009) has spoken of Britain's 'dark side', of sink estates characterised by broken homes and high levels of worklessness, benefit dependency and addiction. This leads Prideaux (2009) to conclude that, on the one level, this Conservatism is little more than a rehash of Charles Murray's idea that extensive state welfare helps to promote a feckless, idle, welfare-dependent underclass (see the earlier discussion in this chapter). Others see something more substantial and argue that the Conservatives have embarked on "a serious attempt to define a new communitarian politics of the right" (Cruddas and Rutherford, 2008a, introductory note), by drawing on the longstanding philosophical tradition of 'one nation Toryism' that has long been advocated by less right-wing elements of the Conservative Party.

Unsurprisingly, many policy documents begin by setting out an extensive and detailed critique of Labour's record in power, particularly in relation to ensuring 'inactive' citizens return to the PLM (Duncan Smith, 2007; Conservative Party, 2008a, 2008b, 2009). A key question remains, however: what are the central elements of the Conservative Party's 'radical' plans for their welfare reform and how different are they from their New Labour predecessors? One area where there appears to be a genuine difference in emphasis is in the extent to which the state will play a direct role in delivering welfare rights and services to citizens in the future. The Right's antipathy towards big government (that is, the state) remains a strong feature of the Conservatives' plans. This old theme is repackaged under a wider appeal for a new politics, suited to the 'post-bureaucratic' age, which is built on individual responsibility rather than collective rights to welfare. "It is all about everyone taking responsibility. The more that we do as a society the less we will need government to do" (Cameron, 2009, p 7).

Duncan Smith's call for a 'new welfare society' is a long way from the post-war welfare society as outlined by Walters (1997) in which the state played a fundamental role (see Chapter Eleven, this volume for a full discussion); rather it is a vision in which welfare is delivered 'beyond the state' by more local voluntary and community sector (VCS) organisations. Top-down, state-led, welfare interventions are identified as promoting welfare dependency among the very communities they were meant to help:

> We believe it is time for an entirely new welfare system, based on an entirely new culture of responsibility, not the state taking responsibility away from people and making them dependent, but people and communities taking responsibility for themselves and achieving the success and satisfaction of independence. (Conservative Party, 2008a, p 9)

Welfare in the post-bureaucratic age is to be driven by a vibrant civil society. Individual volunteers and the VCS are to play a key role in mending broken Britain and in alleviating poverty and social exclusion (Conservative Party, 2008c). New Labour governments have, of course, been more than willing to promote a mixed economy for the delivery of welfare in which the voluntary and private sectors participate as part of 'the social investment state' (rf Dobrowolsky and Lister, 2008, for fuller discussions). However, Pennycook argues that the Conservatives plan to go a step further. They are not looking for the VCS to be a welfare partner of the state but rather a replacement for it:

> The New Conservatives are willing to contemplate undermining the very foundations of fair and accountable collective provision. They are willing to contemplate it because, despite protestations to the contrary, their agenda is driven by ideology and not by a genuine concern for the most disadvantaged in our society. In reality their vision of civil society as panacea represents nothing more than an attempt to return Britain to a Victorian social model in which a haphazard network of philanthropic and private organisations were left to cope – tragically – with acute social dilemmas. Whatever else the experience of state governance in the twentieth century teaches us, it is certainly not that we should return to the nineteenth. (Pennycook, 2008, p 53)

This kind of back to the future philanthropic approach resonates strongly with the active citizenship favoured by the last Conservative governments. However, Pennycook clearly believes that the state must continue to play an important role in meeting the social needs of its citizens and that it is not viable to build future welfare reform around charitable provision for the poor, and presumably, private welfare for the rich.

While differences may exist between the New Conservatives and New Labour on the state's welfare role, both are in agreement about two key issues. First, that paid work is the best form of welfare for the vast majority of people. Second, that rights to social welfare benefits for those who are not in paid employment (including unemployed people, lone parents and many disabled people) should be linked to an individual claimant's responsibility to actively seek work and/or retrain in order to enhance their future opportunities in the PLM. Conditionality is a non-negotiable principle at the heart of the Conservatives' welfare proposals. Those deemed capable of work who refuse to take up work or training options will face sanctions and a reduction or loss of benefit (Dwyer, 2008). In his 2007

Conservative Party Conference speech, David Cameron made explicit reference to the tough welfare-to-work programmes in Wisconsin, US, and stated that those who refuse 'fair' work should be denied rights to welfare. In moves that mirror the government's recent reforms, private companies are also set to play a key role in Conservative plans to activate Incapacity Benefit claimants (Revill, 2008). The key elements of the Conservative Party's plans for increasing conditionality, should they win the election in 2010, are laid out in *Box 4.7*.

The most recent and worked-through account of the welfare reforms envisaged by the Conservatives is outlined in *Get Britain working* (Conservative Party, 2009). Drawing on ideas from Lord Freud, who has previously recommended extending conditionality when advising the New Labour government (see Freud, 2007), the Conservatives are proposing that all out of work benefit claimants (including Incapacity Benefit recipients and lone parents) should be subject to a single integrated 'work programme'. This promises quicker access to personalised support (delivered by private and voluntary sector providers) to help claimants get back into work; claimants who refuse to take up training offers will be subject to benefit sanctions. Reiterating the view that many who claim disability allowances do so unnecessarily, the Conservatives promise more rigorous medical tests to ascertain an individual's capability for paid work. The document also warns that they intend to "reduce payments to those who should not be receiving incapacity benefits" (Conservative Party, 2009), a move that may involve cutting the benefit payments for over half a million Incapacity Benefit claimants by £25 per week.

At the time of writing it remains to be seen if a supposedly new vision, built on the old virtues of responsibility, family, community and country (Cameron, 2009), in which the Conservatives are keen to evoke a moral panic around the idea of a broken Britain (see Stanley, 2008), will be enough to ensure an election victory. In presenting a Centre-Right 'red Tory' (Blond, 2008) policy agenda, Cameron is hoping that the new brand of socially aware Conservatism he preaches fits with the mood of a British public that appears to be disillusioned with New Labour.

Box 4.7: Conservative welfare reforms: a ringing endorsement for conditionality

Real welfare reform to help make British poverty history

1. *Respect for those who cannot work*
   - Those recipients of Incapacity Benefit who really cannot work will receive continued support and will remain outside the return to work process.

2. *Employment for those who can*
   - Every out of work benefit claimant who is capable of doing so will be expected to work or prepare for work.
   - A comprehensive programme of support for jobseekers, including training, development, work experience and mentoring.
   - Welfare-to-work services to be provided by the private and voluntary sector on a payment by results basis, according to their success in returning people to sustainable employment.

3. *Assessments for those claiming out of work benefits*
   - Rapid assessments for every recipient of out of work benefits – for all new and existing claimants.
   - The assessment process will determine how much welfare-to-work providers are paid for placing a claimant in work.

4. *Limits to claiming out of work benefits*
   - People who refuse to join a return to work programme will lose the right to claim out of work benefits until they do.
   - People who refuse to accept reasonable job offers could lose the right to claim out of work benefits for three years
   - Time limits applied to out of work benefit claims, so that people who claim for more than two years out of three will be required to work for the dole on community work programmes.

Source: Conservative Party (2008a, p 8)

Claimants who are capable of work but who refuse to do so

While the majority of out of work benefit claimants would like to work if they could, there is a significant minority who are playing the system. Equally, there are clearly some people who have managed to use Incapacity Benefit registration as a way of avoiding the greater conditionality and lower cash amounts of Jobseeker's Allowance. Our welfare system has tolerated this kind of abuse for too long, and the Government has done little to clamp down on those that exploit the system. In line with our principles, we will deal robustly with those who can work but who refuse to do so, with tough but fair sanctions and time limits meaning that those who refuse to participate in our welfare programmes or accept reasonable job offers will lose their right to claim out of work benefits.

Source: Conservative Party (2008a, p 24)

Summary

- This chapter has outlined six differing approaches to social citizenship. Some key dimensions of each are summarised in *Table 4.1*.
- Each position outlined is concerned to emphasise a particular approach to welfare provision that reflects a wider political/ideological view about the 'good society' and the part that welfare should play in achieving it.
- Welfare is often as much about advancing certain outcomes or particular patterns of behaviour as it is about meeting needs.
- The social democratic vision of welfare citizenship advanced and supported by T.H. Marshall and R.M. Titmuss as part of the PWWS has been subsequently challenged by a range of thinkers from across the Left–Right and liberal–communitarian divides. The position of each approach discussed in this chapter in relation to these varied political standpoints is illustrated in *Figure 4.1*.
- A number of writers (for example, Walters, 1997; Dwyer, 1998, 2008; Goodin, 2000; Gilbert, 2002) have suggested that a new welfare settlement may be starting to emerge. This issue is considered in more detail in Chapter Eleven, this volume.

Further reading

The book by **O'Brien and Penna (1998)** considers the ideological underpinnings of different approaches to social welfare in an accessible manner, as does **Taylor (2006)**. Part II of **Alcock et al (2008)** provides short introductory chapters on a range of key perspectives on welfare, which are worthy of attention. **Deacon's (2002)** book provides a detailed review of the ideas that helped reshape social citizenship in Britain and the US. **Powell's (2008)** edited collection is a good account of New Labour's changes in welfare policy. **Clarke's (2005)** discussion of the ideas that are central to New Labour's particular interpretation of citizenship is also an interesting and informative read. Readers interested in considering the ideas that underpin the contemporary Conservative Party's approach will find that many policy papers and speeches can be accessed via the **Conservative Party's website** at www.conservatives.com/News/Speeches.aspx or via **The Centre for Social Justice** publications page at www.centreforsocialjustice.org.uk/default.asp?pageref=266

The edited collection by **Cruddas and Rutherford (2008a)**, which critiques the emergent 'New Conservatism' from a Centre-Left perspective, also merits consideration.

Figure 4.1: Typology of approaches to social citizenship in relation to the Left–Right and liberal–communitarian axes

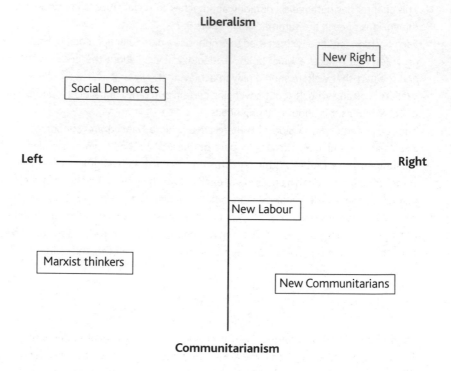

Table 4.1: *Key dimensions of approaches to social citizenship*

Approach	Marxism	Social Democratic	New Labour	New Communitarian	New Right
Central issue for welfare policy	Inequality/ removal of exploitative class relations	Inequality	Welfare dependency	Welfare dependency	Welfare dependency
Primary task for welfare	Radical redistribution of wealth and opportunities	Redistribution of wealth and opportunities	Change individual behaviour	Change individual behaviour	Change individual behaviour
Preferred organisational principles for welfare rights	Universal	Universal Unconditional	Selective Conditional	Selective Conditional	Selective Conditional
Prioritises	Collective economic and social rights	Collective social rights	Individual responsibility	Individual responsibility	Individual responsibility
Preferred provider of welfare	State	State	Individual/market/ state	Individual/market	Individual/market
Basis of claim to public welfare provision	Contribution to national community	Status as a citizen	Prior contribution to PLM	Prior contribution to local community	Prior contribution to PLM

five

Class, poverty, citizenship and welfare

Previous chapters have considered various historical and philosophical/political approaches to social citizenship. The emphasis in this part of the book now changes somewhat to explore relevant debates about *social divisions and citizenship*. This chapter focuses specifically on the issue of class and the closely linked concept of poverty and how they may both impact on citizenship status. T.H. Marshall's seminal account of citizenship was, of course, centrally concerned with how the limited equality of social citizenship would affect or alter ongoing class-based inequalities in society. The following issues are explored and their relevance in relation to class, poverty and welfare are considered:

- defining the problem: basic definitions of class, poverty and social exclusion are offered;
- the advantages and shortcomings of citizenship as a means for meeting the needs of people living in poverty;
- the idea of decommodification;
- the potential and limitations of New Labour's (paid) work-based solution to poverty and social exclusion;
- welfare and social control with a particular focus on the issue of increased conditionality and how this disproportionately affects poor people.

Some definitional issues: class, poverty and social exclusion

Debates about the definition and measurement of class and poverty have a long history within the social sciences. In recent decades, perhaps influenced by academic traditions from Europe, another important concept, *social exclusion*, has also emerged. There is now a vast array of competing literature that offers insights into, and explanations of, the trends and effects of socio-economic differences at local, national and global levels. A consideration of the complexities of such debates is not a primary task of this text. However, before any evaluation of the importance of class, poverty and social exclusion to citizenship can proceed, it is necessary to offer outline definitions of each.

As Giddens' definitions (**Box 5.1**) imply, the unequal and structured distribution of income and wealth is an important aspect of class in contemporary society. In turn these patterns affect distributions of power and opportunities and so impact directly on an individual's social and economic status. The various definitions of poverty offered in **Box 5.1** highlight the fact that poverty remains a highly contested concept that is open to a variety of definitions. This situation is further complicated if the notion of social exclusion is introduced. A comparison of the UN definition of poverty offered in **Box 5.1** with the outlines of social exclusion (**Box 5.2**) highlights the considerable overlap that exists in the way that poverty and social exclusion are defined by various commentators.

For example, it can be stated with some certainty, that in attempting to define relative poverty objectively, Townsend (1979) went some way beyond issues of income and wealth that are traditionally the preoccupation of many poverty theorists, and concerned himself with wider issues of social participation. As Levitas et al's definition in **Box 5.2** shows, social exclusion is a broader concept than poverty that encompasses debates about the ways in which limited material resources may impact negatively on people's lives, but also moves beyond a financial focus to consider how aspects such as "discrimination, chronic ill health, geographical location or cultural identification" (Hills et al, 2002, p 6) may constrain individuals from effective participation in society. However, the continuing importance of poverty in underpinning social exclusion and in particular the deep or severe exclusion noted by Levitas et al needs to be emphasised.

Regardless of the preferred terminology, socio-economic differences organised around class continue to matter greatly. Any talk of a classless society emerging in the UK can be dismissed in light of the mounting evidence of persistent and, indeed, in some cases, unprecedented inequalities (Hills, 1998; Fimister, 2001; Howard et al, 2001). For example, research shows that, while in general terms the health of the nation improved steadily during the past century, inequalities in health between different social classes have 'widened significantly' in the past 20 years (Acheson, 1998; Shaw et al, 2001). In spite of the government's attempt to provide *Opportunity for all* (DSS, 1999), Tony Blair's bold commitment to eradicate child poverty within 20 years (Blair, 1999), and improvements according to certain indicators, the effects of poverty and social exclusion continue to blight the lives of many citizens (see, for example, MacInnes et al, 2009). In light of the continued significance of class, two key questions about citizenship need addressing. First, how does poverty affect an individual's citizenship status? Second, to what extent does social citizenship offer something of worth to those who are living in poverty?

Box 5.1: Defining class and poverty

Class: one of the most frequently used concepts in sociology but there is no agreement about how the notion should be best defined. Most sociologists use the term to refer to socio-economic differences between groups of individuals which create differences in their material prosperity and power.

Class structure: the distribution of classes in society. Classes are based on economic inequalities, and such inequalities are never random.

Source: Giddens (1989, p 581)

Absolute poverty: people are said to be living in absolute poverty when they lack the means for subsistence, that is, they do not have the resources to physically maintain human life, for example, food, shelter, healthcare and so on.

Relative poverty: related to the prevailing standards in the society under consideration at a particular time. Poverty is relative to the standards experienced by other members of society.

Source: Developed from Alcock (1997)

United Nations' definition of poverty: poverty has various manifestations, including lack of income and productive resources to ensure sustainable livelihoods; hunger and malnutrition; ill-health; limited or lack of access to education and other basic services; increased morbidity and mortality from illness; homelessness and inadequate housing; unsafe environments and social discrimination and exclusion. It is also characterised by a lack of participation in decision making and in civil, social and cultural life. It occurs in all countries: as mass poverty in many developing countries, pockets of poverty amid wealth in developed countries, loss of livelihoods as a result of economic recession, sudden poverty as a result of disaster or conflict, the poverty of low-wage workers, and the utter destitution of people who fall outside family support systems, institutions and safety nets.

Source: UN (1995, ch 2, para 19), cited in Howard et al (2001)

Box 5.2: Social exclusion – poverty by another name?

Poverty

The notion of *poverty* is primarily focused on distributional issues: the lack of resources at the disposal of an individual or a household. In contrast, notions such as *social exclusion* focus primarily on relational issues, in other words inadequate social participation, lack of social integration and lack of power.

Source: Room (1995, p 5)

Social exclusion

The term *social exclusion* derives from the idea of a society as a status hierarchy comprising people bound together by rights and obligations that reflect, and are defined with respect to, a shared moral order and can be brought about by many factors, including limited income.

Source: Walker (1995, p 103)

Social exclusion is a complex and multi-dimensional process. It involves the lack or denial of resources, rights, goods and services, and the inability to participate in the normal relationships and activities, available to the majority of people in a society, whether in economic, social, cultural or political arenas. It affects both the quality of life of individuals and the equity and cohesion of society as a whole.

'Social exclusion' itself is universally regarded in the academic and policy literature as involving multi-dimensional disadvantage. 'Deep exclusion' cannot therefore be clearly differentiated from social inclusion on this basis. However, there are degrees of severity of social exclusion. Severe or deep exclusion was therefore defined as follows:

> Deep exclusion refers to exclusion across more than one domain or dimension of disadvantage, resulting in severe negative consequences for quality of life, well-being and future life chances....

It is not clear that 'deep exclusion' is separable from social exclusion more generally, or produced by different 'drivers'. The demonstration of causality in social science is extremely difficult. However, there is overwhelming evidence that poverty is a major risk factor in almost all domains of exclusion that have been explored.

Source: Levitas et al (2007, p 9)

The effect of poverty on citizenship status

Two decades ago Lister (1990) argued that poverty impacted negatively on the civil, political and social rights central to citizenship status; many of her conclusions retain a contemporary validity. In respect of civil rights, she stated that inadequate systems of legal aid and advice constrained the ability of poor people to access justice. This situation was exacerbated (January 2000) by changes to legal aid that have seen a rising number of law firms opt out of the system of legal representation for those with limited means (Dyer, 2002a). Lister also noted that poor people were becoming increasingly marginalised from the mainstream political process. Although the Poll Tax has been consigned to history, its legacy (the absence of a number of poor people from the electoral register who were either unwilling or unable to pay the community charge) lives on. Also, today more than ever, successful political parties concentrate their electoral efforts on attracting the support of crucial middle-class floating voters, a fact that may not be lost on many voters in deprived inner-city constituencies where polling figures are in some cases at historically low levels. When considering social rights, Lister believes that a universal right to a guaranteed minimum of benefits and support, unaffected by a citizen's relationship to the PLM, is a key element of citizenship status. Echoing Townsend (1979) and Barbalet (1988), she also notes that poor people are excluded from the ability to participate fully in their community, that is, a lack of resources means that they cannot fulfil their expected roles as citizens in both public and private spheres. There is little to suggest that this assertion has since become outdated.

As Scott (1994) notes, although Townsend (1979) never mentioned citizenship, he was very much concerned with the extent to which poverty may limit an individual's meaningful participation in society (cf Powell, 2002). This notion of effective membership of society was highlighted in Chapter One as a central aspect of social citizenship and it is certainly something that was important to T.H. Marshall. Townsend famously defined poverty as when people:

> ... lack the resources to obtain the types of diet, participate in the activities and have the living conditions and amenities which are customary or at least widely encouraged or approved, in the societies to which they belong. Their resources are so seriously below those commanded by the average individual that they are in effect excluded from ordinary living patterns, customs and activities. (1979, p 31)

As noted in Chapter Three, Marshall's definition of social rights implies two linked aspects of social citizenship. The first indicates that each citizen can expect a basic minimum of financial support from the state, that is, "the right to a modicum of economic welfare and security" (Marshall, 1949/92, p 8). The second, more expansive, element, "the right to share to the full in the social heritage and to live a civilised life according to the standards prevailing in society" (Marshall, 1949/92, p 8), implies that a citizen can expect to participate fully in society. Interestingly, the way that Marshall defines social citizenship according to minimalist and maximalist elements is mirrored in debates concerning the definitions of poverty and social exclusion previously discussed. Certainly someone who was living in absolute poverty could not be considered a citizen in any meaningful sense. A consideration of relevant evidence (see, for example, Beresford et al, 1999; Howard et al, 2001) also suggests that poverty, when relatively defined, has a serious negative impact on the citizenship status of poor people. Their continued exclusion from many of the day-to-day practices that are taken for granted by the wider population indicates that the full promise of social citizenship remains a distant dream for many, and that Marshall's expansive vision of a 'civilised life' remains an illusion.

Social citizenship: a substantial status for poor citizens?

What, then, does social citizenship offer for those living in poverty? Although the development and availability of a number of welfare services and cash benefits paid for by general taxation does, to a limited extent, involve some redistribution of income between those who are citizens, this slight levelling of inequality was not T.H. Marshall's main concern. The main advantage that accrues from citizenship status is, in effect, a guarantee that no citizen will be allowed to fall into poverty and destitution; their status as a citizen (regardless of class position) gives them access to limited social support. Social rights were seen as helping to abolish class differences because every citizen shared a common status. In this sense Marshall saw citizenship as challenging the class-based inequalities of free market capitalism, offering something of substance for those in poverty.

As Esping-Andersen (1990) has argued, social citizenship represents a challenge to a modern society stratified by social class in which people have to work (that is, sell their labour power), in order to survive. Citizenship, or, more precisely, the social rights element of citizenship, alters or even begins to break down class-based inequalities that are derived from an individual's position in the stratified PLM. Under the class system that operates in many Western contemporary societies, labour markets treat workers as commodities. Each individual sells their labour and receives, in return, some level of financial reward, which varies according to location within a hierarchical PLM, skills and previous training. Ultimately individuals are treated as disposable commodities; we can all be deskilled or made redundant. For the vast majority of people, their status as a worker is vitally important as it provides them with the means to provide for themselves and their families, and exclusion from the PLM is problematic. The advent of social citizenship means that a level of decommodified support becomes available to all citizens, that is, there is a range of benefits and services that people can access because of their status as citizens. Theoretically, where someone fits into the class system is no longer of singular importance. An individual's status as a citizen guarantees them certain rights to welfare that have little to do with status in the PLM, lack of employment or class position. In short, citizenship recognises our worth as human beings rather than as mere workers (commodities) in an economic system. To a limited extent the social rights of citizenship decommodify individuals and grant people a status or worth independent of their market value:

> The outstanding criterion of social rights must be the degree to which they permit people to make their living standards independent of pure market forces. It is in this sense that social rights diminish citizens' status as commodities.... If social rights are given the legal and practical status of property rights, if they are inviolable, and if they are granted on the basis of citizenship rather than performance, they will entail a de-commodification of the status of individuals vis a vis the market. (Esping-Andersen, 1990, p 21)

For Twine (1994), the crucial point to grasp about Esping-Andersen's work is that the balance of class power is fundamentally altered when workers enjoy social rights. These rights empower people through the redistribution of resources, which in turn redistributes power and opens up choices that were otherwise constrained by class position. Arguably, social citizenship offers every citizen something of substantive worth: rights to subsistence, a modicum of welfare independent of their value as workers. In a minimal sense citizenship offers those in poverty an alternative to penury. In certain circumstances social rights can fail to ensure effective participation in society but even minimal welfare is preferable to destitution.

New Labour's solution: 'work for those who can, support for those who cannot'

The centrality of paid work within New Labour's welfare reforms has been widely commented on and certainly a willingness to engage in such work is central to their perspective (Levitas, 1996, 1998; Page, 1997; Deacon, 1998; Plant, 1998; Lund, 1999; Powell, 1999, 2000; Stepney et al, 1999). The government declared that 'work is the best form of welfare', and committed itself to a range of policies to ensure maximum participation in the PLM. Speaking in April 2002 at the national launch of the Jobcentre Plus initiative, the Prime Minister restated the major themes central to his government's welfare reforms. Emphasising an enabling welfare state based on a reciprocal relationship between rights and responsibilities, he reiterated the achievements of the New Deal: 1.25 million people helped into paid work since 1997 and an 18% cut in fraudulent claims for Income Support and Jobseeker's Allowance (JSA). Claiming to have changed the culture of the welfare state, Blair stressed three elements in the government's strategy for reducing dependency on social welfare benefits: first, Jobcentre Plus, which focuses on moving social security claimants off benefits and into work; second, the now well-established 'New Deals'; third, creating new opportunities for higher skilled employment. The idea behind the 'Ambitions' programme is to tackle the present situation where people remain unemployed when certain employers cannot get skilled staff.

As noted in Chapter Four, the government introduced a range of measures to 'make work pay'. These include a system of tapered tax credits for those who work, help with the costs of childcare and the introduction of a national minimum wage. Tax credits especially are an interesting development. Increasingly the taxation system is playing a major role in the delivery of social welfare benefits. Also, in order to be eligible for tax credits, individuals have to be employed. Their expanding role may work to further undermine the idea of a right to unemployment benefit. Hewitt (2000) argues that the government is effectively creating a three-tier system of social security, with those who cannot work reliant on meagre social assistance and those who will not work effectively third-class citizens abandoned by the state.

A number of serious criticisms have been levelled at the government's welfare-to-work strategy. Levitas (1996, 1998) argues that New Labour is guilty of defining social exclusion in very narrow and simplistic terms. She argues that to equate social exclusion with simple exclusion from the PLM, as New Labour does, is problematic for several reasons. First, a simple employed–unemployed dichotomy obscures the real inequalities that continue to exist within the world of paid work. Toynbee (2003) notes that poverty stalks a number of those at the bottom end of the PLM. The working poor remain a reality even with the guarantee of the minimum wage. Second, the unpaid domestic work of many women is rendered invisible by the concentration on paid work alone. Third, New Labour's approach builds on a 'them' (the unemployed underclass) and 'us' (the workers) view of society that was part of their Conservative predecessors' approach. This, Levitas argues, obscures the real cause of poverty, that is, capitalism.

More specifically, Prideaux (2001) argues that New Labour is keen to sell the idea of the New Deal as the means by which people can escape from poverty and join the body of responsible active citizens in paid work. He is, however, sceptical of the view that the New Deal could provide meaningful employment following the initial six-month period of work/training. For Prideaux, the New Deal amounts to false employment, not because the government is involved in some complex conspiracy to provide cheap labour, but because the New Deal actually operates in a way that encourages employers to utilise the pool of subsidised workers on offer:

> At the level of unskilled employment the level of rewards that an employer would receive for recruiting a participant clearly encourages the use of workfare staff rather than full-time employees. When competition is fierce, or during times of economic recession, it hardly makes sense for many entrepreneurs to employ an individual for 36 hours a week at a cost of £133.20 [minimum wage £3.60] when they can pay an individual as little as £73.20 with the difference being made up with a £60 per week New Deal subsidy. Add to this a further grant of £750 for every welfare to work trainee and it becomes clear that the use of a subsidised labour force can offer an employer a substantial financial reward. (Prideaux, 2001, p 108)

A number of commentators have also suggested that the various New Deals may not be as successful as they first appear to be. Gray (2001), Prideaux (2001) and Grover and Stewart (2000, 2002) all make strong arguments that industry and employers rather than unemployed people/lone parents are the real beneficiaries of the New Deals. Peck (2001) argues that the New Deal "joins a list of moderately effective programmes [y]ielding modest outcomes" (p 13). He notes that in March 2000 the job entry rates for the New Deal were modest, with only a third of participants leaving to enter paid work. The schemes were least successful in the great urban conurbations. Peck (2001) also claims that many of those who leave the

New Deals are becoming trapped in 'contingent employment', that is, continually moving from one short-term, low-paid, insecure job to another.

The UK government's own research also indicates some strong reservations about the effectiveness of its chosen approach. Only 27% of companies participating in the 'One' scheme recruited lone parents to their workforce, with even less (20%) taking on the long-term unemployed, while people with mental or physical impairments fared considerably worse (DSS, 2001). More recently the Adult Learning Inspectorate (a government agency) issued a damning appraisal of the New Deal for Young People. The recruitment figures noted for this scheme for the four years up to 2001 appear positive, but the report highlights some serious shortcomings. Sixty per cent of the training for young adults provided by either the government or companies involved was condemned as inadequate. Similarly, although full-time education and training was the most popular option with recruits (40% of 18- to 24-year-olds), only 26% of those participating got a job and 31% a qualification (ALI, 2002).

State welfare: controlling the poor?

While welfare rights can deliver certain tangible benefits to meet the needs of citizens, a number of authors (for example, Dean, 2000; Blakemore, 2003) have argued that state welfare can also be concerned to coerce and control the lives of welfare recipients. The use of welfare systems to intervene in the lives of those in receipt of welfare services has a long history. The Charity Organisation Society in 19th-century London, for example, was keen to ensure that only the 'deserving' poor were able to access their limited conditional support on offer (Fido, 1977). Similarly, Vincent (1991) notes that, "the issue for the new [that is, the 20th] century was not whether but how the principle of interfering in the conduct of the poor could be best attained" (p 24). Chapter Three has already highlighted the ways in which the state sought to use social policy in the early 20th century to prescribe and endorse particular types of behaviour. Attempts by the state to reform, sanction and/or punish those who behave in what is considered to be an inappropriate manner continue in contemporary welfare states. Central to Offe's Marxist critique of social citizenship (see **Box 4.2**) is the claim that state welfare is both repressive as well as potentially enabling.

It has been suggested that two aspects of social control can be identified in relation to state-provided welfare:

• Social control that is directly coercive, such that an individual's autonomy or freedom is deliberately and obviously suppressed.

• Social control that is subtly oppressive and which encourages people to fit into an accepted role or suppresses their individuality in less obvious ways. (Blakemore, 2003, p 101)

Byrne (1999) believes that both aspects are central elements of a social policy built around individualist accounts of citizenship that focus on the 'irresponsible behaviour' of poor people, that has little to offer as a long-term solution to poverty. He notes that "In the hands of politicians we always get the moral argument, the judgement of the poor as unworthy, if redeemable, sinners" (Byrne, 1999, p 22). In a similar vein Jones and Novak (1999) assert that a new ruthlessness characterises contemporary welfare policy with the state increasingly used in a disciplinarian manner, particularly in relation to poor people. They argue that the social democratic state that arose out of the PWWS has long gone, and those living in poverty are now abandoned and demonised. The identification of an 'underclass' is seen as an attempt to present the poor as flawed and unworthy of collective support. Once poor people are seen in these terms it is much easier to prescribe policies that promote neglect and/or more ruthless interventions into individuals' lives (see also Bauman, 1998).

New Labour are keen to promote a particular moral framework and they are not afraid to use welfare policies to encourage and/or compel certain welfare claimants to behave in 'appropriate' ways. As Dean notes, changes to the social security system in recent years have led to more "explicitly coercive behavioural controls" (2000, p 52). The crude application of the 'no rights without responsibilities' mantra is likely to exacerbate this process in the future. The creeping conditionality outlined in the following section illustrates that social control looks set to be an increasingly significant aspect of the 21st-century welfare state (Dwyer, 2004b). Ironically, evidence presented by Dean (2000) suggests that use of coercive measures in state welfare may undermine rather than increase responsible behaviour among claimants.

Poor citizens and the conditional welfare state

The extent to which a 'principle of conditionality', that is, "no rights without responsibilities" (Giddens, 1998, p 65) underpins the British government's general approach to welfare reform was noted in Chapter Four and has been extensively commented on (see Dwyer, 1998, 2000a, 2002; Lister, 1998b; Dean, 1999; Heron and Dwyer, 1999; Powell, 1999; Etzioni, 2000; Heron, 2001; Prideaux, 2001; Deacon, 2002). The implications of this approach to welfare rights, and particularly the rights of poorer citizens, should not be underestimated. As noted in Chapter Three, Marshall's (1949/92) theory of citizenship implied an equality of status universally enjoyed by all deemed to be citizens. For Marshall, it was the addition of the third social rights element that made the citizenship status of the social democratic PWWS both distinctive and substantive when compared to that which had gone before. Although Marshall saw citizenship as a status that entailed both rights and duties, a general concern with social rights, rather than responsibilities, characterised his approach. Many (for example, Giddens, 1994; Selbourne, 1994; Etzioni, 1997, 2000; Mead, 1997b) have subsequently criticised his work for placing the idea of unconditional entitlement to welfare at the centre of his account. Marshall was, of course, not alone in asserting this view. The belief that rights to welfare should be both universal and unconditional was shared by others (for example, democratic socialists), who were also concerned to ensure that public welfare would lessen inequalities and foster a sense of social solidarity between citizens (Cox, 1998; Deacon, 2002). Sixty years on, such ideas are considered by many to be both outdated and likely to exacerbate passive welfare dependency. The 'new' politics embraced with some enthusiasm by New Labour in Britain (Blair, 1995, 1998) can be seen as a fundamental challenge to the idea of the 'entitled citizen' that was central to the PWWS (Mullard, 2002). New Labour now argues that only those who 'take charge' of their own lives and behave as responsible 'active' citizens are worthy of welfare rights (Wetherly, 2001), and that, if necessary, reluctant individuals should be compelled to act responsibly by the application of benefit sanctions (Dwyer, 2000a).

Very few, if any, welfare rights are, of course, totally unconditional. In many ways, a significant number of social rights, that is, the benefits and services that we associate with the welfare state, are and always have been, to some extent, conditional. Principles of (contingent) universality, contribution and social assistance have long been a feature of most European welfare states (see Chapter One). It has also been argued that conditionality features throughout the history of British welfare (Powell, 2002). The vital point to note, however, is the extent to which a principle of conditionality has become central to the organisation of contemporary public welfare in the UK in a relatively short time. As Deacon (2002) noted, the wholehearted endorsement of this approach by a British Labour government would have been unthinkable less than a decade previously, but it is now fundamental to their vision of a 21st-century welfare state.

The examples in *Box 5.3* illustrate the extent to which conditionality is now established in a wide range of policy areas and is being systematically applied to increasing numbers of people who are inactive in the PLM. New Labour is not afraid to use a mix of incentive and sanction in order to cajole people into the PLM or to compel them to behave in a more 'responsible' manner. Those who refuse are subject to punitive benefit sanctions.

Box 5.3: Conditionality and New Labour's welfare reforms

Social security

Since 1997: The various 'New Deals'

There is now a range of New Deals on offer to particular groups of claimants where benefit rights come only with attendant responsibilities. Groups covered include young people, the long-term unemployed, lone parents, disabled people and partners of unemployed people (see www.newdeal.gov.uk for details).

Young and long-term unemployed people who refuse to take up one of four work/training options offered (a job with the private sector, a job in the voluntary sector, a place on an environmental task force or full-time education and training) lose some or all of their benefit for a period of between 2 and 26 weeks, depending on circumstances (DWP, 2002a; TUC, 2002). In the period January-March 2002 approximately 15% of participants on the New Deal for Young People were subject to sanctions (CESI, 2002). In May 2002, 21,000 JSA claimants were subject to sanctions (DWP, 2002a, Table 3.5).

Lone parents. Since April 2001 work-focused interviews (WFIs) have been compulsory for most lone parents claiming Income Support with children aged over 13. From 7 April 2003 all lone parents claiming Income Support will be required to attend (Treolar, 2001). In the period between 30 April 2001 and 29 March 2002 1,531 lone parents were sanctioned for failing to attend the compulsory interview without good cause (*Hansard*, 2002b).

April 2002: Jobcentre Plus

Anyone claiming working-age benefits including JSA, Income Support, Incapacity Benefit, Maternity Allowance, Bereavement Benefits, Industrial Injuries Disablement Benefit, Care Allowance and the Social Fund must take part in a WFI with an adviser to be eligible for benefit (Treolar, 2001).

2002/03: Housing Benefit sanctions

In a policy U-turn in 2002 the government announced it was going to support proposals outlined in Frank Field's (Minister for Welfare Reform, 1997–98) 2002 Housing Benefit (Withholding of Payment) Bill, which linked benefit rights to behavioural conditions. The Bill proposed that the right to Housing Benefit be withdrawn, for a maximum of 12 months, from individuals who had (or whose children had) been convicted twice by the courts within a three-year period of anti-social behaviour (Field, 2002). In June 2003 the Department for Work and Pensions announced its intention to press ahead with sanctions in this area (Labour Party, 2003).

April 2002: Withdrawing Child Benefit?

Perhaps the most controversial conditionality discussions to emerge were proposals for the withdrawal of Child Benefit from parents whose children persistently truant from school and/or engage in anti-social behaviour (Finch, 2002; Hinsliff, 2002; Wintour and Smithers 2002). In the face of intense debate and criticism from both within and beyond the Labour Party, this idea has been dropped for the time being. Nonetheless, it is indicative of the distance that the government has travelled in a relatively short time and the extent to which conditionality now informs much social security policy.

2007: *Reducing dependency, increasing opportunity*, aka the Freud Report

Freud aimed to instigate a further 'step-change' in the delivery of social security provision. He recommended achieving this by, first, applying stronger JSA-type conditionality to the vast majority of out-of-work benefit recipients, including most lone parents and disabled people. Second, allowing private and voluntary sector organisations to tender for contracts to deliver the intensive back-to-work support packages necessary to reconnect long-term (that is, 12 months plus) benefit recipients with paid employment. Third, the introduction of a single, 'safety net' benefit for working-aged people that clearly linked signposts that rights come with attendant responsibilities to seek paid work.

> Achieving the changes on the scale recommended in this report implies much more than purely tinkering with benefit rates, conditionality and the provision of support. The whole system is predicated on a cultural context which changes in line with people's perceptions and expectations. A system based on a presumption of robust self-reliance will require an entirely different set of rules than one in which significant parts of society are not given the opportunity of, or expected to, work. The difficult heritage of the passive labour market policies of the 1970s is one of welfare dependence rather than self-reliance. One of the objectives of this reform must therefore be to generate clear signals around independence, respect and mutual obligations. (Freud, 2007, p 46)

See Freud (2007) for further details and Grover (2007) for more critical discussions.

2007: Welfare Reform Act

New rules were introduced to phase out Incapacity Benefit and Income Support, previously paid on the basis of incapacity for work. From October 2008 the Employment and Support Allowance (ESA) has been paid to new claimants who are unable to work because of illness or disability. Aside from a minority with severe impairments, most are expected to attend WFIs or undertake work-related activity as a condition of continued receipt of ESA. The Act also allows for non-payment (or reduction of Housing Benefit) when someone is evicted for anti-social or criminal behaviour, or has failed to comply with a local authority warning to improve behaviour. Sanctions range from an initial four-week, 10% reduction, to total loss of entitlement (for up to a five-year period) for those who continue to behave in an anti-social manner and fail to engage with rehabilitation services (CPAG, 2007).

2008: *Realising potential: A vision for personalised conditionality and support,* aka the Gregg Report
Gregg recommended a 'personalised conditionality' regime tailored to an individual and the support that they may require to enable them to undertake paid work. Following a screening process, benefit claimants would be allocated to one of three groups:

- *Work-ready group:* for those immediately ready to enter paid work; individuals to be subject to current JSA-type arrangements/rules.
- *Work progression group:* for those who may not be immediately able to work but where, with the necessary support, there is 'a genuine possibility' of a future return to the PLM; Gregg proposes that the overwhelming majority of lone parents and ESA recipients should be allocated to this group.
- *No conditionality group:* reserved for lone parents with *very* young children, carers and those with the most severe impairments; there would be no requirements for work search or work-related activity as a condition of receipt of benefit.

This also endorses Freud's call for a single working-age benefit regime (see Gregg, 2008).

2008: Green Paper, *No one written off: Reforming welfare to reward responsibility: Public consultation*
2008: White Paper, *Raising expectations and increasing support: Reforming welfare for the future*
These two documents draw on many of the recommendations of the Freud and Gregg reports. In the White Paper the government reiterates the reciprocity at the heart of its preferred approach to social security, promising to "increase the support we offer and the obligations we expect in return" (DWP, 2008c, p 10). The Secretary of State for Work and Pensions talks of entering a third phase of welfare reform, where "no one is left behind, that virtually everyone should be required to take up the support that we know helps people overcome barriers to work" (DWP, 2008c, p 8). The government commits to piloting the Gregg model of 'conditionality and support' for new ESA and lone-parent claimants from 2010 and also escalating sanctions.

All Incapacity Benefit claims are to be moved to the new ESA regime by 2013 (see DWP, 2008c for more details).

2009: Welfare Reform Act

This legislation makes good on many of the promises in respect of conditionality noted above. A 'Work for Your Benefits' (WfYB) programme was introduced for the long-term unemployed. Lone parents' entitlement to Income Support ends once their youngest child reaches seven years old, with a switch to JSA or ESA regimes as deemed appropriate. A pilot scheme was introduced for those drawing JSA or ESA who have serious heroin or crack cocaine drug dependency problems for whom the receipt of benefit becomes conditional on signing up to a drug rehabilitation programme (OPSI, 2009a).

Housing

1998: Crime and Disorder Act

Building on the agenda of their Conservative predecessors, the Labour government introduced Anti-Social Behaviour Orders (ASBOs). These civil court orders grant a local authority or the police the power to prohibit an individual from acting in a specified anti-social manner and/or the power to exclude an individual from their home or other specified locality. It is a criminal offence (potentially punishable by imprisonment) to break the conditions set out in such an order. In the period from 1 April 1999 to 31 December 2001, 518 ASBOs were served (*Hansard*, 2002a).

2002: Police Reform Bill

2003: White Paper, *Respect and responsibility: Taking a stand against anti-social behaviour*

These two documents outline Home Office proposals to expand and enhance ASBOs in the future and set out the government's strategy for dealing with anti-social behaviour (Home Office, 2002a, 2002b, 2003a).

2003: Anti-social Behaviour Act

2003: Criminal Justice Act

This legislation introduced a host of new instruments to promote good behaviour, including dispersal orders, parenting contracts, demoted tenancies, individual support orders and acceptable behaviour contracts (rf NAO, 2006 for details).

2006: *Respect action plan*

This contains an abundance of initiatives aimed at tackling anti-social behaviour, many of them focused on addressing the lifestyles of 'problem families' and the most excluded individuals. Proposals include enhanced personal support schemes for individuals with specific or multiple issues, and the linking of government regeneration funding to systems of behaviour management and sanctions for problem families (see RTF, 2006).

Education
March 2001: Adult Literacy and Numeracy Strategy Unit

In a series of pilot projects established across England, conditionality again informed the government's approach to tackling the problem of adult illiteracy. As part of the government's 'Skills for Life' strategy, nine localised schemes were set up to test the effectiveness of a variety of 'carrot and stick' approaches in persuading JSA claimants to learn basic skills. In Wearside appropriate individuals were referred to a full-time basic education scheme, given £10 per week extra benefit for attending and £100 bonus for successful completion of the course. In contrast, since 17 September 2001 the right to JSA of other claimants aged 25-49 in north Nottinghamshire/Leeds was made subject to removal if they refused, or gave up, an allocated place on a basic educational skills programme. Initially benefits were withheld for two weeks and this period would be doubled for a second 'offence' (Kingston, 2001; Treolar, 2001). The government has not ruled out the possibility of a national roll-out of this approach, even though the Social Security Advisory Committee (SSAC) stated it was against sanctions in this area (SSAC, 2002).

Healthcare
2001: Violent patients to be refused care?

Faced with approximately 65,000 violent actions being perpetrated against health service staff (many involving patients under the influence of drink and/or drugs), a zero tolerance policy towards violent and disruptive patients became part of UK health policy. Although guidelines state that refusing treatment is a last resort and that ordinarily verbal and written warnings should be issued, the government declared that it would support staff who (under the threat of immediate danger) made on-the-spot decisions and refused treatment for violent patients (see DH, 2001, 2002a). Borrowing from the range of powers discussed in the 'Housing' section above, the Queens Medical Centre in Nottingham has also used court injunctions and ASBOs to ban three people from entering hospital grounds, unless in need of life-saving treatment (Carvel, 2001).

2001: Sure Start Maternity Grant
This increased in value from £100 to £500 over two years, and is available to new mothers who are (or whose partners are) recipients of various means-tested benefits and tax credits (DWP, 2002b). Payment of the grant "will be conditional on a parent providing evidence [that is, a certificate signed by a specified health professional] that health advice has been received from an approved healthcare professional" (DH, 2000, p 3). This may well be an example of the least punitive

type of conditionality, but those who do not have the relevant approval are not eligible for the grant. In the period 2001/02 8,433 claims for the grant were initially refused because the required certification was not provided by the applicant (DWP, 2002c).

2002: Modernisation of the Welfare Food Scheme
Plans to modernise this scheme (which provided milk tokens and vitamins to mothers, babies and toddlers in 800,000+ low-income families) indicated that the government was considering a further extension of the conditional approach that it introduced for the Sure Start Maternity Grant (DH, 2002b). Under the proposals, in order to be eligible to receive vouchers exchangeable for a wider range of healthy foods (including fruit) mothers would have to register with certain healthcare professionals on three specified occasions before and after the birth of a child (see Brindle, 2002; CPAG, 2002a; DH, 2002b). Conditionality in this area has now been abandoned since the Healthy Start Scheme (introducing the new vouchers) replaced the Welfare Food Scheme in 2005. Health professionals are now prompted to encourage breastfeeding and generally healthy lifestyles among recipients.

The Welfare Reform Acts of 2007 and 2009 indicate that the Labour government's commitment to conditionality remains strong. The 2007 Welfare Reform Act builds on the approach of the 'Pathways to Work' scheme and Freud's (2007) call for greater conditionality. Changes instigated under it will see increasing numbers of disabled people having to attend work-focused interviews (WFIs). Those with less severe impairments will be required to be actively involved in seeking work (Corden and Nice, 2007). Employment Support Allowance (ESA) will replace Incapacity Benefit and Income Support paid in relation to sickness or incapacity. During an initial 13-week 'assessment phase', all new ESA claimants will be paid a basic allowance and expected to undergo a work capability assessment (WCA). Once WCA requirements are satisfied, the majority of claimants will be able to access a work-related activity element of ESA. However, receipt of this 'main phase' component (paid at a higher level than basic allowance) is conditional on clients drawing up individual return-to-work action plans, attending regular WFIs, routinely undertaking 'reasonable steps' to manage their condition and/or accepting specified training or basic skills support, to facilitate their return to paid work. Refusal carries the threat of benefit sanctions and an enforced return to the lower basic benefit. Disqualification from ESA for up to six weeks is possible where someone is:

> ...limited in their capability for work because of their own misconduct, because they remain someone who has limited

capability for work through failure, without good cause, to
follow medical advice, or because they fail, without good cause,
to observe specified rules of behaviour. (2007 Welfare Reform
Act, Section 18)

The small number of people who, following their WCA, are identified as
having severe conditions and 'limited capability for work-related activity'
will qualify for a 'support component'. This will be set at a higher level
than the work-related activity element of ESA, and such claimants will
not need to participate in work-related activities (CPAG, 2007). Critics
argue that the assumptions and conditions that underpin this change in
approach in providing social security to disabled people are inappropriate,
particularly as their lack of paid employment may be due to "the disabling
structures and practices of society rather than any individual deficits" or
lack of desire to work (Patrick, 2009, p 48).

A second Welfare Reform Act received Royal Assent on 12 November
2009. This drew on many of the recommendations and sentiments
expressed in the independent reviews by Freud (2007) and Gregg (2008).
In a press release accompanying the 2009 Act, the Minister for Work and
Pensions, Yvette Cooper, re-emphasised the familiar refrain that individuals
had to be prepared to take steps to re-engage with the PLM in return for
collective welfare support:

> It [the Act] makes clear that almost everyone should be on a
> journey to work – either looking for work now or preparing
> for work in the future. It will mean more support for people
> who face difficulties getting jobs but also greater responsibilities
> on people to take up that help. (DWP, 2009, p 1)

Overall the Act allows for more 'personalisation of benefit conditionality',
and several new initiatives make new demands on particular groups of
citizens. Building on incremental changes over the past decade that have
lowered the age at which lone parents are expected to consider paid
work, the Act requires lone parents with children aged from one to three
to attend periodic Jobcentre interviews. Lone parents whose children are
aged between three and six will be required to undertake training or other
appropriate preparation to enable a return to paid work. From 2010, once
their youngest child is over seven, lone parents will be required to look for
work that is available while their child(ren) are attending primary school.
Entitlement to Income Support on the grounds of being a lone parent will
also end and those able to work will be subject to JSA rules, while others
with qualifying impairments will be expected to apply for ESA. Echoing

the community jobs approach championed by Etzioni (see Chapter Four, this volume), long-term unemployed people will be required to enter a 'Work for Your Benefits' (WfYB) programme. This will offer additional intensive support alongside an expectation that individuals will have to agree to take part in compulsory, full-time work experience. Another new scheme will require JSA or ESA recipients who are crack cocaine and heroin users to agree to undertake personalised drug rehabilitation programmes as a condition of continued benefit receipt (OPSI, 2009a).

Successive New Labour governments have significantly distanced themselves from the notion of (largely) unconditional welfare rights and are increasingly embracing, in both principle and practice, the idea that public welfare provisions are conditional entitlements. This diminishes the limited equality that the citizenship of the British PWWS promised. Furthermore, the principle of conditionality is not imposed in a uniform manner on all citizens. Essentially, it is the welfare rights of poor people that are being reduced or removed. The diminution of such rights will have the greatest negative effect on those living in poverty, or on the margins of it. Simultaneously, the state is demanding that they accept increased individual responsibility for their future welfare and well-being (Dwyer, 1998, 2000a; Bryne, 1999; Lister, 2001). Under Tony Blair, New Labour has institutionalised a new form of social citizenship in which conditional entitlement now dominates (Dwyer, 2004b, 2008). Although some differences in focus exist under his successor Gordon Brown, the principle of conditionality per se remains unchallenged. It is firmly embedded at the core of New Labour's modernised welfare state and, as the more recent policy developments discussed in this chapter indicate, an enthusiasm for extending its reach further clearly exists.

Whatever the outcome of the next general election (due in 2010), it remains highly unlikely that an incoming Conservative or Labour government will challenge the now widely accepted, highly reciprocal approach to welfare delivery that has become the norm for mainstream political parties in the UK. Gordon Brown stated that New Labour had "not done enough to promote a philosophy which emphasises rights and responsibilities together" (Brown, 2006, p 5), and more recently that, "we will combine tough sanctions for those who refuse to work or train with better and more targeted support for those most in need, to give them the skills and advice they need to get back onto the jobs ladder" (DWP, 2008a p 2). Similarly, in his 2007 Conservative Party Conference speech, David Cameron referred to the tough welfare-to-work programmes in Wisconsin, US, stating that those who refuse 'fair' work should be denied rights to welfare (see p 81, this volume). Peter Hain (Secretary of State for Work and Pensions) (2008) remains convinced that real differences remain between the current government's 'human capital' approach to activation (which emphasises training and opportunity), and what he sees as Cameron's more punitive 'work first' option (see Levy, 2004, for further discussions regarding such distinctions). Conditionality is, however, a non-negotiable element of both visions; those who refuse to take up work or training options will face sanctions and a reduction or loss of benefit.

Conditional welfare rights are openly endorsed by politicians and commentators from across the mainstream political spectrum, including the Centre-Left (White, 2007), as a necessary element of the 21st-century 'active' world of welfare. A new consensus about the role and purpose of the welfare state has emerged. As this conditional welfare state, with its stress on individual responsibility, becomes embedded and institutionalised, there is a danger that the social, economic and political causes of unemployment, poverty and family breakdown will cease to be recognised (Dwyer and Ellison, 2007). Influenced by right-wing ideas about the causes of welfare dependency, the principle of conditionality emerged as a key theme in welfare reform under the Conservative administrations of Margaret Thatcher and John Major. The subsequent consolidation and expansion of the conditional welfare state under New Labour, and perhaps a future Conservative government led by David Cameron, may yet prove to be one of Tony Blair's most enduring legacies. Arguably the trend towards increasingly conditional welfare noted in this chapter is not limited solely to the UK but is part of a wider shift in welfare policy in many Western nation states (Dwyer, 2004b). The significance of this change for social citizenship will be addressed more fully in Chapter Eleven, the concluding chapter to this volume.

Summary

This chapter has looked at the continued importance of social class, and more specifically, poverty in relation to citizenship. Scott notes that:

> Under a fully established system of citizenship the vagaries of the market and of individual circumstances, such as disability, ill health, unemployment, old age, and family size do not prevent people from enjoying what is believed to be appropriate for a citizen. (1994, p 130)

In the UK and elsewhere there remain a substantial number of individuals who, in spite of the existence of the welfare state, are living in poverty and are unable to access the resources necessary to enjoy a minimum standard of living and/or exercise fully their rights as citizens. It may be reasonable therefore to argue that the continued existence of poverty signals the failure of citizenship (Vincent, 1991). Nonetheless, the availability of certain decommodified social rights is of positive value to all citizens and perhaps of particular value to those living in poverty. This chapter has noted the following:

- The definition and measurement of poverty and social exclusion is contentious and the subject of much debate.
- New Labour's assertion that 'work is the best form of welfare' is too simplistic. The welfare needs of many citizens in advanced capitalist economies are indeed best served by activity in the PLM, but others in paid employment continue to work long and hard and, yet, experience poverty.
- Rights to social welfare remain vitally important to those outside the PLM.
- The minimum that social citizenship alludes to has been reduced and constrained in recent decades.
- Social control is an important aspect of welfare states. Conditionality can be seen as an attempt to intervene and control the lives of poor people.
- The ongoing application of a principle of conditionality is likely to result in the increased social exclusion of certain marginalised groups, for example, those in poverty.

Further reading

Alcock (2006), **Lister (2004a)** and **Howard et al (2001)** all provide interesting, accessible and comprehensive introductions to debates about the definition, measurement and effects of poverty touched on in this chapter. **Beresford et al (1999)** is also of merit as it presents the views and analyses of poor people themselves on the definition, causes and solutions to poverty. Two books from The Policy Press Understanding Welfare series are also very useful. The edited collection by **Ridge and Wright (2008)** discusses the impact of poverty and, also importantly, wealth on citizens' lives. **Millar's (2009)** book is a good place to start for those looking to explore many of the changes in social security policy under New Labour. Readers seeking an overview of rights and responsibilities in the UK social security system should access Social Security Advisory Committee Occasional Paper number 6, authored by **Griggs and Bennett (2009)**.

Website resources

Interested readers should also refer to the following websites that contain a wealth of relevant information, resources and debates:

Child Poverty Action Group (CPAG), a campaigning organisation that works towards the eradication of poverty and is involved in the promotion and protection of welfare rights: **www.cpag.org**

Joseph Rowntree Foundation (JRF), commissions research into a range of social issues including poverty, income and wealth. Of particular relevance is the series of annual New Policy Institute studies (since 1999), monitoring government progress in the reduction of social exclusion and poverty according to a set of fixed indicators. This work is regularly updated and is available at **www.poverty.org**. The JRF site also has a 'Findings' section that presents succinct summaries of completed research funded by the organisation. The work of **Hills (1998)** into patterns of inequalities in income and wealth in the UK since the 1950s is sobering reading: **www.jrf.org.uk**

Department for Work and Pensions (DWP) holds the government's own policy documents and research on many aspects of welfare reform and poverty/social exclusion. *Opportunity for all* (updated annually since 1999) presents the government's analysis of its progress towards the target of eradicating child poverty in 20 years: **www.dwp.gov.uk**

Gender, citizenship and welfare

This chapter considers *gender* and how it relates to citizenship. Two linked questions are central to the subsequent discussions. First, to what extent can citizenship be regarded as a gendered concept? Second, how does gender impact on citizenship? The following themes and debates are explored:

- the gendered construction of citizenship;
- the relationship between gender and citizenship;
- social change, gender, paid work and care;
- contemporary initiatives and legislation aimed at promoting family-friendly policies and a 'work–life balance';
- sexuality and citizenship;
- transforming citizenship.

Is citizenship gender-specific?

A number of feminist writers (for example, Pateman, 1989; Vogel, 1991; Lister, 2003a, 2003b, 2003c) have argued that citizenship is essentially a gendered concept that reflects the wider patriarchal oppression of women within society. Lister (2003c) believes that two intertwined constructs, namely, the abstract disembodied individual and the public–private divide, lie at the heart of citizenship, and are central to an understanding of women's past and continued exclusion from full citizenship status. She notes that citizenship has, in the past, been largely defined according to a stereotypical male vision. Abstract individual citizenship has been built around gendered notions of what a man should be, while women, and any activity deemed to be incompatible with the public exercise of citizenship, have typically been relegated to a secondary private sphere.

As *Figure 6.1* illustrates, Lister is arguing that the characteristics seen as synonymous with being a citizen are essentially those that have come to be regarded as masculine. She is critical of this approach and emphasises the need to see people as embedded within particular historical, social and gendered locations. Arguing that the public–private dichotomy is a theoretical and practical barrier to women's citizenship and that the private duties characteristically assigned to women have a negative impact on women's ability to be active in the public sphere, she notes that a key issue for feminists is how informal care is viewed in relation to the obligations that citizenship entails.

In a similar vein, Vogel (1991) argues that historically citizenship has been

Figure 6.1: The gendered dichotomy of citizenship

The 'male' – public citizen	The 'female' – private non-citizen
Abstract, disembodied, mind	Particular, embodied, rooted in nature
Rational, able to apply dispassionate reason and standards of justice	Emotional, irrational, subject to desire and passion; unable to apply standards of justice
Impartial, concerned with public interest	Partial, preoccupied with private, domestic concerns
Independent, active, heroic and strong	Dependent, passive, weak
Upholding the realm of the freedom of the human	Maintaining the realm of necessity, of the natural and repetitious

Source: Lister (1997, p 69)

seen as the masculine domain and that the exclusion of women should be seen as one example of the tendency for citizenship to exclude individuals who, in various ways (because of a different racial and ethnic identity, an inability to exercise defined rights and responsibilities, a particular ascribed social status and so on), deviate from the institutionalised male ideal of the 'citizen'. Although she views T.H. Marshall's approach as generally advantageous in that it places social rights at its core, she believes that in outlining the theoretical construction of the PWWS both Marshall and Beveridge condemned women to a marginalised second-class citizenship status. Central to this marginalisation was the taken for granted assumption that women, especially married women, would naturally take on the unpaid domestic care role within a defined nuclear family unit while the benevolent male breadwinner would provide for the family through paid employment.

For Vogel (1991), marriage as an institution is especially relevant to women's exclusion from citizenship status. It is the device by which men, as citizens, dominate female non-citizens:

> Marriage, which begins as a voluntary association between two
> citizens – two agents capable of valid contractual undertakings –
> turns into a permanent house arrest for one of them. (1991, p 73)

Vogel argues that once married, a woman's ascribed identity is often centrally based on her identity as a wife rather than as a citizen. The fact that marriage is seen very much as a private relationship and, therefore, largely beyond the public concerns of citizenship has two functions. First, it (literally) reproduces civil society and also allows for the orderly movement of property over generations. Second, it serves to subordinate women. The dependence of women on their male partner is taken for granted and it is assumed that he will ensure her welfare in return for the care offered in the private sphere. Such assumptions underpin welfare systems that continue to afford limited or non-existent social security rights to those engaged in informal care work. Vogel is clear that women's exclusion and marginalisation is not simply a matter of personal bigotry but that the systematic subordination of women is itself "an integral part of men's citizenship status" (Vogel, 1991, p 75).

The patriarchal welfare state

Pateman's (1989) discussion of the patriarchal welfare state is perhaps one of the most influential discussions of gender, welfare and citizenship. Patriarchy can be defined as the dominance of men over women, or the structures and practices through which men are able to dominate women. Pateman argues that the welfare state constructs and deals with citizens in different ways depending on whether or not they are male or female, and that it is necessary to analyse how gendered assumptions about the respective roles of men and women affect social rights (see **Box 6.1**). A central issue is the connection that is made between access to full citizenship rights and participation in paid work and how this negatively impacts on the rights of women who provide unpaid familial care. For Pateman, it is ironic that, while the public worlds of (paid) work and (state) welfare are fundamentally underpinned by the unpaid private care work of women, women are systematically disadvantaged in terms of their welfare rights by performing such care work. Male claims to welfare are regarded as legitimate because of prior activity in the PLM and their attendant tax and NI contributions. In contrast, the ongoing reluctance of the state to recognise that the provision of informal support within a familial setting is as valid a form of social contribution as paid work serves to entrench female dependency and undermine their claims to welfare rights. Although the welfare state offers women services that may be of real value to individuals, Pateman believes that its emergence means that many women merely exchange dependence on an individual man for dependence on a patriarchal state. The welfare state does little to challenge the structures and practices that define women as dependants rather than as autonomous citizens.

> ## Box 6.1: The patriarchal welfare state
>
> Theoretically, and historically, the central criterion for citizenship has been 'independence', and the elements encompassed under the heading of independence have been based on masculine attributes and abilities. Men, but not women, have been seen as possessing the capacities required of 'individuals', 'workers' and 'citizens'. As a corollary, the meaning of 'dependence' is associated with all that is womanly.... (p 134)
>
> As participants in the market, men could be seen as making a public contribution, and were in a position to be levied by the state to make a contribution more directly, that *entitled* them to the benefits of the welfare state. But how could women dependants of men, whose legitimate 'work' is held to be in the private sphere, be citizens of the welfare state? What could, or did, women contribute? The paradoxical answer is that women contributed – welfare.... (p 138)
>
> Women's citizenship is full of contradictions and paradoxes. Women must provide welfare, and care for themselves, and so must be assumed to have the capacities necessary for these tasks. Yet the development of the welfare state has also presupposed that women necessarily are in need of protection by and are dependent upon men. The welfare state has reinforced women's identity as men's dependants both directly and indirectly, and so confirmed rather than ameliorated our social exile.... (p 139)
>
> *Source:* Pateman (1989) (page numbers refer to an abridged version entitled 'The patriarchal welfare state', in Pierson and Castles, 2006)

Gender and citizenship

Like Lister (1997), Walby (1994) argues that the public–private dichotomy is critical to understanding women's citizenship status and facilitates a differential access to citizenship rights for women in comparison to men. It is not simply a case of women being slower to gain the rights that male citizens enjoy, but that they have a different relationship to citizenship. A key issue for many women is that access to full social citizenship rights is usually dependent on individuals being full-time workers. The work of Ginn et al (2001), for example, illustrates how caring has a detrimental impact on social security in old age. A central question then is whether or not caring can become compatible with full citizenship status. Should women only be entitled to full citizenship status if they behave like men and engage in male patterns of work in the PLM?

Drawing on the work of Lister (1990), Walby (1994) highlights a central tension at the heart of many feminist critiques of mainstream citizenship theory. Women could either:

(a) look to enter the public sphere of paid work as a way of ending their status as second-class citizens; or
(b) seek to change the dominant male notion of citizenship and look to have their contribution as informal carers positively recognised within an altered notion of citizenship.

Option (a) requires women to behave like men and mimic male patterns of paid employment. If option (b) is taken instead, the dilemma is that women may then possibly be reinforcing their own disadvantage as their informal caring role has undermined their status as citizens in the past. "Women's greater commitment to caring is simultaneously positively valued and a source of disadvantage to women" (Walby, 1994, p 387).

A number of writers have consistently argued that women endure a second-class citizenship status in respect of the civil, political and social rights central to citizenship. Pascall (1997) argues that the civil rights of women are undermined by a lack of consistent state protection from domestic violence in private relationships and the "workfare of compulsory altruism" (1997, p 239) in marriage. The shortcomings, disadvantages and discrimination inherent in the criminal justice system have also been noted (Kennedy, 1992; Carlen, 2002). While today there is no formal distinction between men and women in terms of political rights, women's participation in formal politics remains low. Figures from 2001 indicate that in the UK only one third of cabinet ministers were women, 18% of Members of Parliament were female and men made up 66% of appointments to non-departmental public bodies (Dench et al, 2002). Previous discussions have noted that the social rights of women are often undermined by a social security system that treats women as the dependants of men and also undervalues, and then systematically penalises, those who engage in informal care work in the home. In terms of social rights, women have fared better in areas of public welfare where universalist rather than contributory (that is, where rights are dependent on previous NI contributions from wages) principles are dominant, for example, healthcare and education (Pascall, 1997).

Evidence suggests that gender difference has an important negative effect on women's citizenship status; so has citizenship offered anything of substantive worth for women? Walby (1994) notes that in terms of a general redistribution of money via social security benefits, the welfare state disproportionately benefits women rather than men. Although social insurance negatively discriminates against women and many end up reliant on more meagre social assistance benefits, overall women gain more in benefits but pay out less in taxes than men. The operation of the welfare state represents a shift from private to public patriarchy. Instead of women having to rely solely on an individual patriarch, social rights give many an option of relying on limited public welfare provisions. Walby (1994) argues, therefore, that citizenship has profoundly affected gender relations throughout the last century.

Social change, gender, paid work and care

The extent to which, in the past, individuals' lives reflected the gendered stereotype of male breadwinner–female carer which theoretically underpinned the PWWS, is open to debate. Today, given the dramatic changes in partnering and parenting that have occurred, and mothers' increased employment within the PLM, it is clear that the lived reality of many men and women no longer conforms to such standards (Millar, 2003). Certainly the family and PLM are two arenas in which women's roles and expectations have shifted in the past 50 years. However, within a more heterogeneous mix of contemporary families it may be reasonable to argue that gender roles in the home have undergone modification rather than transformation. Women continue to do the bulk of domestic and caring work in families and working fathers appear to be reluctant to take up options of paternity leave even when it is an accepted part of state policy, as in certain Scandinavian nations (Crompton, 2002).

Against this backdrop of change, Walby (1999) notes that the ongoing changes affect both men and women, but "some longstanding dimensions of gender inequality still prevail and in changing social circumstances need to be addressed anew" (1999, p 1). For Walby, 'affirmative action' strategies retain a contemporary validity because the structured inequalities and disadvantages of the past continue to impact negatively on many women's lives in the present. Initially it may require positive policies that begin from the premise that women's citizenship status remains qualitatively inferior to men's, in order to ensure that women achieve the substantive equality that citizenship implies.

Walby then explores two aspects of social change of particular relevance to women's citizenship. First, she notes both change and continuity within the PLM. In spite of the unprecedented levels of female paid employment, accompanied by a wider restructuring of paid work (that is, an increase in the service sector and a reduction of heavy manufacturing industries), Walby notes that the world of work remains gendered, with occupational and hierarchical segregation entrenched. Also, although there has been a gradual reduction in the 'earnings gap', full-time women workers in the UK earned 82% of men's full-time hourly earnings in 2000. Furthermore, in 2001 44% of women (as opposed to 9% of men) were engaged in part-time work; much of it poorly paid and of low status (Dench et al, 2002). Second, Walby discusses the significant changes in family life that have occurred since the 1950s (for example, new ways of parenting and partnering, increased demand for care in later life as citizens in developed nations enjoy longer lives). She believes that the state needs positively to embrace these changes rather than simply condemn working women to a future double shift of work and care. She is, however, clear that the duty to engage in paid work should be a central part of the 21st-century citizenship deal. Strongly asserting that "supporting strategies which do not involve [paid] employment do women no favours in the long run" (1999, p 5), Walby notes that growing levels of paid employment among women have improved the individual finances of many and also benefited the wider economy.

Although generally positive about the potential for women to engage with ongoing social change successfully, Walby concludes with a note of caution. While many women are increasingly well educated and able to move forward positively, she notes that other dimensions of social division cut across gender and impact negatively on the lives of others. Real, and at times stark, inequalities exist between rich and poor women, women of different ethnic origins, younger and older females, women with impairments and their able-bodied counterparts (cf Yuval-Davis, 1997).

For Lister (1999), women's citizenship is too often presented as a simplistic choice between promoting women as either citizen-workers or citizen-carers. She believes that more fundamental issues will have to be tackled if women are to become full citizens. There is an essential need to change the sexual division of labour within society. Although the situation is changing slowly, the overwhelming burden of domestic work and care continues to fall on women (ONS, 1998). This domestic role continues to impact on women's ability to enter the public arena as equal citizens and Lister argues that, if the subordinate citizenship status of women is to be eradicated, then the private as well as public behaviour of men will need to change. This will require a range of tactics, for example, the introduction (as in many

Scandinavian nations) of policies to promote a work–life balance such as parental leave. However, the long hours culture that is particularly prevalent in the British PLM will also need to be challenged.

As previously noted, informal, familial care work presents the dilemma of whether or not campaigns to place such care work on an equal footing with paid work further entrench women's role as family carers and so help to cement the barriers that prevent them from becoming full citizens. For Lister (1999), a number of options exist. First, the state could make more generous NI payments on behalf of people engaged in the long-term provision of care for disabled relatives or infirm elders. This would ensure that carers had access to benefit rights of similar value to those contributing through paid work. Another approach may be to provide more substantial benefits for carers in recognition of their social contribution – a form of participation income (see Chapter Eleven, this volume) could, for example, be introduced. This approach is not without dilemmas itself. The move towards direct payments for disabled people (see Chapter Seven, this volume) potentially hands more control over personal support packages to the person receiving care rather than the caregiver; this may undermine the claims of carers for enhanced benefits. Also, enhancing carers' benefits may, arguably, lock those who provide such care into long-term dependency on state benefits.

Considering the care of young children, Lister (1999) notes that good quality, affordable childcare, alongside policies for adequate parental leave, are prerequisites if women are to be expected to take up paid work. This will again require a change in the culture of the workplace. Men taking time off to care for sick children, for example, is still routinely frowned upon by many employers who continue to view such tasks as 'women's work'. Parental leave remains a non-starter for many men who may wish to spend some time with their children. As Crompton (2002) also makes clear, for many career women the contemporary rhetoric of work–life balance rings hollow; for some, choosing not to have children remains a prerequisite of professional success.

A consideration of lone parenthood further highlights the gendered tensions underlying policies to encourage women into the PLM. As Lister (1999) asserts, most lone-parent families, the vast majority of which are headed by a female, are especially susceptible to poverty. Citing evidence which suggests that most lone parents want to work once their child is established in primary school, Lister believes that it is right to use a variety of measures to encourage lone mothers into paid work, as potentially this provides them with the best route out of poverty. However, this approach may undermine the social value of mothering. It can be argued that raising children is as valid and necessary a form of social contribution as paid work, and that it should, when necessary, be supported by the state. The UK has been very liberal in enforcing paid work responsibilities on lone parents in the past, but as previous discussions (see Chapter Five, this volume) indicate, the balance between the rights of lone parents to draw on collective welfare provisions to support their family and their responsibility as individuals to provide for their family's needs through paid work is currently being renegotiated. Consequently, the informal care contribution of lone mothers may be rendered invisible and those who continue to draw welfare benefits rather than work are at risk of being labelled 'partial', dependent citizens (Burns, 2000).

For Hancock (2000), the devaluation of the informal care work of women has been central to the past marginalisation of women, but under New Labour she argues that a significant shift has occurred. Where once the role of women was constructed primarily around their duties as 'mothers/carers', they are now viewed as 'worker/citizens'. Lewis (2001) similarly argues that an 'adult worker model' rather than a male breadwinner–female carer approach is now central to contemporary policy. As New Labour asserts this approach, it has been keen to promote a range of family-friendly policies so that both men and women can combine their responsibilities as parents and workers. These are discussed in the next section.

Family-friendly policy and the 'work–life' balance

It has previously been noted (Chapters Four and Five, this volume) that New Labour strongly believe that paid work is the best form of welfare for the vast majority of citizens. Given this stance, it is not too surprising to find that the government is keen to facilitate increased participation in paid work through the implementation of 'family-friendly' policies (HMT/DTI, 2003; Oliver, 2003). A central focus of its approach has been to encourage employers to offer flexible working arrangements that will allow employees to combine paid employment with any care responsibilities that they may have in the home. Convincing employers of the advantages that ensue to businesses that promote flexible working was also evidently part of the government's agenda (DTI, 2002). It is women, as providers of the majority of informal care, who have embraced flexible working arrangements (Oliver, 2003).

As *Box 6.2* illustrates, in recent years a range of new rights has been introduced. These include rights to parental leave, a right to time off work for care of dependants, new rights for part-time workers and working time regulations. These have been combined with enhanced financial support for families and increased public support of childcare provision. The government has been, and remains, keen on driving the work–life balance agenda forward. Indeed, it believes it to be of particular importance for its long-term objectives of increasing productivity, enhancing employment opportunities and eradicating child poverty (HMT/DTI, 2003; OPSI, 2009c). Arguably, taken as a whole the range of measures introduced equate to a significant change in the government's approach to work and family policy (Lewis and Campbell, 2007).

Utilising the work of Iverson and Wren (1998), Dean (2002b) is more critical of New Labour's approach in this area. He believes that New Labour's work–life balance stance was an attempt to resolve the three linked questions of "how is it possible to sustain functional families while maximising labour force participation, yet minimise social spending?" (2002b, p 6). He argues that, in order to maximise the potential of all parents to combine their family and work roles, the government was attempting to resolve this 'trilemma' by initiating policies such as those outlined in **Box 6.2**, alongside a national minimum wage. Dean notes, however, that to date government action has amounted to little more than compliance with European Union (EU) directives on working hours and parental leave and part-time working. A reluctance to interfere in the operation of big business has meant that the minimal positive impacts of the government's approach have been limited to well-placed workers and little of consequence has changed for low–income families active in the more insecure and low-paid sectors of the job market. This has restricted the extent to which low–income families in particular are able successfully to combine paid work and caring roles. Dean concludes that this will only become a reality if and when the government "places unequivocal social obligations on business" (2002b, p 9). More recently he has also argued that a lack of awareness of their work–life balance entitlements among poorer families, and a scarcity of independent welfare rights advice, limits the positive potential of family-friendly policy for those on low incomes (Dean, 2007).

The mainstreaming of gender equality has long been a part of the EU's agenda (Hantrais, 2000), and Hancock (2002) believes that the EU has the potential to outline a more woman- and, indeed, family-friendly notion of citizenship. This, however, remains a highly questionable assumption given the EU's preoccupation with paid work and the fact that many of the social rights implied by 'citizenship of the (European) Union' derive from an individual's status as a paid worker, rather than as a carer or a citizen (Ackers, 1998; Levitas, 1998; Ackers and Dwyer, 2002, 2004; see Chapter Nine, this volume, for further discussions).

Box 6.2: Policies aimed at promoting a work–life balance

2002 Employment Act
Flexible working: parents with children under six years of age (for disabled children the age limit is 18) have the right to apply to work flexibly, for example, reduce overall hours, change hours of work and/or other aspects of their terms and conditions of employment. The employer must consider the request seriously.

Maternity pay/leave: statutory maternity pay to increase from £75 to £100. The maximum period of maternity leave increased to one year (to include six months' unpaid leave).

Paternity leave: fathers have a new right to two weeks' paternity leave to be taken within eight weeks of a child's birth. Statutory paternity pay set at same level as statutory maternity pay.

Paid adoption leave: the above rights extended to parents who adopt children.

2006 Work and Families Act
Flexible working: extended the right to request that an employer considers putting in place flexible working arrangements for those acting as carers for adults.

Maternity pay/leave: also lengthened the maximum period for which statutory maternity pay, maternity allowance and statutory adoption pay are payable, from 26 weeks to 52 weeks.

Paternity leave: established a new scheme to give certain employees (generally fathers) a new entitlement to take care leave to look after a child and receive pay while they are on leave, subject to certain conditions.

Childcare provision
2002 Spending Review: doubled the government's overall financial commitment to childcare; 1.6 million childcare places to be created by March 2004. Sure Start initiatives to be enhanced with Children's Centres to be established in disadvantaged areas.

1998 National Child Care Strategy: established to enhance the availability of good quality, affordable childcare.

Other initiatives

1998 Working Time Regulations: basic rights for workers introduced including the right to work no more than, on average, 48 hours a week (although a worker may choose to work longer hours); the right to one day a week off and four weeks' annual paid leave. Some employment sectors are excluded.

1999 Parental leave: parents of any child born/adopted on or after 15 December 1999 are entitled to take 13 weeks (maximum of four weeks per year) of unpaid leave before the child's fifth birthday.

1999 Time off to care for dependants: employees have a right to take a 'reasonable' amount of unpaid time to deal with an emergency involving a dependant.

2000 New rights for part-time workers: part-time workers gain the same rights (pro rata) as their full-time counterparts, for example, annual leave, company pension schemes, rights to maternity and sick pay etc.

2003 Working Tax Credit and Child Tax Credit: both credits offer some financial support for parents. Working Tax Credit includes a means-tested childcare element to meet up to 70% of the cost of childcare for poor working parents. Child Tax Credit is a tapered means-tested benefit.

Source: HMT/DTI (2003, ch 4)

Sexuality and citizenship

Certain parallels can be drawn between feminist attempts to re-gender citizenship and the struggles of gay men and women to assert their rights. The public–private dichotomy is particularly salient. Sexual practices have long been confined to the private sphere and this in itself can render the needs and rights of lesbian and gay citizens invisible (Isin and Wood, 1999; Lister, 2003c). In line with the radical 'claims-based' approach to understanding the origins and development of rights (in Chapter One, this volume, see the discussion of Dean's work, 2001, 2002a), Plummer (2006) notes that rights are both socially constructed and contested, and that it is only relatively recently that gay rights have been forced onto the agenda by the campaigning and lobbying of gay men and women. Noting that, "finally, then, by the early twenty first century hitherto marginalised discussions of sexual rights start to assume prominence in citizenship theory" (2006, p 163), he traces the ways in which debates about 'intimate' or 'sexual citizenship' have been used by both feminists and gay and lesbian people to demand social inclusion. For Plummer, the articulation of gay rights across the globe remains uneven and he reminds us that many gay men and women are actively denied rights and/or openly persecuted in certain places. Nonetheless, he believes the very fact that issues of sexuality and sexual politics have become part of contemporary citizenship debates is indicative of a measure of progress, and that "a new visible culture of lesbian rights, gay rights, transgender rights – indeed intimate citizenship or even queer citizenship – are in the process of being created even as they are contested" (Plummer, 2006, p 166).

For Weeks (2001), the feminist and lesbian and gay movements are united in the ways in which they force their agendas into the public realm. A moment of 'transgression', a public assertion of the right to be different, precedes the claim to citizenship:

> Without the transgressive moment, the claims of the hitherto excluded would barely be noticed ... transgression appears necessary to face the status quo with its inadequacies, to hold up a mirror to its prejudices and fears. But without the claim to full citizenship, difference can never find a recognised place. The sexual citizen makes a claim to transcend the limits of the personal sphere by going public, but the going public is, in a necessary but nevertheless paradoxical move about protecting the possibilities of private life and private choice in a more inclusive society. (Weeks, 2001, p 60)

Citizenship, however, is not without its particular problems for lesbians and gay men. Richardson (1998, 2000) argues that alongside the 'male' ideal discussed previously, citizenship status has been constructed around a norm of heterosexuality. She considers how homosexuality impacts on the lives of gay individuals in relation to Marshall's triumvirate of civil, political and social rights, and argues that lesbians and gay men are partial citizens. In the past, the lack of legal protection from discrimination or harassment because of sexuality, and the denial of a formal right to marriage for gay couples, has denied sexual minorities equal civil rights. Furthermore, although there are no formal distinctions between the political rights of homosexual and heterosexual individuals, the legitimacy of lesbian and gay men's claims to recognition and, when necessary, appropriate resources, are often subject to a hostile response from the mainstream (Isin and Wood, 1999). Due to homophobic attitudes, being openly gay can also be a hindrance (at worst, effectively acting as a bar) when standing for political office. Many lesbians and gay men are further disadvantaged in terms of social rights because same-sex relationships are not recognised by various institutions that provide welfare (Richardson, 1998; Lister, 2003c).

Towards formal equality?

The present UK government has made some steps towards the realisation of formal equality for gay people, most notably the equalisation of the age of consent. In June 2003 the government also responded to years of sustained pressure from gay rights groups and announced its intention to grant homosexual couples the same rights as married heterosexual partners. Under the 2004 Civil Partnership Act lesbians and gay men are able to declare their partnership legally and acquire the new legal status of 'registered civil partners'. The government was keen to emphasise that the Act fits with similar legislation in a range of Western nations (cf Stonewall, 2003), and that it was illustrative of its wider commitment to the promotion of formal equality. However, as Tatchell (2009) notes, the Act remains discriminatory as same-sex couples cannot be legally married and heterosexual couples are not permitted to request a civil partnership. Opinion among gay couples as to whether or not the specific category of civil partnership, which is effectively reserved for same-sex couples, is preferable to extending legal rights to marriage to gay and lesbian couples, appears to be equally split. However, qualitative research has shown that many welcome the legal protections civil partnership brings (Smart et al, 2006).

In line with the general tone of many reforms emerging from New Labour, prior to enacting the civil partnership legislation the stress was very much on the rights *and* responsibilities that would ensue for civil partners. New rights include: joint treatment for income-related benefits and state pensions, parental rights over each other's children and recognition for immigration purposes. In the event of a civil partnership being dissolved in the courts, both partners share responsibility for a fair division of property and must ensure that appropriate arrangements for contact with children are put in place where necessary. Partners who are bereaved will also enjoy the same legal rights (for example, the right to register the death of their partner, equal recognition under inheritance laws), and social benefit rights, as a surviving spouse. Following their legislation on registered civil partnerships, the government also enacted the 2004 Gender Recognition Act, which gives transsexual people who have undergone full gender transformation the right to have their gender changed on their birth certificate and the legal right to marry. Individuals who successfully apply to the Gender Recognition Panel for a full Gender Recognition Certificate are subsequently legally recognised according to their acquired gender (OPSI, 2009b).

Certain commentators (Waites, 1999; Stychin, 2001) have noted the positive potential of the EU in outlawing discrimination on grounds of sexuality. Recent developments appear to confirm this view. For example, Article 13 EC expressly outlaws discrimination on the grounds of sexual orientation. The 2004 Gender Recognition Act followed a European Court ruling in 2002 which stated that the British government was acting unlawfully in failing to recognise the rights of people who had undergone gender transformation (Ahmed, 2003). In another case in 2002 appeal court judges in the UK House of Lords invoked Article 14 of the European Convention on Human Rights (ECHR) in ruling that a gay man had the same rights as a heterosexual spouse or cohabitee to take over a deceased partner's tenancy (Dyer, 2002b). The 1998 Human Rights Act, which incorporated the ECHR into British law, appears to be driving forward policy to extend equal citizenship rights to sexual minorities.

In the past, sexual orientation has been used to exclude certain individuals from the equality of status inherent in citizenship (see, for example, Waites, 1999). Today certain commentators are more optimistic about the possibility of promoting 'sexual rights' as an adjunct to civil, political and social rights (see Richardson and Turner, 2001). They believe that the exclusive, hegemonic heterosexual normality of the past has been challenged by a combination of social change, the emergence of vocal lesbian and gay communities and radical queer theory (Waites, 1999; Weeks, 2001). In spite of such progress, homosexuality has been, and arguably remains, variously conceived as a threat to national security, traditional family values and the wider social fabric of the nation (Richardson, 1998). One further change brought about by New Labour, the repeal, in 2003, of Section 28 of the 1988 Local Government Act which banned schools from 'promoting' homosexuality, is indicative of recent progress in curtailing legally sanctioned discrimination against gay and lesbian citizens. The strong lobbying from some quarters against the repeal of Section 28 and the fact that the government continues to refuse to grant cohabiting homosexual couples the same right to marry as heterosexuals, indicates that there is some way to go before such discrimination is fully overcome (Dillon, 2003; Tatchell, 2009).

Transforming citizenship?

Given the problematic nature of citizenship for women in the past, a number of feminist scholars remain ambivalent about the future usefulness of the concept (see Lister, 2003b). For some, however, a re-gendered notion of citizenship is seen as an important part of any wider attempt to positively transform gender relations and the social institutions of welfare. Fraser (2000a) locates such aims within in the wider context of oppressed minority groups' cultural and symbolic struggles for recognition and equality. As Lewis (2009, pp 258–9) notes,

> Fraser (1997, 2000a) identifies three dimensions to these recognition denials: *non-recognition*, the rendering of invisibility as a result of dominant cultural forms; *misrecognition*, being seen as lacking value and as inferior; and *disrespect*, being maligned or disparaged in everyday interactions or representations. A politics of recognition therefore aims towards seeing and valuing individuals, groups, identities, experiences, knowledges and expertise, (potential) contributions, humanity and personhood; upholding citizenship status and rights; and affording people dignity and respect (Fraser, 2000a; Lister 2004b, 2007).

A reconsideration of the public–private divide is, therefore, central to the future transformation of citizenship in the work of both Fraser (2000b) and Lister (1997, 2003b), two feminists who have been keen to outline ways forward.

Fraser (2000b) points out that the gendered assumptions which continue to underpin many contemporary welfare states increasingly do not reflect the reality of modern life. Indeed, she argues that the breadwinner–caregiver dichotomy is a powerful myth that has disadvantaged women and long failed to fit with many people's patterns of parenting and partnering. Fraser is attempting to articulate a framework for thinking about how gender equity may be achieved in future welfare arrangements. For her, gender equity is a complex idea that encompasses seven normative principles that move away from the sterile equality versus difference debates that have been a feature of past feminist thinking. Utilising her seven principles, Fraser (2000b) considers four important issues: the social organisation of care work, the principles that underpin welfare provision, differences that occur among women as a generic group and, finally, the other goals, beyond gender equity, that would properly be central concerns for a new welfare state. She then initially outlines two idealised models: the 'universal breadwinner' model and the 'caregiver parity' model (see **Box 6.3**).

According to Fraser, both the universal breadwinner and the caregiver parity models represent significantly different feminist visions of the future, but in certain respects both represent a measure of progress towards gender equity. The universal breadwinner model proves to be especially useful for childless women and/or those without domestic care responsibilities. The caregiver parity model certainly makes life better for those with significant

Box 6.3: Towards gender equity in welfare

Seven normative principles crucial for gender equity

1. *The anti-poverty principle:* preventing poverty is crucial to achieving gender equity now, ... given the high rates of poverty in solo mother families ... a welfare state should at least relieve suffering by meeting otherwise unmet basic needs. (p 6)

2. *The anti-exploitation principle:* needy women with no other way to feed themselves and their children, for example, are liable to exploitation ... the availability of an alternative source of income enhances the bargaining power of subordinates in equal relationships ... support must be provided as a right. When aid is highly stigmatised or discretionary, the anti-exploitation principle is not satisfied. (p 7)

3. *Income equality:* [this] principle requires a substantial reduction in the vast discrepancies between men's and women's incomes. (p 8)

4. *Leisure time equality:* [this] principle rules out welfare arrangements that would equalise incomes while requiring a double shift of work from women, but only a single shift from men. (p 9)

5. *Equality of respect:* rules out social arrangements that objectify and depreciate women – even if those arrangements prevent poverty and exploitation, and even if in addition they equalise income and leisure time. (p 9)

6. *The anti-marginalisation principle:* requires provision of the necessary conditions for women's participation, including childcare, elder care and provision of breastfeeding in public. It also requires the dismantling of masculinist work cultures and woman hostile environments. (p 10)

7. *The anti-androcentrism principle:* requires decentralising masculinist norms – in part by revaluing practices and traits that are currently undervalued because they are associated with women. It entails changing men as well as women. (p 10)

Two feminist models for a new welfare state?

The breadwinner model: aims to achieve gender equity principally by promoting women's employment. The point is to enable women to support themselves and their families through wage earning. The breadwinner role is to be universalised, in sum, so that women, too, can be workers. (p 13)

The caregiver parity model: aims to promote gender equity principally by supporting informal care work.... The aim is not to make women's lives the same as men's but rather to make the difference costless.... The caregiver role is on a par with the breadwinner role, so that women and men can enjoy equivalent levels of dignity and well-being. (pp 18-19)

Source: Fraser (2000b)

familial care responsibilities; but both fail to provide full gender equity, according to Fraser's seven principles (see ***Table 6.1***).

Table 6.1: *Relative merits of universal breadwinner and caregiver parity models*

Principle model	Universal breadwinner model	Caregiver parity model
Anti-poverty	Good	Good
Anti-exploitation	Good	Good
Income equality	Fair	Poor
Leisure time equality	Poor	Fair
Equality of respect	Fair	Fair
Anti-marginalisation	Fair	Poor
Anti-androcentrism	Poor	Fair

Source: Fraser (2000b, p 25)

Fraser (2000b) notes that, in effect, the universal breadwinner model is asking women to be more like men, while the caregiver parity model does little to challenge the current gendered roles of men and women, but at least reduces the costs of care for women. She concludes that the only way to ensure that gender equity will become a reality in future is to strive towards a third model, the 'universal caregiver'. This approach envisages a radical reordering of the institutions of work, care and welfare:

> A universal caregiver welfare state would promote gender equity by effectively dismantling the gendered opposition between breadwinning and caregiving. (Fraser, 2000b, p 26)

This would, of course, require men to change their whole approach to work and welfare. Paid work and informal care work would be given parity on both a personal and an institutional level.

The work of Lister (1997, 2003b) is also concerned with outlining a women-friendly citizenship. She notes that three approaches to re-gendering citizenship have been outlined by feminist scholars. 'Gender neutrality' approaches focus on equality and aim to make gender irrelevant to citizenship rights and responsibilities. Those who argue for 'gender differentiation' often look for a formal recognition of women's roles and contributions as carers within a reformulated theory of citizenship. The emphasis here is on a politics that recognises women's difference and the validity of female forms of contribution. A 'gender pluralist' approach accepts the continued importance of gender, but recognises that other factors, such as ethnicity, class, sexuality and disability, are also significant in shaping individual identity and citizenship status. According to Lister (2003b, 2003c), it is this third approach that offers most for the positive reformulation of citizenship. She believes that feminists should look to:

> ... reconstruct citizenship along pluralist rather than dualist lines. In place of the male standard, masquerading as universalism, citizenship will then embody a differentiated universalism which gives equal status to women and men in their diversity. (Lister, 1997, p 197)

For Lister the challenge that citizens face today is to find the correct balance between diversity and common values (cf Weeks, 2001). While this may not be an entirely new problem for a progressive theory of citizenship (refer to the dilemma outlined by Titmuss, in *Box 4.1*, Chapter Four), the acknowledged complexities of contemporary social life demand that differences of gender, sexuality and a range of other dimensions (and any inequalities that may then subsequently accrue) are considered alongside class–based divisions in a reformulated notion of citizenship.

Summary

Although discussions of gender inequality (and this chapter) have tended to focus on women, it is important to recognise that gender issues also relate to men. The male breadwinner (myth) and the lived experiences of men are profoundly gendered. Connell's (1995) approach to hegemonic masculinity has been especially influential in raising questions about how men both benefit from 'the patriarchal dividend' and, for marginalised masculinities (for example, black, gay, working-class men), incur specific penalties. For example, young working-class men are seen to be under-achieving in schools and are more likely to be imprisoned and/or attacked in the streets, while black and gay men have long been subject to abuse and discrimination. Likewise older men may experience feelings of dislocation and exclusion following redundancy or retirement, emotions that derive, in part, from their learnt gender identity. Of course, the experiences of men who lose out in these masculine contests does not detract from the broader issue of gender inequalities between men and women. Nevertheless, many contemporary social policy commentators now recognise that the problems men face, and those they cause, are themselves gendered (Mann, 1998b; Scourfield and Drakeford, 2002).

This chapter began by asking two linked questions, 'To what extent can citizenship be considered as a gendered concept?' and 'How does gender impact on citizenship?'. It has attempted to answer these questions by engaging with feminist critiques and also by highlighting the contemporary issue of family-friendly policy. Several conclusions can be drawn:

- Citizenship is a gendered concept. Many writers have been critical of the male assumptions that underpin citizenship.
- Much feminist criticism of citizenship has highlighted the extent to which women, as a group within the boundaries of the nation state, are excluded from full citizenship status.
- Patriarchal structures and ideologies continue to have a negative impact on women's ability to act as citizens.
- The 'private' world of informal care (and gendered assumptions made about women's role to provide such care) constrains many women's ability to act within the 'public' world traditionally associated with citizenship.
- In terms of social citizenship, women also face disadvantaged treatment and access to social benefits because many welfare systems continue to assume female financial dependence on men and are largely biased towards traditionally male work patterns.
- There are commonalities but also important differences in the ways that sexuality and gender may affect citizenship status.
- In spite of its many limitations, certain feminists believe that a reformulated notion of citizenship that moves beyond the public–private, (male) breadwinner–(female) caregiver dichotomies of the past has the potential to deliver gender equality and enable men and women to achieve a real balance between family life and paid employment in the future.

Further reading

Readers interested in the issues discussed in this chapter should start with **Pateman's (1989)** discussion of the patriarchal welfare state. **Lister's (2003c)** book (2nd edition) is also an excellent and wide-ranging discussion of feminist critiques and perspectives on citizenship. **May and Brunsdon (2005)** offer a fuller consideration of work–life balance issues. The review article by **Richardson and Turner (2001)**, and **Plummer's (2006)** chapter, are both good starting points for those who wish to consider debates about sexuality and citizenship.

Website resources

Relevant material and links to other potential sources can be found at the following sites.

Women and Equality Unit, Department of Trade and Industry, which holds many of the UK government's publications on work–life balance: **www.womenandequalityunit.gov.uk**

For those interested in issues around sexuality and citizenship the websites of **Stonewall (www.stonewall.org.uk)** and **OutRage! (www.outrage.org.uk)**, two campaigning groups that work towards social justice and equality for gay men, lesbians and bisexuals, are good places to start. The Economic and Social Research Council (ESRC) CAVA (Care, Values and the Future of Welfare) study group also have a web page which has access to a number of relevant discussions and publications: **www.leeds.ac.uk/cava**

seven

Disabled citizens?

In the past, many theorists from a wide range of mainstream political positions (for example, liberal, communitarian and Marxist) have been content to follow 'commonsense' ideas about disabled people lacking the capacities required to function as 'normal' citizens (Handley, 2003). T.H. Marshall's famous account of citizenship, for example, fails to consider issues of impairment and disability. However, his emphasis on the rights and responsibilities of able-bodied males, and the fact that many disabled people fail to enjoy basic citizenship rights in any substantive sense (Oliver and Barnes, 1991; Barton, 1993; Barnes et al, 1999; Barnes and Mercer, 2003), suggest that it would be premature to consider many disabled people as equal members of the community of citizens that Marshall envisaged. Issues of impairment and disability continue to raise a number of important questions about the potential for and limitations of citizenship. The following three areas are discussed:

* individual/medical models of disability;
* disabled people as active citizens;
* disability and welfare policy: progress under New Labour?

A social understanding of disability

Disabled people and their organisations have long articulated demands for a recognition of their rights as equal citizens (Oliver, 1996). Angered by a dominant, professionally constructed and administered 'medical model' of disability (intrinsically linked to ideas of dependency), they have challenged by developing, alongside like-minded intellectuals, a *social model* of disability which focuses on the disabling attitudes, environments, practices and policies that are prevalent in contemporary society (Oliver, 1990, 1996; Barton, 1993; Barnes and Mercer, 1997, 2003). In *Box 7.1* Barnes et al

(1999) discuss how the *medical model* reinforces ideas of abnormality based on presumptions of individual biological and/or physiological inferiority.

> ## Box 7.1: Individual/medical and social models of disability
>
> ### The individual model
> The focus is on bodily 'abnormality', disorder or deficiency, and the way in which this in turn 'causes' some degree of 'disability' or function limitation. For example, people who have quadriplegia cannot use their arms and are therefore unable to wash or dress themselves. However, this functional 'incapacity' is used as the basis for a wider classification of the individual as (an) 'invalid'. Once they have been categorised in this way, the 'disability' becomes their defining characteristic and their incapacity is generalised. This forms the basis for a 'personal tragedy' approach, where the individual is regarded as a victim and someone who is in need of 'care and attention', and dependent on others – a perspective which has been at the heart of contemporary social welfare policies designed to help disabled people cope with 'their disability' (Oliver, 1983, 1990; Finkelstein, 1993).
>
> The recommended solution lies in curative and rehabilitative medical intervention, with an increasing involvement of allied health practitioners, psychologists and educationalists. To acquire an impairment is to become the object of professional attention.... The basic concern is to diagnose the bodily or intellectual 'abnormality' and advise on appropriate treatment.
>
> ### The social model
> In developing what became known as a social approach to disability, disabled people in Britain argued that it is society which disables people with impairments, and therefore any meaningful solution must be directed at societal change rather than individual adjustment and rehabilitation. The social model riposte to the individual medical approach is that 'disability is not the measles' (Rioux and Bach, 1994).
>
> The Union of the Physically Impaired Against Segregation (UPIAS) was in the vanguard of those calling for an alternative model of disability. In its manifesto document *Fundamental principles of disability* (1976), UPIAS placed the responsibility for disability squarely on society's failures. 'In our view it is society which disables physically impaired people, disability is something imposed on top of our impairments by the way we are unnecessarily isolated and excluded from full participation in society. Disabled people are therefore an oppressed group in society' (UPIAS, 1976, p 14) ... the meaning of disability was turned on its head:

- *Impairment:* lacking part or all of a limb, or having a defective limb, organ or mechanism of the body.
- *Disability:* the disadvantage or restriction of activity caused by a contemporary social organisation which takes no or little account of people who have physical impairments and thus excludes them from participation in the mainstream of social activities. (UPIAS, 1976, pp 3-4)

Subsequent discussions among disabled people and their organisations have amended reference to physical impairments so that any impairment (including sensory and intellectual examples) falls within the potential scope of disability.

Whereas impairment is regarded as an individual attribute, disability is not. Instead, it is described as 'the outcome of an oppressive relation between people with ... impairments and the rest of society' (Finkelstein, 1980, p 47).

Source: Barnes et al (1999, pp 21, 27-8)

In contrast to the individual/medical model, the social model locates disability firmly in the social sphere. Central to this approach is the assertion that people with impairments are no different from everyone else in that, as individuals, they differ in the range of things that they can and cannot do. Impairment affects the ways in which an individual's body and mind functions, but the quality of life enjoyed by disabled citizens is determined by a society's reaction to impairment (Williams, 1995). According to the social model, disability comes from:

> The failure of a structured social environment to adjust to the needs and aspirations of citizens with disabilities rather than from the inability of disabled individuals to adapt to the demands of society. (Hahn, 1986, p 132)

This failure to consider fully the needs of individuals with impairments denies disabled people their citizenship rights. Barnes (1991, 1992; Barnes et al, 1999) outlines how disabled people have long faced institutionalised discrimination in most areas of their lives. Pointing to a combination of enforced segregation within the education system, the labour market and various welfare services, and a hostile physical environment, Barnes argues that disabled people are effectively denied the civil, political and social rights that are central to the notion of citizenship. As Oliver (1996) notes, the state has played a central role in this marginalisation. Disabled people have identified structures, policies and professional practices within state welfare provisions that have exacerbated their social exclusion and promoted dependency. Arguably the citizenship rights for disabled people remain firmly anchored in rhetoric rather than reality (Barnes and Oliver, 1995).

The medical and social models of disability have been the subject of much subsequent debate. Morris (1991) and other feminist critics have, for example, questioned the extent to which the social model may obscure the different personal experiences of disabled people. A good short basic overview of these debates and critiques is offered in Handley (2003); Priestley (1998) also provides a useful discussion.

Active citizens

The struggles of disabled people for equality and recognition, and for their right as people with impairments to exercise full and effective membership of society, are ongoing (Priestley, 2003). In Chapter Four it was noted how a particular type of active citizenship has been constructed by the New Right that, to a certain extent, has been subsequently adopted by 'third way' thinkers and governments. Central to this notion of the *active citizen* is the idea that individuals should, whenever possible, assume responsibility for their own and their family's welfare via paid employment. Such responsible, active citizens also accept that charitable works, that is, the giving of private time and/or money to deserving, less fortunate members of the community, is also necessary. The collective struggle of disabled people's organisations and their allies provides an alternative model for active citizenship, one that is arguably more positive.

A number of authors (Oliver, 1996; Oliver and Barnes, 1998; Barnes and Mercer, 2003) outline and discuss the important role played by coordinating organisations run by disabled people themselves (for example, UPIAS [Union of the Physically Impaired Against Segregation], Disabled Peoples International, British Council of Organisations of Disabled People [BCODP]) in the long struggle for rights. As *Box 7.1* indicates, organisations such as UPIAS were at the forefront of the development of the social model of disability that refocused debates around impairment on issues central to citizenship. Indeed, organisations run and managed by disabled people (often referred to by the shorthand term the Disabled People's Movement [DPM]) have become an integral part of the wider challenge, by various new social movements, to the exclusive and paternalistic citizenship of the PWWS (see Chapter Four, this volume).

Marginalised by mainstream politics, the DPM has combined lobbying and direct action to force the claims of disabled people onto the welfare agenda (Barnes and Mercer, 2003). It has denounced the ways in which disabled people's welfare services have often been couched in the language of 'special needs' and instead has sought to articulate a challenge that combines the language of equal citizenship with an active struggle for rights. They have contested the traditionally dominant image of disabled people as passive recipients of welfare, who lack both the competence to make decisions about their own needs and the ability to act as citizens in their own right (Oliver and Barnes, 1998). Increasingly, disabled people and their organisations have called for the right to define their own needs and for the autonomous definition and control of any welfare services that they may require to facilitate independent living (Oliver, 1996). The status of disability activists as 'active citizens' is thus confirmed through their ongoing acts of dissent and participation in a collective struggle for the rights that full citizenship should entail. In turn, the extension of such rights will offer many new possibilities for meaningful participation and increase both the individual and collective autonomy of disabled people within society. It is important to remember, however, that the struggles of disabled people are not solely about rights. Disabled people are also seeking to assume relevant responsibilities on a par with non-disabled citizens. They are looking to assume control of their own lives. Campaigns around independent living and the right to meaningful paid work are about empowering people with impairments and enabling them, whenever possible, to assume increased responsibility for their own welfare. The extent to which changes in welfare policy since the 1990s have helped to facilitate this process are considered next.

Disability and welfare policy in the UK: progress under New Labour?

The introduction of a number of UK policy reforms of significance for disabled people has been a feature since the 1990s. This section focuses on policy changes in three important areas, namely: social security benefits, 'community care' and anti-discrimination legislation. In part changes in policy and/or the organisation and delivery of welfare in these sectors can be seen as evidence of the success of the disabled people's organisations in getting their concerns onto the political agenda (Handley, 2003). Certainly, many of the assumptions made in relation to the respective rights and responsibilities of the state in meeting the needs of disabled people are being increasingly questioned. This is particularly evident when reforms of the social security benefit system are considered.

Work, welfare and disability

Disability is typically characterised by high levels of unemployment, poverty and social exclusion (Howard et al, 2001, ch 3). Research suggests that more than half of the disabled people who do not work would like to engage in paid employment, with many also believing that they are discriminated against in the PLM (Heenan, 2002). As Hewitt (1999) notes, the New Labour government is keen to emphasise the right of disabled people to play a full role in society (DSS, 1998a). This crucially includes the right to work, which, as previously noted, the government now regards as *the* central duty of citizenship. Since its return to power in 1997, a central part of New Labour's approach has been to challenge certain assumptions about paid work, welfare and disabled people that have long been taken for granted. In 1997 the Social Security Advisory Committee (SSAC) reviewed policy options in relation to disabled people and the government's desire to promote work as the best form of welfare. It came up with four issues for further consideration (SSAC, 1997, pp 2-3, quoted in Hewitt, 1999, p 158):

1. The extent to which the benefit system should make provision for long-term sickness or disability (other than the additional costs directly attributable to disability) at a different rate from that of long-term unemployment benefit.
2. Whether ... the benefit system should reward those who have previously worked to a greater extent than those who have not, or have been unable to work.
3. Whether it is practical to develop a structure that provides greater incentive for those currently treated as incapable of work ... to move from benefit dependency into work, to at least some extent, without unfairly penalising or stigmatising those who are incapable of work.
4. Whether ... a structure can be developed that encourages those who can work, either for a part of a week or episodically, or can work full-time but with a limited capacity, but does not penalise those who, having attempted to do so, cannot, for good reason, sustain the attempt.

The backdrop for these deliberations was the increasing amount of social security expenditure going on benefits for sick and disabled people. Figures indicate that costs rose from £5 billion in 1979 to around £24 billion in 1996/97, although arguably they had peaked by this date (Hyde, 2000).

In the past both governments and citizens have generally tended to support the claims of long-term sick and disabled people for social security for two reasons. First, because disabled people meet commonly held views about legitimate need for the provision of financial support and care through the public welfare system. Second, because the cause of their inactivity in the PLM is seen by many as being beyond their control. In short, questions about whether disabled people are choosing to be idle are generally perceived as having little relevance because their inability to work is 'obviously' linked to an individual impairment (see Dwyer, 2000a). These views may reflect wider ideas about disabled people being a 'deserving' case for largely unconditional collective support. It is important to note that such views have been identified as disabling by disabled people's organisations. Barnes (1992), for example, discusses how disabled people have challenged such discriminatory views and demanded the eradication of disabling attitudes and environments, so that they can realise the right to paid employment. Indeed, New Labour could possibly claim that their social security benefit reforms are motivated by a desire to encourage disabled people into work and support the wider right to work agenda of the DPM. Alternatively, perhaps they are indicative of a broader attempt to diminish the welfare role of the state, reduce costs and redefine social citizenship, so that entitlement to benefit becomes, whenever possible, conditional on accepting the obligation of paid work (Dwyer, 1998, 2000a; Hewitt, 1999; Hyde, 2000).

Certainly disabled people's access to benefits has been subject to a number of significant changes as part of a more general restructuring of social security provision in Britain (see Chapter Five). The previously noted approach of the SSAC appears to be focused on encouraging as many people as possible, who are currently in receipt of disability benefits, back into paid work, without simultaneously penalising 'genuine' claimants who cannot work because of impairment. As Hyde (2000) notes, in the past the system of disability benefits has been criticised for being expensive and failing to lift those disabled people dependent on benefits out of poverty. Also, prior to recent reforms (see *Box 7.2*), it could be argued that arrangements for the payment of special benefits to those who were long-term unemployed because of impairment created an administrative category of disability which effectively exempted those labelled in this way from having to take up the responsibility of paid work. The more rigorous approach to the administration of long-term out-of-work benefits by New Labour has attempted to tackle what it saw as the perverse incentives of the disability benefit system that it inherited.

Both 'carrots' and 'sticks' are part of New Labour's reforms. The carrots take the form of a range of incentives to encourage disabled people into work. These include benefit enhancements (see *Box 7.2*) to ease the transition from welfare to work and tax credits specifically for disabled people who enter the PLM. The accompanying reductions in eligibility for benefits (people who fail the capability assessment are deemed capable of work and excluded from entitlement to benefit), and the requirement that claimants attend a job-focused interview as a condition of eligibility, help to ensure compliance. The abolition of Incapacity Benefit and its replacement with Employment and Support Allowance (ESA) under the 2007 Welfare

Box 7.2: Carrots and sticks: disability benefit reforms under New Labour

New Deal for Disabled People (first piloted in 1998)
- Targeted at those in receipt of Incapacity Benefit or Severe Disablement Allowance who must attend a work-focused interview.
- A guarantee that people can return to their previous level of benefit at any time within 12 months of taking a job.
- Job finders grant of £200 for each client.
- £50 a week top-up of pay for those taking part-time jobs for a period of six months.
- £75 per week to employers for six weeks following recruitment.

1999 Welfare Reform and Pensions Act
- A strengthening of the link between work and entitlement. Only those who have recently been in work and paid NI contributions are now eligible for Incapacity Benefit.
- New claimants of Incapacity Benefit must see a personal advisor for an interview about routes back into work as a condition of eligibility.
- The 'all work test' (since renamed the capability assessment) is introduced. This refocuses the medical examination used to determine eligibility for incapacity benefits to emphasise a claimant's capacity for work rather than their impairments.
- Introduction of the means testing of Incapacity Benefits. People in receipt of occupational or private pensions will have the benefit reduced by 50p for every pound these pensions rise above £85.

2007 Welfare Reform Act
- New rules introduced to phase out Incapacity Benefit.
- From October 2008 Employment and Support Allowance (ESA) paid to new claimants who are unable to work because of illness or disability.
- The majority of ESA claimants placed on a lower (that is, JSA rate) benefit for 13 weeks while their claim is assessed.
- The majority of ESA recipients expected to attend WFIs or undertake work-related activity as a condition of continued receipt of ESA.
- A minority of ESA recipients with severe impairments not subject to conditionality.

Sources: for more detailed discussions, see Hewitt (1999); Hyde (2000); Heenan (2002)

Reform Act (see Chapter Five, this volume, for more discussion) further emphasises the government's view that the vast majority of disabled people in receipt of disability benefits should be actively looking for paid work. Hyde (2000) identifies three ways of understanding the shift in approach that has occurred in relation to disabled people's rights to social security benefits. First, changes can be seen as part of a wider ideological shift towards conditional welfare inspired by New Right thinkers and taken up as part of 'third way' welfare reform, as discussed in Chapters Four and Five, this volume. Second, as previously noted, they may be part of a cost-cutting exercise. Third, the process can be understood as part of a wider economic strategy in which labour market policy aims to regulate workers, in order to promote low-paid work and provide a reserve army of cheap labour that meets the needs of capital (cf Grover and Stewart, 2000, 2002; Prideaux, 2001).

Although she acknowledges the concerns of critics (Barnes, 2000; Drake, 2000; Hyde, 2000; Roulstone, 2002), and recognises that the New Deal for Disabled People (NDDP) has its shortcomings, Heenan (2002) offers a more positive appraisal of the scheme. She points out that the NDDP has four main elements: schemes to explore pathways into employment, a personal adviser for each client, an information and research campaign to educate both clients and employers and an evaluation of initiatives. Informed by a qualitative user-focused study, Heenan argues that the NDDP is underpinned by an enabling, rather than coercive, ethic, which provides opportunities for disabled people to enter paid work if they wish. Overall Heenan's respondents were positive about the scheme, particularly the work of client advisers and the involvement of the voluntary sector. The voluntary organisation that won the contract through competitive tender for running the scheme was seen by respondents as more trustworthy and approachable than the state. A number of clients reported problems with government benefit personnel in the past. The personal adviser's role was seen as a fundamental factor in the successful transition to work. Respondents noted that emotional as well as practical support was offered, and many highlighted the importance of a period of 'in-job' support following employment.

Critics such as Drake (2000) and Hyde (2000) remain unconvinced. Both believe that satisfactory opportunities for the meaningful employment of disabled people are few and far between. They argue that the current benefit system fails to provide genuine social citizenship rights for disabled people who do not work:

> In sum, the government has restructured social security
> so that the system focuses more narrowly on people with

severe impairments, older disabled people (that is, those over
pensionable age) and disabled children. (Drake, 2000, p 430)

The latest reforms of social security provision (that is, the Welfare Reform
Acts of 2007 and 2009) appear likely to herald an era in which benefit
recipients (including many disabled people) will increasingly be subjected to
the personalised conditionality regimes championed by Gregg (2008). The
promise of more intensive individualised support alongside this to enable
individuals back into paid work may not be enough to ensure meaningful
employment for many. As Barnes (2000) reminds us, personal advisers and
schemes to change employers' attitudes have been tried before and failed.
Throughout their period in office successive New Labour administrations
have introduced a complex range of reforms for disability benefits. The
main outcomes of these reforms will be an increase in the number of
disabled people who will face cuts in their social security benefits and/or
have little choice but to return to paid work in the future. Disabled people
have long struggled for the right to work, but it should be remembered
that citizenship also involves the right to adequate social security. Recent
reforms diminish rather than enhance that right.

Disabled people and community care

The community care policies of today have been fashioned by a range
of changes and concerns that have emerged since the 1980s. A political
desire to enhance consumer choice and promote a *mixed economy of care*
was an essential part of the Conservative government's welfare agenda in
the 1980s. A general recognition that state-run long-stay care institutions
were outdated and inappropriate, and economic concerns about their costs,
combined to bring community care to the fore. The basic idea behind
community care is that older and/or disabled people who require care should
be supported in their own homes whenever possible. In many cases this
translates into familial carers (often, but not exclusively, women) caring
for other members of their family (for a fuller discussion, see Parker and
Clarke, 2002; Blakemore, 2003, ch 10).

The 1990s saw some significant care legislation enacted (see **Box 7.3**).
The 1990 NHS and Community Care Act sought to rationalise the
management of care. Local authority social services departments were
charged with assessing and providing a package of care tailored to the needs
of individual clients. The idea behind the creation of an internal market
was, theoretically, to promote greater choice. Rather than a local authority
having a duty to provide services directly, they were charged with making
an assessment of an individual's needs and then putting together a package

of services (provided by a range of public, private or voluntary agencies) to best meet those needs. In reality many needs remained unmet due to the budgetary constraints placed on local authority social services departments (Blakemore, 2003). However, the ability of a majority of disabled people to exercise any consumer choice was also virtually non-existent, as those reliant on welfare benefits had to take what they were given by local social services departments (Barnes et al, 1999). Furthermore, feminist scholars had begun to highlight the contribution of familial carers in providing care in the home. The 1995 Carers (Recognition and Services) Act placed carers' needs at the centre of community care policy, a development that is not without pitfalls as far as those in receipt of care are concerned (Parker and Clarke, 2002). A conflict between the rights and agendas of disabled people and those of familial carers is a distinct possibility. Furthermore, conflicts of interest may also occur between disabled people who purchase care and the individuals they employ as personal assistants to provide it (Spandler, 2004).

Box 7.3: Significant community care legislation

1990 NHS and Community Care Act
The aims of the Act were to promote/prioritise the option of people being cared for in their own homes and the enhancement of consumer choice.

Created an internal (or quasi-) market system of social services. Local authorities required to act mainly as purchasers of services provided by a range of other private or voluntary organisations.

Local authorities required to draw up care plans that were based on 'client/ needs-led' assessments.

1995 Carers (Recognition and Services) Act
Carers who provide 'care on a regular basis' to a person who has been, or will be, assessed for community care services are entitled to an assessment of their own situation.

Local authorities have to take into account the results of the carer's assessment when making decisions about services to be provided to the user.

1996 Community Care (Direct Payments) Act

Allows direct payment to be made to a disabled person so that they may purchase a package of care from a range of providers.

Local authorities have a choice of providing this option, rather than a duty to provide it.

2001 Health and Social Care Act

Extends the approach of the 1996 Community Care (Direct Payments) Act. Disabled people aged 16-18 are eligible to apply for direct payments, as are persons with a parental responsibility for a disabled child.

Concerns about such issues have informed the fundamental critique of community care developed by disabled people's organisations and certain academics. First, these critics argue that the very notion of 'care' may enhance the negative view of the person being cared for as 'dependent'. Second, they note that there is a tendency for community care to favour the language and approach of an individualised medical model of disability in which disabled people are seen as 'deserving' but rather unfortunate recipients of support. Third, they point out that the rhetoric of empowerment and choice may hide a reality in which a right to a measure of collective support is giving way to a norm of individually purchased and/or familial care (Morris, 1993; Barnes et al, 1999; Ackers and Dwyer, 2002; Parker and Clarke, 2002).

These issues have been central to the critique of community care developed by disabled people involved with the Independent Living Movement (see Morris, 1993). In many respects the 1996 Community Care (Direct Payments) Act can be seen as an outcome of sustained campaigns by disabled people for empowerment and increased control over their own lives. As *Box 7.3* illustrates, the Act gives local authority social services departments the power to make direct cash payments to individuals in lieu of community care services. The emphasis is on enabling users of services (that is, disabled and/or older people) to achieve maximum choice and control over their support services. Once a disabled person receives the payment directly they can purchase their care from any suitably qualified provider. However, local authorities are not duty bound to provide direct payments, but rather have the option of providing direct payments to users if requested. The legislation is also problematic in a number of other ways. The provision of direct payments still remains reliant on professional judgements about a person's needs and abilities. The requirement that a person 'possesses the mental capacity' to manage direct payments can rule out certain people. For example, Roulstone and Morgan (2009) note that many people with learning difficulties are deemed to be ineligible to receive direct payments. Nonetheless, direct payments do help to facilitate independent living and empower significant numbers of disabled people, some of whom have been able to employ personal assistants for the first time. The government has been keen to endorse and expand this approach. In 1997 they extended the scheme to cover people aged 65 plus and the 2001 Health and Social Care Act further expanded its scope (see *Box 7.3*). In spite of the government's enthusiasm, it needs to be borne in mind that in the decade following the 1996 Community Care (Direct Payments) Act under 5% of those eligible for a direct payment were receiving one (Davey et al, 2007).

The various advantages and disadvantages of direct payments are noted in *Table 7.1*. Pearson (2000) discusses further the tension that exists between the two discourses commonly used to interpret direct payments, that is, empowerment and social justice and market-based consumerism. He notes the positive potential of direct payments, but questions whether they may yet be another example of the state attempting to distance itself from its welfare responsibilities and reduce its overall costs. A great deal also depends on how direct payment policy is implemented in different localities. The quasi-market system now in place encourages diversity between localities and this has important implications for the idea of social citizenship. Differing opportunities and rights to care, dependent on locality, ensue; some users will be able to access and make use of a range of options/providers and others will not. This may well be problematic for the idea of common citizenship and the notion of equality of status.

Individual budgets and 'self-directed' support: the next steps?

New policies are currently being implemented in England to further extend the choice and control available to disabled people and older people, in respect of the care and support they receive. As Glendinning (2008) notes, the language involved in several influential government policy statements has shifted with the term 'direct payments' being replaced by discussion of 'individual budgets', for example, *Improving the life chances of disabled people* (Cabinet Office, 2005), *Independence, well-being and choice: Our vision for the future of social care for adults in England* (DH, 2005) and *Opportunity age* (HMG, 2005). 'Individual budgets' moves things a step further on from 'direct payments'. The idea is that an individual budget would allow the various resources and funds to which an individual is entitled to be pulled together to enable people to secure a flexible range of care goods and services from a wider range of providers than those that are available under direct payment schemes. "For example an individual budget may be used to pay informal carers (including close relatives living in the same household), or to purchase goods and services from local authorities" (Glendinning, 2008, p 454), both of which are not normally allowed under direct payment rules. A series of pilot schemes was established between 2006 and 2008 to explore how individual budgets may work in practice and these are currently being evaluated.

Table 7.1: Advantages and disadvantages of direct payments

Disadvantages	Advantages
The disabled person has to take on the responsibilities of an employer	Personal support is controlled by the disabled person
It can be time-consuming and complex; need to open and manage a dedicated bank account as required	A cost-effective way to provide care
Problems in interactions with local authority, for example late payment to dedicated account so no money to pay wages	Choice is enhanced
	Control over who enters your home
	Flexibility
In times of high employment it can be difficult to recruit people with the correct range of skills and attitude	Evidence to suggest improvements in quality of care
	Promotes autonomy/reduces dependency of disabled people

In a similar vein to earlier discussion around direct payments (see **Box 7.1**), underpinning the enthusiasm of those who advocate individual budgets is a belief that they enhance the control and choice available to older people and disabled people in need of care. As she makes clear in her discussion, Glendinning is, in principle, in favour of user choice and control, but she also recognises that their promotion within a quasi-market system may not be entirely straightforward for several reasons. First, choices in any real sense may be unavailable in particular areas. This point is endorsed by Roulstone and Morgan (2009), who argue that a 'lottery of provision' alongside localised 'professional ambivalence' may combine to deny individuals choice and control in any meaningful sense. Second, any access to choice, where it exists, may depend on the availability of relatives or friends who are willing and able to act as advocates to negotiate a suitable package care and support on behalf of a disabled or older person. Third, many of the current providers of home social care who hold large block contracts with local authorities may be reluctant to become involved with a plethora of individuals, each holding a personalised direct payments account, particularly if they feel it reduces their capacity to service bigger and potentially more profitable contracts. Fourth, and linked to the previous point, it is possible that individuals who are seen as either troublesome or having complex or problematic care needs will effectively be excluded by providers who decline the opportunity to service particular older and/or disabled purchasers' needs.

Arguably the consumerist foundations on which the personalised direct payments approach is based undermine more traditional notions of collectivised citizenship. As previous discussions in this chapter have illustrated, it needs to be remembered, however, that such traditional notions of citizenship often excluded and stigmatised disabled people in the past. Where they are available and work well, the advent of direct payments and, more latterly individual budgets, not only enables disabled people to manage personalised care packages that meet their needs, but also offers a further significant advantage in respect of wider citizenship debates. Such policies offer disabled people real opportunities to exercise the duties associated with active citizenship which run counter to negative discourses that routinely associate disabled people with welfare dependency (Rummery, 2006). Nonetheless, as welfare policy looks to promote self-directed support by looking to promote the choice and control of disabled people and older people, care must be taken to ensure that the baby is not thrown out with the bathwater.

> Policy has to account for a diversity of disabled people who may be at very different vantage points in terms of their readiness for self determination. Ironically, in moving away from the enforced collectivities of day services and the absence of a Centre for Independent Living or user-led organisation in every locality there is a risk of individual support solutions fostering enforced individualism and isolation. (Roulstone and Morgan, 2009, p 343)

Towards equal citizenship rights for disabled people?

The 1995 Disability Discrimination Act gives individuals the legal right to take employers to court if they feel they have been discriminated against because of their disability. However, a number of critics (Barnes, 2000; Gooding, 2000; Woodhams and Corby, 2003) have reservations about the ability of the Act to challenge wider disabling institutional practices and cultures. They note four main drawbacks. First, the Act is underpinned by, and reinforces, the dominant medical model of disability. Impairment is seen as the cause of disability rather than wider social structures and organisation. Second, disabled people have to prove that they are disabled, as defined by the Act. A person is only considered disabled if they have:

> A physical or mental impairment which has a substantial and long-term adverse effect on his [sic] ability to carry out normal day-to-day activities. (Section 1[1], cited by Woodhams and Corby, 2003, p 63)

If they fail to convince a tribunal on any one of the 'substantial', 'long-term' or 'normal' requirements, a claim against an employer is likely to be dismissed. Third, as the individual has to prove categorically that discrimination exists, only limited protection is provided. Fourth, the majority of employers are not covered by the Act. Although critics recognise that there needs to be a system for individual complaint, they also hold that a positive duty on employers to promote equality should be prioritised in anti-discrimination legislation.

Initially there was no official body to enforce, monitor and police the Act, but this changed with the establishment of the Disability Rights Commission (DRC) in April 2000. The Commission had the power to take up cases on behalf of disabled individuals or groups; however, it appeared to be more concerned to educate employers rather than challenge those with discriminatory employment practices. Barnes believes that:

> Given the nature and extent of discrimination encountered by disabled people there is little here to suggest that the DRC will be any more successful than its contemporaries for gender and race. (2000, p 449)

He also argues that certain fundamental issues need to be tackled if the world of paid work is to become the norm for many disabled people. First, there is a need to tackle the issue of disabling environments. Workplaces, buildings and transport systems need to be made accessible to people with a variety of impairments. Second, there is a need to provide work that is 'socially and financially rewarding', rather than low-paid, low-status work that characterises the employment of many disabled people at present (cf Drake, 2000). Barnes (2000) believes that there is a need to enforce employment quotas on companies and that government could take the lead by setting targets for all state departments and agencies to employ disabled people. It could also ensure that only those private sector companies that employ a set quota of disabled workers are awarded government contracts. The government could further help to facilitate an increase in disabled people's paid employment by shifting its funding priorities from mainstream voluntary sector organisations to those that are controlled and run by disabled people themselves. Many of these already actively recruit and employ a high number of disabled staff; the majority of charitable bodies that serve disabled people do not. Drake (2000) similarly argues that a league table of employment statistics could be set up by the DRC as part of a social inclusion audit, so naming and shaming employers who are not employing disabled people. Whatever the tactic, the government could, and should, be more proactive in setting the agenda for increasing disabled people's employment by tackling institutional prejudice and inertia. In October 2007 the government established the Equality and Human Rights Commission, which took on the work of its three predecessors which previously dealt separately with equality issues in relation to: gender (the Equal Opportunities Commission, or EOC), 'race' and ethnicity, (the Commission for Racial Equality, or CRE) and disability (the DRC). It remains to be seen if this umbrella body will be any better at advancing the rights and opportunities of disabled people in the future.

Tackling their systematic exclusion from full enjoyment of their rights as citizens has long been a key concern of the DPM. The legislation of the last decade, particularly in relation to direct payments and, perhaps, anti-discrimination, indicates that disabled people's organisations and their allies have enjoyed some success in influencing welfare policy. Nonetheless, disabling attitudes, practices and policies continue to exist in many public and private settings. While these remain, it is too soon to consider disabled people as full and equal citizens.

Summary

- A dominant medical model of disability that focuses on individual impairment and personal tragedy serves to individualise the causes and solutions of disability.
- The social model challenges this approach and shows how social and economic structures and institutionalised practices work to disable people with impairments and deny them their rights as citizens.
- Faced with exclusion and prejudice, disabled people and their organisations and allies have used the concept of citizenship to argue for equal rights.
- The DPM presents an alternative model of *active citizenship*. Their active participation in a collective struggle for recognition and equality contrasts with the dominant contemporary notion of active citizenship that emphasises individual responsibility and charitable works.

- The provisions and practices of the welfare state have served to deny or infringe the social citizenship of generations of disabled people (Oliver, 1996).
- Legislative changes (for example, the introduction of direct payments) since the 1990s indicate that disabled people and their allies have made some progress in challenging the oppressive practices and policy of the past.
- Disabling attitudes, environments and policies continue to impinge on the ability of many disabled people to exercise their rights and responsibilities. They are thus denied the equality of status that citizenship implies.

Further reading

Disability by **Barnes and Mercer (2003)** provides the best up-to-date, short introduction on disability and the issues discussed in this chapter. The chapter by **Morris (2003)** in Ellison and Pierson's book *Developments in British social policy 2* is especially useful for those interested in developments in community care under New Labour.

Website resources

The journal *Disability & Society* is published six times a year. Available at **www.tandf. co.uk/journals/carfax/09687599.html** it is a good place to keep up to date with recent debates and developments.

The Centre for Disability Studies at the University of Leeds has an excellent website that has links to a large range of other sites and an extensive literature archive: **www.leeds.ac.uk/disability-studies/**

eight

Race, ethnicity, citizenship and welfare

This chapter raises a number of important questions about the links between formal (legal) citizenship and social citizenship (that is, access to welfare rights). The following areas are discussed:

- the formal and substantive dimensions of citizenship;
- beyond a simple black–white divide;
- nationality and immigration legislation in the UK: exclusive citizenship;
- refugees, asylum seekers and welfare policy in the UK;
- New Labour and 'race'.

Formal and substantive citizenship

The definition of citizenship outlined by Faulks (1998) in Chapter One implies that citizenship works on many levels. This section illustrates how formal legal aspects of citizenship relate to issues of membership, and how 'race' and ethnicity may in turn be significant in terms of inclusion and exclusion. Citizenship is a formal legal status but also has a substantive dimension to it. Brubaker (1992) distinguished between these *formal* and *substantive* elements of citizenship status and concluded that many minority ethnic groups were disadvantaged in relation to both. *Formal citizenship* designates in a legal sense 'membership of a nation state' and also, therefore, access to rights and duties that accrue to citizens. Questions about *substantive citizenship* deal with the extent to which those who enjoy the formal legal status of citizen may, or may not, enjoy the rights (including rights to welfare) that ensure effective membership of a national community. Brubaker concluded that many minority ethnic citizens faced exclusion in terms of both formal membership and substantive rights. This may be due to deliberately racist policy or because individuals from minority ethnic groups were defined as not belonging to a particular imagined community of citizens (see Anderson, 1983) as a result of their cultural/religious practices differing from an idealised, and often racially constructed, national norm (Bottomore, 1992; Ahmad and Husband, 1993; Mason, 2000).

The relationship between formal membership and substantive rights is, however, more complex than a simple process of exclusion:

> That which constitutes citizenship – the array of rights or patterns of participation – is not necessarily tied to formal state membership. Formal citizenship is neither a sufficient nor necessary condition for substantive citizenship….That it is not a sufficient condition is clear: one can possess formal state membership yet be excluded in law or in fact from certain political, civil or social rights … that formal citizenship is not a necessary condition of substantive citizenship is perhaps less evident…. Often social rights, for example, are accessible to citizens and legally resident non-citizens on virtually identical terms. (Brubaker, 1992, pp 36-8)

As the above quotation makes clear, the interplay between formal and substantive citizenship is far from straightforward. Certain individuals who, as Brubaker (1992) notes, are '*legally* resident non-citizens', may be able to access substantial welfare provisions in spite of a lack of formal citizenship status. Many migrant workers enjoy welfare rights comparable to those of citizens of their host state on the basis of their contribution as workers within the PLM. When welfare rights are organised according to a social insurance principle (see Chapter One, this volume), the legal right to live and work in a particular location may effectively override shared formal citizenship status. It is, therefore, possible to be an 'outsider' or non-citizen (that is, excluded from formal legal membership of a nation state), and yet simultaneously be included in collective welfare arrangements.

The subsequent discussions in this chapter indicate, however, that issues of 'race' and ethnicity continue to have a salience in debates about citizenship. Formal nationality and immigration legislation can be used to construct an exclusive national identity that is problematic for 'outsiders' looking for legal rights of entry/residence. In turn, this can have a negative effect on the substantive citizenship status and welfare rights of those 'insiders' who enjoy equal formal citizenship but who are, nonetheless, "intractably different" (Mason, 2000, p 133), in terms of racial characteristics or ethnic practices from the dominant majority population. A report by the British government's Social Exclusion Unit (2000), cited in Howard et al (2001, p 143), notes:

> In comparison to their representation in the population, people
> from minority ethnic communities are more likely than others
> to live in deprived areas; be poor; be unemployed, compared
> to white people with similar qualifications; suffer ill health
> and live in overcrowded and unpopular housing. They also
> experience widespread racial harassment and racial crime and
> are over represented in the criminal justice system. ... But there
> is much variation within and between ethnic groups in all of
> these areas. (SEU, 2000, p 17)

Ethnicity and racialisation continues to affect the everyday life and
opportunities available to individual citizens in Britain (Howard et al, 2001;
Ahmad and Craig, 2003), but, as the last sentence of the above quotation
implies, in order to understand the complex effects of ethnicity it is
important to move beyond a simplistic black–white dichotomy.

Beyond the black–white divide

The work of Modood (1992; Modood et al, 1997) has challenged a
number of assumptions that underpinned certain simplistic approaches
to understanding the relationship between ethnicity and inequality. Keen
to argue that a crude division of citizens into inadequate and patronising
categories of black or white is an inappropriate way of theorising ethnic
difference and disadvantage, Modood argues that in the past the British
approach to 'race' relations has been heavily influenced by this naive
racial dualism. He believes that experts and academics need to respect
the principle of ethnic self-identity and promote a more complex and
differentiated approach, if we are to build a more genuinely pluralist notion
of citizenship, that has meaning for all Britain's minority ethnic groups.

As Modood (1992) points out, many individuals of Asian descent do not
consider themselves black. Indeed, the term 'Asian' is itself contentious. In
Britain it is commonly associated with people whose families originally
migrated from the Indian subcontinent and subsequently settled in the
UK. In the US, however, people of Korean descent are widely labelled as
Asian. The main point to grasp here is that 'black' and 'Asian' are blanket
terms that hide all sorts of differences that exist between diverse ethnic
groups. For example, individuals who may previously have been crudely
described as 'black people' can be variously differentiated between those
of Caribbean and those of African origin. The category 'Asian' similarly
can be broken down into more distinct communities: Indians, Pakistanis,
Bangladeshis, East African Asians, Bengalis, Gujaratis and so on. If religion
is also considered, differences between Hindus and Muslims (and then

perhaps Sunni Muslims and Shiite Muslims) may also have some salience. Modood's central argument is that major differences exist within any crudely applied, hegemonic black–white divide, and that such differences are of similar significance as any that may exist between white and non-white populations. Evidence indicates (Modood et al, 1997; Berthoud, 2000) that disadvantage is differentially experienced across various groups of minority ethnic citizens. For example, an analysis of Labour Force Survey statistics over time illustrates that:

> Young white men have the lowest risk of unemployment and the highest earnings power, but Indians are very close to them on both indicators. The three other groups included in the analysis [Caribbean, African and Pakistani/Bangladeshi] are all much worse off than either white or Indian individuals, with substantially higher risks of unemployment and lower average earnings. (Berthoud, 2000, p 389)

To understand fully the exclusion from full citizenship that many minority ethnic communities face, it is necessary to develop a more complex sociology than one based on biological differences such as skin colour. For Modood (1992), 'cultural racism', which may include oppression around differing religious practices, is often as fundamental an aspect of racism as one based on colour. He argues that "colour, class and culture are the three distinct dimensions of race" (Modood, 1992, p 54), with those who suffer from a negative mix of all three aspects effectively excluded from many of the potential benefits of citizenship. He asserts that this exclusion is directly related to the degree of difference exhibited by an individual or group from the norms and values inherent in T.H. Marshall's thinking. "The more distant an individual or group is from a white upper middle class British, Christian/agnostic norm, the greater the marginality or exclusion" (Modood, 1992, p 54).

A major problem for minority ethnic groups is the extent to which 'Britishness' has been constructed around a colonial past that emphasised white superiority. Modood (1992) argues that the way forward is to acknowledge and develop a hyphenated British identity in the future. This would enable different individuals to construct categories of belonging that reflect their geographical, religious and cultural origins and identities, for example, Black-British, African-Caribbean-British, British-Muslim, British-Pakistani-Muslim and so on. At the same time, commonalities between different groups of minority ethnic British citizens should be explored, so that a more positive notion of shared national identity can be affirmed.

British Muslims: common citizenship or segregated lives?

Aspirations to affirm a positive, inclusive notion of citizenship are to be supported, but a consideration of work looking at citizenship, ethnicity and inclusion/exclusion in relation to British Muslims raises a number of issues. Increasingly, Islam is evoked in European states as an alien presence, with Muslims often perceived as a direct threat to the liberal norms and values that are seen as central to Western notions of citizenship (Ahmad and Husband, 1993; Werbner, 2000). Arguably the events of September 11th 2001 in New York have prompted a policy shift that promotes a more open and potent hostility towards citizens who follow Islam, citizens who were already particularly susceptible to Islamophobia and social exclusion (Runnymede Trust, 1997).

Ahmad and Husband's (1993) work raises a number of important questions in relation to citizenship and difference. They point out that an Islamic lifestyle has policy implications, as the religion makes specific demands about diet, and ways of educating, praying and burying people. Mainstream policies, at both national and local level, may fail to meet these particular requirements, and the welfare needs of Muslim minority ethnic groups may remain unmet until new culturally sensitive policies are introduced. Wider racist discrimination against minority populations on the basis of ethnic or religious identities also provides an agenda for discriminatory action against Muslim populations in Britain. For example, the establishment of separate Muslim faith schools was only approved in January 1998, in spite of the fact that Catholic schools had long been supported by the state (Werbner, 2000). Ahmad and Husband (1993) also discuss the negative interplay between formal and substantive aspects of citizenship, and note that immigration and residency status is linked to enjoyment of many social rights (see also Howard et al, 2001; Lister, 2003a). Local welfare agencies can also, in effect, operate as the surveillance instruments of central state immigration controls (Cohen, 2002a, 2002b) and/or deny, due to direct and indirect racism, minority ethnic citizens benefits and services to which they are entitled (NACAB, 1991; Law et al, 1994; Ahmad and Craig, 2003).

The Cantle Report (2001) was charged with investigating community cohesion in light of the urban unrest in Oldham, Burnley and Bradford in the summer of 2001. All three towns have significant populations of citizens with Pakistani/Bangladeshi origins. Initially many migrants travelled from Pakistan in the 1950s and 1960s to these northern towns to work in the then thriving cotton and wool mills (McLoughlin, 1998), and many subsequently married and settled in the UK. The demise of the cotton and wool industries led to a fall in general regional prosperity, with the Asian communities in particular, but not exclusively, experiencing unemployment and socio-economic deprivation.

Against this backdrop, Cantle found that Asian, black and white communities often lived segregated lives in different districts of the towns. This physical separation was compounded by separate educational, social, cultural and employment networks. In making his recommendations (**Box 8.1**), Cantle criticised the media for inflammatory reporting of disturbances and was also damning of those clinging to an outdated mono-culturalist view of British nationality.

Box 8.1: The main recommendations of the 2001 Cantle Report

- New citizens to swear/agree formal allegiance to the UK.
- Fluency in English to be a precondition of citizenship.
- 'Faith' schools to allow 25% of pupils from other faiths.
- Police to be proactive in banning racist marches.
- Local government to do more than establish links with self-appointed community leaders.
- Myth-busting campaign.

Source: Cantle (2001)

In July 2003 it was announced that a group of Members of Parliament (MPs) were to revisit these three areas to assess any progress in bringing different communities together. Echoing earlier recommendations by the Runnymede Trust (1997), Cantle believed that *citizenship education* recently introduced into the national curriculum was an important tool that could help to overcome xenophobia and segregation on all sides. As Ahmad and Craig (2003) note, if all Britons are to share a common status, it is essential that the disadvantages faced by many minority ethnic populations are overcome and that a *mutual respect for difference and diversity* becomes a central feature of any future vision of citizenship.

UK nationality and immigration legislation: exclusive citizenship?

The early connections between nationality, national identity and citizenship, and their exclusive implications for those who fail to measure up to a racially constructed notion of Britishness, have already been noted in Chapter Three. Arguably, the nationality and immigration legislation enacted following the Second World War (see ***Box 8.2***), which defined and redefined formal British citizenship in a number of complex ways, continued this process (Paul, 1997; Mason, 2000). Evidence suggests that post-1945 the state began to play a major role in constructing an ideological framework in which minority ethnic communities and particularly non-white people were seen as a threat to the 'British' identity and way of life.

Throughout the 1950s central government was closely involved in the surveillance and control of labour migrants newly arrived from the West Indies. Reports deemed these migrants as suitable only for mundane manual work, susceptible to high levels of unemployment and criminal activity, and likely to be reliant on state welfare (Carter et al, 1987). The state has played a major role in constructing British racism and informing both media and public debate; both mainstream political parties were not averse to playing the 'race' card if deemed necessary. Much immigration legislation has been introduced following moral panics mobilised around inherently racist assumptions. For example, the 1958 'race riots' in Nottingham and Notting Hill were followed by the 1962 Commonwealth Immigration Act. The Thatcher years also saw legislation enacted that undermined the position of minority ethnic citizens (Gordon, 1989).

An analysis of British post-war immigration legislation illustrates that the British state has implemented a series of Acts that have negatively impacted on the citizenship rights and status of legally resident minority ethnic citizens, and simultaneously sought (literally) to exclude non-white people from beyond the geographical boundaries of Britain attaining formal legally defined citizenship. Much immigration legislation has helped to define the presence of black people in Britain as problematic and racialised the notion of 'Britishness' (Gordon, 1989; Mason, 2000). Immigration and nationality legislation did not develop in a vacuum but must be evaluated in light of Britain's imperial past. Labour market issues are also significant. Britain openly invited many migrants from the Empire (and subsequently the Commonwealth countries) to the UK to fill labour market shortages in the past (Lewis, 1998). Overall, however, it is hard to avoid the conclusion that much post-war UK immigration legislation "sought to close the door on dark skinned potential migrants while keeping it open to white.... The underlying theme of this aspect of official policy, then, is that difference is a problem" (Mason, 2000, p 29).

'Earned citizenship': emphasising the rights and responsibilities of new migrants

The recent expansion of the EU in 2004 (see fuller discussions in Chapter Nine, this volume), and the unprecedented numbers of forced migrants seeking asylum (see below), has led to significant, new and diverse populations of migrants entering the UK in the past decade. Against this backdrop, recent policy has become focused on the 'integration' of migrants and the promotion of cohesive 'communities' built around common 'British' values (Cantle, 2001; Commission on Integration and Cohesion, 2007; Osler, 2009). Following recommendations in the Crick Report (2003), since 2005 migrants who want to apply for UK citizenship under the

---

Box 8.2: Significant UK nationality and immigration legislation (1948–88)

1948 British Nationality Act: established three categories of citizenship all with rights to reside in the UK:
* citizens of UK and the colonies;
* citizens of the Commonwealth countries;
* citizens of Eire.

1957 British Nationality Act: individuals with 'pure European descent' given five years to register as citizens of the UK.

1962 Commonwealth Immigration Act: for the first time entry into Britain was limited to those who held UK-issued passports and work vouchers. Until this Act, migrant black Commonwealth workers had the same right of entry/residence as other British citizens.

1968 Commonwealth Immigration Act: a Labour administration further tightened controls in the face of the so-called 'Ugandan Crisis'.

1971 Immigration Act: replaced all previous legislation, created two different classes of British subjects with different rights:
* *patrials:* broadly those with family ties in Britain, were essentially white, had rights of entry and residence;
* *non-patrials:* overwhelmingly non-white, born in the Commonwealth. Lost their rights to enter and settle in Britain.

1981 British Nationality Act: removed the ancient right of *jus soli* and created three levels of British citizenship with British Overseas Citizens having no real rights of abode anywhere.

1986 New visa requirements: introduced for visitors from five named Commonwealth countries, all with predominately black populations.

1988 Immigration Act: broadened the definition of illegal entry; detention and deportation made easier. Appeals against removal reduced and to be lodged after the event.

Sources: for further details see Carter et al (1987); Gordon (1989); Cesarani (1996); Paul (1997); Lewis (1998); Mason (2000)

---

naturalisation process have had to pass the formal 'Life in the UK' test (more usually referred to as the 'citizenship test') and also demonstrate knowledge of the English language (rf Osler, 2009, for fuller discussions). Although debate continues as to whether it is possible, or indeed reasonable, to try and inculcate common 'British' values within what is now an ethnically and culturally diverse national community, the government is fully committed to pursuing this approach in the future and has set out plans for the reform of immigration policy that emphasises 'stronger borders' and 'firm but fair' managed migration (UKBA, 2008).

The now departed Secretary of State for Communities and Local Government, Hazel Blears, set out the core elements of New Labour's approach to managing these new waves of migration by stating an intention to "maximise the benefits of migration and minimise the impacts at local level" (CLG, 2008, p 5). Where she invokes the language of citizenship, it is emphasised that:

> We are making a series of changes to set out more clearly the expectations on newcomers: to work to pay taxes and to support themselves without recourse to public funds; to learn English and to obey the law. Citizenship will no longer follow automatically from staying in Britain for a number of years, instead it must be earned. (CLG, 2008, p 6)

Subsequent changes introduced in the 2009 Borders, Citizenship and Immigration Act emphasise compulsory periods of 'temporary residence' and 'probationary citizenship' that are to be steps on the way to earned 'citizenship'. Future entry into the UK, for the purposes of labour migration, will be under a points-based system where only highly skilled migrants required to fit specified gaps in the PLM will be able to apply. Those migrants who contribute to the community through 'active citizenship' (for example, voluntary work in charities) will be able to have their citizenship applications fast tracked. In contrast those who engage in criminal activity which attracts a custodial sentence will have their citizenship application stopped and will potentially face enforced removal from the UK. Migrants will have no rights to access social assistance benefits, local authority housing or homelessness assistance until they have 'earned' the right to British citizenship or permanent residence. In effect permanent residence and access to full welfare rights will be conditional on migrants proving economic self-sufficiency over a number of years. Finally, the government plans to introduce a new Transitional Impacts of Migration Fund, with money to be raised by increasing fees for immigration applications (UKBA, 2008; Home Office, 2009). Critics have argued that, the supposedly new approach to managed migration that the 2009 Act lays out is, in many ways, at least as exclusive as the preceding immigration and citizenship legislation that it replaces.

> Under the aegis of New Labour Policy, 'managed migration' policy is operationalized through the enforcement of reduced quotas, visas and surveillance administration that are aimed particularly certain immigrant groups, including those who are non-English speaking and perceived to be 'low-skilled' and 'unskilled'. These measure may be seen as rendering an illiberal top-down attempt to socially engineer democracy and community cohesion. (Cheong et al, 2007, p 42)

Refugees, asylum seekers and welfare in the UK: two decades of exclusion

The number of displaced migrants entering Britain has grown steadily throughout the 1990s and seeking asylum has become one of the most sensitive and controversial immigration issues in recent years. For example, published statistics indicate that 110,700 asylum applications were received by the Home Office in 2002 (Home Office, 2003b). As the number of individuals seeking asylum in the UK has risen, increasingly restrictive immigration and asylum legislation/policy has been introduced (Mynott, 2000, 2002; Craig, 2001; Cohen, 2002a, 2002b; Sales, 2002a). Indeed, it can be argued that, as more stringent attempts to keep people out have been put in place (for example, Blunkett, 2001), simultaneously, successive governments have sought to limit the welfare entitlements of those asylum seekers who enter the country (Bloch, 2000; Zetter and Pearl, 2000; Bloch and Schuster, 2002; CPAG, 2002b; Morris, 2002).

Since 1990 five consecutive pieces of legislation have impacted negatively on the welfare rights of asylum seekers:

- 1993 Asylum and Immigration Appeals Act
- 1996 Asylum and Immigration Act
- 1999 Immigration and Asylum Act
- 2002 Nationality, Immigration and Asylum Act
- 2004 Asylum and Immigration (Treatment of Claimants etc) Act.

The 1993 and 1996 Acts combined to remove (with few exceptions) any rights of asylum seekers to permanent accommodation provided by the local authority. A major outcome of this policy was a fragmentation of provision (Zetter and Pearl, 2000). Furthermore, the 1996 Act withdrew the right for in-country asylum applicants (and those in the appeal process) to many social security benefits and shifted the duty of support from the national social security system onto local authority budgets. This resulted in many asylum seekers, especially single people, being placed in temporary hostel accommodation and being given vouchers to spend (Sales, 2002a).

The introduction of the 1999 Immigration and Asylum Act saw the New Labour government consolidating the approach of their Conservative predecessors. The Act widened the gulf between the social rights enjoyed by UK citizens and those available to asylum seekers. It removed the duty to meet basic housing and social security needs from local authorities and placed it with the newly created National Asylum Support Service (NASS),[1] which was charged with coordinating and funding the accommodation and financial support of all asylum seekers arriving in the UK after 1 April 2000, and the majority of those already in the UK who had not previously accessed support under earlier legislation. The 1999 Act also excluded all persons subject to immigration control from a right to access social assistance benefits. In their place, destitute asylum seekers became entitled to receive vouchers worth 70% of basic Income Support and £10 cash.

NASS meets its housing requirements by subcontracting to a mixture of accommodation providers, including local authorities, private landlords, and, to a lesser extent, refugee community organisations (Sales, 2002a). Following an initial period of induction spent in emergency accommodation, NASS rules for asylum seekers permit individuals to choose one of three support options: accommodation only, accommodation and subsistence or subsistence only. The right to NASS support is, however, highly conditional. In line with current policy, asylum seekers are dispersed to cluster areas around the country. Finch (2001) argues that the selection of cluster areas is driven largely by the availability of housing, rather than the official desire to group individuals according to common language. Failure to comply with dispersal or certain other specified conditions could see the right to housing and financial support withdrawn (Zetter and Pearl, 2000; Disson, 2001; Finch, 2001; CPAG, 2002b).

The 1999 Immigration and Asylum Act was superseded by the 2002 Nationality, Immigration and Asylum Act and a basic system of conditional NASS support was retained. But the Act again initiated important changes in relation to the prospective provision of basic welfare. In response to widespread condemnation (Mynott, 2000; Refugee Council, 2002a) and associated problems (Eagle et al, 2002), the voucher system was phased out and replaced with 'entitlement cards' which would allow holders to access cash benefits to the same value (Refugee Council, 2002b; Sales, 2002a). Most controversially Section 55 of the 2002 Act left thousands of forced migrants who, on entering the UK did not apply for asylum 'as soon as is reasonably practicable' (originally defined as within 48 hours of entering the UK but subsequently extended to 72 hours), effectively homeless and destitute (GLA, 2004; IAP, 2004; Refugee Council, 2004). The Act also gave the Home Secretary the power to withdraw/deny NASS support for all in-country applicants who: (a) could not provide a clear and coherent account of how they came to be in the UK; (b) could not provide clear and accurate information on their circumstances, for example, how they had been meeting their basic needs to date; and (c) had failed to cooperate with the authorities' further enquiries.

The 2004 Asylum and Immigration (Treatment of Claimants etc) Act further curtailed forced migrants' rights. New powers to terminate NASS support for failed asylum seekers with dependent children were introduced. A new obligation on adult failed asylum seekers with young families to accept voluntary repatriation or face the possibility of destitution and their children being taken into care was also instigated. Access for failed asylum seekers to 'hardcase' accommodation (see further below) also became conditional on them performing specified community activities.

Displaced migrants and welfare: a tiering of entitlement

The legislative changes of the 1990s and 2000s have consolidated a long-established link between immigration/residency status and welfare entitlement (see Williams, 1989; Cohen, 2002a; Hayes, 2002). The situation is further complicated due to the stratified system of entitlement that exists within the generic population of asylum seekers/refugees, who enjoy differential entitlements to housing and social benefits depending on formal immigration status (Bloch, 2000; CPAG, 2002b; Morris, 2002; Sales, 2002a). Four basic groups, each with different rights to welfare, can be identified (see *Box 8.3*).

Individuals granted humanitarian protection status are asylum seekers who are not expelled from the UK following the failure of their application because it is dangerous for them to return to their country of origin at that time. The status can be withdrawn if the danger in a migrant's homeland is perceived to have ceased. An unknown, but substantial, number of the failed asylum seekers referred to in *Box 8.3* 'disappear' and/or assume other identities. Morris (2002) notes that in 1998 between 11,000 and 14,000 people received a negative decision but stayed in the UK with no rights to social welfare and no obvious way of supporting themselves. Failed asylum seekers must leave NASS accommodation within 28 days of notification by the Home Office. Such migrants, under specified circumstances (for example, no safe route for return, illness), may be able to access 'hardcase' support under Section 4 of the 1999 Immigration and Asylum Act. This support is highly conditional and intentionally offered, "in the most basic way possible" (HMG, 2004, p 25), while arrangements to remove failed asylum seekers are finalised. The tight eligibility criteria for receipt of Section 4 provisions and administrative deficiencies in NASS have resulted in substantial numbers of failed asylum seekers in urgent need of accommodation being denied support (CAB, 2002). Many others have simply left NASS accommodation and effectively disappeared. Parliament has recognised that there are 'considerable numbers' whose claim has failed, living in unknown locations without any rights to shelter or basic welfare (HAC, 2004). The impact of rules which permit local authorities to provide 'hardcase' accommodation to failed asylum seekers who are unable to leave the UK remains unknown, but homelessness and destitution continue to be a reality for many (ICAR, 2006).

Box 8.3: The rights of displaced migrants in the UK

Refugee status: legally resident under the 1951 Geneva Convention, able to claim full social rights on the same basis as citizens, have the right to work and enjoy rights to family reunion.

Asylum seekers: that is, those making a claim for refugee status. Welfare rights vary considerably; those lodging new in-country claims effectively have no rights to public support under the 2002 National Immigration and Asylum Act, previously entitled to apply for permission to work but this was removed in July 2002; no rights to family reunion.

'Humanitarian protection' status: (previously known as exceptional leave to remain) granted for periods of up to three years; same rights to social welfare as citizens, they may work, but they lack rights to family reunion.

Failed asylum seekers: asylum seekers whose claims have been turned down and who have no legal right to remain and thus routinely no recourse to public support.

The combined effect of the tiering of entitlement and successive changes in the law already noted is a situation whereby different categories of displaced people within the UK have widely different rights. The spectrum ranges from those with refugee status, who have the same formal rights to welfare as full citizens, to 'overstayers', who effectively have no recourse to publicly provided accommodation or financial support. This complex and chaotic situation is summarised by Morris (2002, p 421):

> Alongside the national welfare system we have dispersal and vouchers under NASS (to be replaced by reception centres), a small number of instances of 'hard cases' support and provisions of last resort for the vulnerable under the NIAA [National Immigration and Asylum Act]. Excluded from any support are rejected asylum seekers who are legitimately present but do not meet the hard cases criteria, the able-bodied whose leave is conditional on 'no recourse to public funds', and those who are unlawfully present and simply destitute – until perhaps the conditions of their existence produce the vulnerability which might qualify them for help.

There is strong evidence to suggest that the statutory provisions available are failing to meet the needs of many displaced migrants (Dwyer, 2005; Dwyer and Brown, 2008). The benefits available are insufficient, and many (including those eligible to some additional support because they fall into recognised 'vulnerable' categories, for example, disabled migrants) fail to receive full benefits (see ILPA, 2001; CAB, 2002; Eagle et al, 2002; Penrose, 2002; Roberts and Harris, 2002). Furthermore, the problem of substandard housing, highlighted initially by Finch (2001) and Lukes (2001), appears to be a lingering problem as does homelessness, which is often triggered by a change in an individual's status as their claim is processed (Dwyer and Brown, 2008).

As the role of the state in meeting basic needs diminishes and the ability to take paid employment is curtailed, many asylum seekers are forced to rely on non-state bodies for support. Non-statutory bodies such as refugee agencies, charities, churches, refugee community organisations (RCOs) and even friends and family, have to assume an increasing role (Bloch and Schuster, 2002; Dwyer and Brown, 2005). The potential for individuals to draw on these sources of support may, however, be seriously limited. Dispersal makes it unlikely that RCOs and informal community networks will be available as they remain concentrated in the South East and London, and are often in a precarious financial position (Zetter and Pearl; 2000; Wilson, 2001). Similarly, as most asylum seekers and refugees are single and displaced from close family, informal familial support is often not available.

The present Labour government is clear in its assertion that welfare rights come with attendant responsibilities, and that claims to access state support properly imply a willingness to contribute to the welfare of the wider community, most notably via engagement with the paid labour market (see Chapter Four, this volume). Asylum legislation in recent years has not only reduced the welfare entitlements of many displaced migrants and marginalised their claims for state support, but has effectively also denied many such people the right to work. It is something of a paradox that present policy leaves many displaced migrants dependent on state provisions, while simultaneously denying them the opportunity to escape such entrenched dependency by entering paid employment. One option may be to move towards a policy that allows displaced migrants to engage in paid work while their asylum claims are being considered. There may well be drawbacks linked to the promotion of paid work. Duvell and Jordan (2002) note that many displaced migrants who are currently able to work legally are often to be found in low-paid, low-status employment. For others, injured or traumatised by their previous experiences, work may be inappropriate. Nonetheless, a policy that allows paid employment has potential benefits. First, it would allow a majority of asylum seekers to contribute to their own, and the wider community's, welfare, and thus help to challenge the negative stereotyping of displaced migrants as passive welfare claimants. Second, it could potentially reduce the need for some to seek exploitative, illegal employment in the shadow economy. Third, it may allow employers to make use of the skills and capabilities that many asylum seekers possess. This could also provide individual asylum seekers with enhanced possibilities to meet their needs. While racist and xenophobic attitudes certainly fuel the contemporary hostility towards displaced migrants, the twin issues of a lack of prior contribution and a scarcity of resources may also be part of the wider fears of certain citizens, who seek to justify restrictive notions of citizenship and exclude the claims of outsiders, no matter how great their needs (see Dwyer, 2000a, 2005).

New Labour and 'race'

A number of commentators have identified a contradiction central to New Labour's policies in relation to 'race' and ethnicity (Mynott, 2000; Craig, 2001; IRR, 2001). It has been argued that the government's record in highlighting and tackling the disadvantage and social exclusion that affects many members of minority ethnic communities is, at best, patchy. Craig (2001) notes that, generally, issues of 'race' and ethnicity had a low priority in the government's first term in office. For example, the head of the Social Exclusion Unit stated that 'race' was not a priority in its work and only one of the poverty indicators outlined in *Opportunity for all* (DSS, 1999) explicitly mentioned minority ethnic groups. On a more positive note, Craig acknowledges that the setting up of the Macpherson Inquiry (1999) into the racist murder of Stephen Lawrence and the police handling of it not only led to a general debate about institutional racism, but also resulted in the requirements in the 2000 Race Relations (Amendment) Act that public authorities examine their outlook and practices in relation to equality of opportunity and set employment targets for under-represented groups. He also recognises that the government may be beginning to appreciate the need to address issues of ethnicity more explicitly in future. On issues of immigration and asylum, he is, however, scathing:

> The government's response to the growth in the numbers of refugees and asylum seekers over the past four years shows at best a schizophrenic attitude to issues of 'race' and ethnicity. This is demonstrated by the populist – and racist – stance of the government towards immigration. On the one hand, it is prepared to consider extensive immigration of professional workers over the next few years to fill what it regards as significant gaps in the UK labour market. On the other hand, it has taken a punitive and at times quite vicious position towards refugees and asylum seekers arriving without economic leverage. (Craig, 2001, p 98)

This condemnation echoes that of Mynott (2000), who believes that New Labour's recognition of a distinction between undeserving 'economic migrants' and genuine persecuted asylum seekers fails to recognise the realities of migration in the modern world and reinforces racist agendas. He also finds it incongruous that the Home Office is charged with the task of engendering positive community/'race' relations and the promotion of equal opportunity and tolerance for minority ethnic groups, while at the same time it is actively promoting exclusive and intolerant immigration and asylum policy.

Note

[1] In April 2007, following reorganisation within the Home Office, the Borders and Immigration Agency (since renamed the UK Border Agency, or UKBA), assumed responsibility for asylum support. The old acronym of NASS is retained in these discussions as the UKBA has simply taken over NASS support functions.

Summary

* Formal and substantive aspects of citizenship are both important if an individual is to achieve effective membership of a national community and enjoy the equality of status that full citizenship promises.

- The notion of 'Britishness' has been racialised in nationality, immigration and asylum legislation and this has proved to be particularly problematic for members of minority ethnic communities who differ from an outdated white mono-culturalist view of British nationality.
- It is important to acknowledge and develop a more complex understanding of ethnic difference that goes beyond a simplistic black–white divide, to include religious and cultural practices.
- Contemporary debates about asylum policy illustrate that national citizenship, and the rules that govern it, are of central importance in defining an individual's welfare rights. The right of a displaced migrant to obtain entry to and/or formal membership of a particular (national) community is crucial if that person is to gain access to adequate welfare provision.

Further reading

Mason (2000) is an excellent introductory text on 'race' and ethnicity and related aspects of citizenship. Two special journal editions, *Critical Social Policy* **(2002)**, vol 22, no 3 and *Social Policy and Administration* **(2001)**, vol 39, no 3 look at asylum policy/debates in the UK and also in the wider European context.

Website resources

The Runnymede Trust is an independent think-tank that produces a wealth of work relating to ethnicity: **www.runnymedetrust.org/index.html**

The Refugee Council (**www.refugeecouncil.org.uk**) and the UK Border Agency (**www.bia.homeoffice.gov.uk**), often on opposing sides of the general debate about asylum, provide an extensive range of relevant materials and links.

nine

Social Europe

The European Union (EU) is now an established system of supranational government. After briefly discussing the establishment, expansion and key institutions of the EU, this chapter moves on to explore some important debates that relate to the EU's social policy role. The following areas are addressed:

- the expansion of the EU and its key institutions;
- the development of the EU's social dimension;
- the expansion of the EU: proactive and defensive citizenship in action?
- citizenship of the Union: a differentiated status;
- different worlds of welfare or a European social model;
- a more expansive vision of EU social rights.

The establishment and expansion of the EU

Box 9.1 outlines the development of the EU since the founding of the European Economic Community (EEC) in the Treaty of Rome in 1957. Subsequent waves of expansion have seen the EU develop considerably. After the first wave of integration of Eastern European nations (and Malta and Cyprus) since 2004, there are now a total of 27 member states, with the EU covering a population of approximately 501 million people.

Box 9.1: The establishment and expansion of the EU

1957 EEC established. Founder members are Belgium, France, Federal Republic of Germany, Italy, Luxembourg and the Netherlands.

1973 Denmark, Ireland and the UK join.

1980s Greece (1981), Spain and Portugal (1986) join.

1995 Austria, Finland and Sweden join.

2004 Cyprus, the Czech Republic, Estonia, Hungary, Latvia, Lithuania, Malta, Poland, Slovakia and Slovenia join.

2007 Rumania and Bulgaria join.

2015? Talks accepting, in principle, that Turkey will become a member have already taken place.

Key institutions of the EU

The EU is best viewed as a system of multilayered government in which policy, including social policy, frequently develops as the product of compromise. The policy-making process is a complex one, with legislation often emerging from attempts to balance the varied interests of different EU institutions and the different national interests of member states. *Box 9.2* outlines the key institutions and their role in the policy-making process of the EU.

In many ways the Commission provides the impetus for closer cooperation between member states. Commissioners are appointed by the governments of member states but each commissioner has to take an oath that states that they will put EU interests before those of their national government. The various heads of member state governments routinely come together as the European Council four times a year, but may meet more frequently if a pressing issue needs to be discussed. The Council's meetings often set the broad direction of policy within the EU. The Council of Ministers is made up of the relevant ministers of state from each member state. It meets periodically to decide on legislation that falls within a particular policy remit. For example, if a piece of agricultural legislation is being implemented or amended, all the agriculture ministers from the various member states come together as a Council of Ministers to discuss relevant issues.

Box 9.2: Key institutions of the EU

The Commission: the Executive. It initiates, implements and monitors policy and legislation.

The Council of the European Union: there are two elements to the Council:

* *European Council:* this is where the heads of state and government meet to discuss EU policy issues;
* *Council of Ministers:* made up of the various member states' ministers who meet periodically to decide on legislation that falls within their remit.

European Parliament: has budgetary and supervisory powers.

European Court of Justice: the judicial arm of the EU.

The European Parliament is unique among the institutions of the EU in that its members are directly elected by citizens in member states across Europe. The members of all other EU governmental institutions are appointed by member state governments. It is mainly a deliberative body, and cannot initiate legislation, but it can object to and cross-examine the Commission's proposals. It does, however, also have certain important powers and is able to dismiss the Commission if a 60% majority vote of Members of the European Parliament is secured. The European Court of Justice (ECJ) acts as the constitutional court of the EU. Its role is to ensure that European law and the national laws of the member states do not contravene EU treaties. It also acts to interpret legislation by ruling on cases. In terms of social policy, it has an important role in that it has set out a number of judgments that have led to an expansion of the social rights enjoyed by EU citizens (Cram, 1998; Hantrais, 2003).

A new treaty, the Lisbon Treaty (or Lisbon Agenda), which came into force in 2010, abolished the pillar structure introduced under the Maastricht Treaty (Treaty of the European Union, or TEU) (1992). In addition to this, the new Treaty has introduced a number of provisions to simplify decision making within the EU by extending the use of qualified majority voting to new areas of policy. In institutional terms, the most significant innovation of the Lisbon Treaty has been the introduction of a permanent President of the European Council. The new President will work alongside the similarly newly established European Foreign Minister. Additionally, the Charter of Fundamental Rights of the EU, which combines in a single text for the first time civil and political rights with social and economic rights, has been fully integrated into the Treaty, theoretically making it legally binding for all member states (rf Europa, 2009). However, uncertainty remains as to how this measure will be implemented in individual member states. For social policy, the importance of the changes in the EU institutional framework noted above therefore remain uncertain in the immediate future.

The development of the EU's social dimension

A gradual and growing interest in social policy has emerged at the EU level as it has developed and redefined its scope and purpose since the 1950s (Geyer, 2000; Hantrais, 2000; Threlfall, 2002). The Treaty of Rome (1957), which saw the establishment of the EEC, was concerned primarily with promoting economic objectives, such as increased trade and the free movement of workers, rather than directly developing an extensive social policy role. Nonetheless, member states agreed to common social security provision for migrant workers and close cooperation on matters such as employment law, working conditions and so on. They also agreed to the setting up of a European Social Fund to promote retraining of workers and labour force mobility in order to combat unemployment (Geyer, 2000; Hantrais, 2000).

By the mid-1970s, the Council of Ministers was advocating a slightly more ambitious approach to social policy. Their Social Action Programme (1974) noted that closer integration and economic expansion would be of limited value unless any economic progress could be used to enhance the lives of Europe's citizens. The action plan outlined three broad social policy objectives: the attainment of full and better employment, an improvement in living and working conditions and increased involvement of management and workers in economic and social decisions. It should be noted that the plan was not legally binding on member states, but was more a statement of intent about how the Council wished to proceed. The Social Action Programme set in progress a number of EEC initiatives in areas such as education, women's rights, health and safety at work and so on, and set the tone for further developments.

Throughout the 1980s EU social policy continued to emerge as an adjunct to employment and economic policy. The creation of a *European social space* was debated and the decade also saw the notions of 'social dialogue' (between workers and management) and a 'social plinth' (that is, a guaranteed minimum of social rights) being put forward as ideas around which to further advance EU social policy. The Community Charter of the Fundamental Social Rights of Workers (1989) asserted that social issues should be afforded the same importance as economic ones. It also triggered two important debates. The first was whether or not it was right and proper for the EU to get involved directly in social policy at all. To what extent should the EU intervene to establish a set of common social provisions to protect the interests of workers and, therefore, regulate the relationship between labour and management in individual member states? Should such matters be left to individual member states? The second debate was concerned with how the EU should intervene. A wide range of differing welfare standards and welfare practices exist in different member states (see the section 'Worlds of welfare or a European social model?', pp 185-9). Should the EU recommend minimum or maximum standards of social provision across member states? Although the Charter brought these questions to the fore, as it was not a legally binding document its implementation was left largely in the hands of individual member states (Hantrais, 2000).

Arguably, the Charter illustrates that an increased concern for the social rights of 'citizens' rather than workers gained momentum throughout the 1980s (Threlfall, 2002). This process was further enhanced in the Agreement on Social Policy, which (at the insistence of a hostile UK Conservative government who refused to adopt it) was annexed to the Maastricht Treaty (1992) (Geyer, 2000). The subsequent Social Action Programmes from the Commission (1995–2000), and the incorporation of the Agreement on Social Policy into the Amsterdam Treaty (1997), illustrate the EU's desire to extend the scope of its remit in relation to social welfare. Nonetheless, the EU continues to look to member states largely to find their own ways forward, guided by two important principles, namely, subsidiarity and non-discrimination.

Over the past decade much contestation around social policy in the EU has centred around the Lisbon Agenda (2000), which aimed to make the EU "the most competitive and dynamic knowledge-based economy in the world" (Presidency Conclusions, 2000). Under the Lisbon Agenda a number of important initiatives have been undertaken (using the so-called Open Method of Coordination, or OMC), which impact within areas such as labour market policy, pension reform and social exclusion and healthcare policy across the EU. Much of the literature has regarded the Lisbon Agenda as a move towards greater flexibility and lower levels of social protection (see, for example, Dwyer and Papadimitriou, 2006). The OMC approach is essentially an intergovernmental forum of consultation. The purpose of the exercise is not full-scale harmonisation or the production of 'hard law'. Instead it aims at spreading best practice across member states and assisting the emergence of national policies on the basis of agreed EU goals (Presidency Conclusions, 2000). The non-legally binding nature of the OMC, which relies heavily on benchmarking and peer pressure between member states, has led some to question its effectiveness as a policy-making tool.

Principles underpinning EU social policy

The EU's power to intervene directly in the welfare systems of member states was limited by the principle of subsidiarity introduced in the TEU (1992). This principle allowed member states to enact measures to meet the legislative requirements of the EU in ways that reflected their institutional and cultural custom and practice. Effectively this amounts to an acceptance that, in the first instance, social policies should be made at the national or sub-national level, with the EU only intervening when its objectives cannot (or are not) sufficiently met by policies instigated by lower-level political institutions. The implementation of social policy therefore remained very much a national prerogative (Geyer, 2000). An end result of this principle was the continuing existence of a diversity of welfare states across the EU.

For EU citizens who choose to exercise their right to move and reside in other member states, this diversity of provision across the EU assumed a further importance, because formal equality in the context of EU law rested on the principle of non-discrimination and referred simply to the abolition of discrimination on grounds of *nationality*. EU citizenship status does not provide a guaranteed minimum standard of welfare provision for EU migrant citizens, but merely grants some, depending on their status as citizens (see below), the right to the same benefits and services as would ordinarily be enjoyed by a national of that member state. Put simply, an individual's location has a major influence on the extent and quality of the social rights available to them (Ackers and Dwyer, 2002, 2004).

There has been cautious but progressive movement by the EU into the social policy arena since 1957, and arguably social issues came more to the fore in the 1990s. It would appear that in contrast to its economic policy, most recently signified by the establishment of a single common currency and European Monetary Union, the EU is content to outline minimum standards of welfare for member states to meet. The development of a single European welfare system imposed by institutions of the EU appears to be a long way off. The Commission is in the business of trying to establish a consensus on social policy objectives, so that member states may be encouraged to improve and modernise their welfare systems. At the same time the principles of subsidiarity and non-discrimination indicate that, at present, member states retain ultimate responsibility for organising and delivering welfare within their borders.

The expansion of the EU: proactive and defensive citizenship in action?

As noted in *Box 9.1*, the EU underwent considerable enlargement in 2004 and 2007. Consequently, formal EU citizenship status was granted to nationals of the so-called Accession 8 (A8) countries (that is, Poland, Lithuania, Estonia, Latvia, Slovenia, Slovakia, Hungary and the Czech Republic) and then subsequently Rumania and Bulgaria (sometimes referred to as the Accession 2, or A2, countries). This expansion of the EU is significant in that it has opened up possibilities for new EU citizens from Central and Eastern Europe to live and seek work in other EU member states for the first time. As Ryan et al (2009) recognise, the enlargement of the EU has opened up a range of new options for A8/A2 migrants from which a diversity of migratory movements may ensue; from permanent residence at one end of the scale to more fleeting, circulatory and multiple short-term moves at the other. Using A8 migration into the UK as a case study, alongside the theoretical insights of Ellison (2000), discussions below consider the ways in which the expansion of the EU has facilitated opportunities for the 'proactive engagement' of citizenship status among A8 migrants on the one hand, while often triggering more 'defensive engagement' among some members of local host communities in the UK on the other.

It is estimated that in excess of one million Central and Eastern European migrants have arrived in the UK since 2004 (Pollard et al, 2008). The UK has proved to be a popular destination for these new European citizens for several reasons. First and foremost, although transitional arrangements allowed old member states a seven-year phasing-in period for the extension of full EU citizenship rights to A8 nationals, the UK was one of only three (the others being Sweden and Ireland) among the existing 15 EU member states that granted A8 migrants immediate access to their PLM. The UK government's requirement that those who wished to seek paid work must first enrol on the Worker Registration Scheme (WRS) does not appear to have acted as an impediment. Between 1 May 2004 and 30 September 2007, 715,000 A8 migrants' requests to work in the UK were approved by the Home Office (Lemos and Portes, 2008). Additionally, a long sustained period of economic growth (which has now ended), a favourable disparity in wage-earning potential between A8 migrants' countries of origin and the UK, alongside a comparatively low and differentiated (regressive) tax system, all helped to make the UK an attractive proposition for A8 migrants looking to exercise their new right to freedom of movement as EU citizens (Stenning et al, 2006).

The positive economic benefits of increased migration into the UK in recent years have been widely recognised and should not be easily dismissed (for example, CLG, 2008; Pollard et al, 2008; Rutter et al, 2008). The availability of A8 workers was welcomed by the majority of British employers who, prior to the current economic downturn, struggled to fill such "3D (dirty, dangerous and dull) jobs" (Favell, 2008, p 704) with locally available workers (Dench et al, 2006). However, the impact of increased migration on the UK labour market remains the focus of much debate. Some commentators are keen to emphasise, "there is very little either in economic theory or in the recent empirical work to suggest that migration is having a significant negative impact on the UK labour market" (Coats, 2008, p 5; see also Lemos and Portes, 2008). Although many would agree that there is limited evidence to suggest that migration has a significant, general long-term negative impact on the employment rates or wages of 'native' workers, A8 migration may, in the short term, have more damaging effects for the most disadvantaged groups within the established workforce (TUC, 2007; HoLSCEA, 2009; Jurado and Bruzzone, 2009; Reed and Latorre, 2009). The availability of A8 migrant labour is also likely to make it harder for low-skilled members of established communities, particularly those with histories of long-term unemployment, to re-enter the PLM (Coats, 2008).

Allied to fears among some among host communities in the UK about jobs is a parallel view that "competition over scarce resources, and specifically housing, in socio-economically deprived neighbourhoods is at the heart of tensions between established communities and new migrant groups" (Amas, 2008, p 17). Media scare stories undoubtedly play their part and the sale of former council housing stock to private landlords, which is subsequently privately let to new migrants, may also fuel misconceptions (Rutter and Latorre, 2009). Much available evidence on the allocation and occupancy of social housing appears to counter such fears and very few A8 migrants are likely to have sufficient housing needs priority to qualify for social housing (ICoCo, 2007). Robinson's (2007) review of CORE data[1] identifies a 'yawning gap' between rhetoric that asserts that EU migrants are being given preferential treatment in respect of social housing, and a reality in which less than 1% of social rented lettings across England are allocated to A8 nationals. A recent evaluation also found, unambiguously, "there is no evidence that social housing allocation favours foreign migrants over UK citizens" (Rutter and Latorre, 2009, p ix). However, because the amount of available social housing stock has diminished while simultaneously increased migration has played a part in increasing local demand, some members of established white and minority ethnic communities now perceive themselves to be competing with more recently arrived migrants (including in some instances A8 migrants), for scarce housing and welfare resources (see Cook et al, 2008, 2010: forthcoming). Such perceptions have been highlighted as promoting resentment and intergroup tensions across the UK, particularly in relatively deprived urban settings (Amas, 2008; Jurado and Bruzzone, 2008).

A question of citizenship?

A8 migration into the UK came about as a direct result of the enlargement of the EU in 2004. This, for the first time, afforded many Central and Eastern Europeans opportunities to exercise their newly acquired supranational EU citizenship status to reside and work in other member states. In the past citizenship status and the social rights that subsequently ensue have been closely tied to membership of a nation state. But as Faist (2001) points out, increasingly, local, national and supranational communities are all important sites in which people seek to exercise their citizenship status in contemporary society. Any meaningful understanding of the fears of host communities and tensions that A8 migration may engender between established British, white and minority ethnic locals on the one hand, and A8 migrants on the other, needs to take into account both the plurality and contested character of current-day citizenship.

As Ellison notes, contemporary citizenship is characterised by changing modes of participation and belonging, where citizen engagement is played out in a range of spaces from local to global.

> Rapid change transforms the nature of citizen participation and 'encourages' engagement, willing or not, in the pursuit, or defence, of particular interests and/or social rights. In short, both the capacity to engage, and the differential nature of engagement itself, are rapidly becoming the most significant features of a citizenship conceived as a series of fractured 'contiguous belongings. (2000, para 1.1)

Ellison goes on to make a distinction between two different types of citizen activity. First, *proactive engagement* occurs when specific groups are able to utilise a particular set of social resources and conditions to enhance their interests (or those of others) at a given time. In contrast, *defensive engagement* demands that citizens must, in certain circumstances, "defend themselves against the erosion of their social rights [which is] created by the persistent and occasionally dramatic demands of rapid economic, social and political change" (Ellison, 2000, para 1.4). In short, defensive engagement routinely occurs when citizens are looking to preserve or maintain their existing entitlements and interests, while active engagement is often linked to attempts to expand the reach of citizenship status as individuals or groups compete for the often finite social resources that are central to any substantial notion of social citizenship.

The expansion of the EU was a significant and dramatic change in the European political and social landscape that enabled A8 nationals to utilise their EU citizenship status for the first time. In spite of the limitations inherent in EU citizenship status (for fuller discussions see Ackers and Dwyer, 2004; Currie, 2008), mobile A8 nationals are proactively engaging with their newly acquired rights to free movement within the EU. As mobile workers they are, quite properly, looking to exploit the tangible benefits that their new opportunities for mobility may bring by living and working in Britain. The unprecedented and largely unpredicted numbers of A8 citizens who subsequently chose to exercise their newly acquired rights caught the government by surprise and in certain locations had a significant impact on local job markets, housing and certain public services (ICoCo, 2007; TUC, 2007).

It is against this backdrop, where A8 migrants are utilising their supranational rights, that some members of established local host communities have started to engage defensively to protect what they perceive to be *their* local rights to jobs, housing and welfare. In doing so they consistently seek to justify their stance by legitimatising the exclusion of newly arrived A8 migrants on the basis that jobs and welfare should be reserved primarily for fellow national citizens who have previously contributed to the (national) common good. It is important to remember, however, that racism, particularly white racism, may also be a central cause of tensions between majority populations and different minority ethnic communities. Cultural and economic factors have been identified as key issues for those white Britons who seek to justify prejudice (Valentine and McDonald, 2004). Recent work also highlights that racially motivated harassment is part of the backdrop against which darker-skinned A8 migrants of Roma origin live their lives in England (Cook et al, 2010: forthcoming). The intention of this discussion is not to marginalise debates about the ways in which certain physical or cultural differences may be exaggerated to suit the needs of racists in any society. Rather, this discussion of proactive and defensive citizenship engagement is designed to illustrate how the aspirations of different groups of citizens, each with valid rights to assert, may clash as citizenship evolves over time and is played out in a variety of spaces and locations.

'Citizenship of the Union': a differentiated status

The gradual shift in language from an emphasis on workers' rights towards a more general enunciation of concern for the rights of citizens that characterised the 1980s came to formal fruition with the declaration of the 'Citizenship of the Union' (that is, EU citizenship) in Article 8a of the TEU, now Article 17 of the consolidated Treaty of the European Communities (TEC) (see **Box 9.3**). The rights which this status confers are outlined in Articles 18-21 of the TEC and can be summarised as follows: the right to move and reside freely in the EU, the right to vote and to be a candidate in both municipal and European-level elections, the right (as necessary) to claim diplomatic protection under the authority of another member state and the right to petition the European Parliament.

When considering these rights, two points are evident: their limited scope and the apparent lack of a social dimension. Indeed, Weiler (1998) has suggested that European citizenship is little more than a cynical public relations exercise and that the most important right, that is, the right to free movement and residence laid out in Article 18, is not granted according to an individual's status as a citizen, but rather "in their capacity as factors of production" (Weiler, 1998, p 13). Such differential rights to residence among various groups of European citizens assume further importance because they impact on an individual's right to access social provisions when resident in a host state.

Box 9.3: Citizenship of the Union

Article 17

1. Citizenship of the Union is hereby established. Every person holding the nationality of a Member State shall be a citizen of the Union. Citizenship of the Union shall complement and not replace national citizenship.
2. Citizens of the Union enjoy the rights conferred by this Treaty and shall be subject to the duties imposed thereby.

Article 18

1. Every citizen of the Union shall have the right to move and reside freely within the territory of the Member States subject to the limitations and conditions laid down in this Treaty and by the measures adopted to give it effect.

Source: TEC (1997)

A number of commentators (Pollard and Ross, 1994; Ackers, 1998; Weiler, 1998; Dwyer, 2000b, 2001; Reich, 2001; Ackers and Dwyer, 2002, 2004; Kleinman, 2002; Warnes, 2002) have recognised that European citizenship is a highly stratified status built around an exclusive ideal of the citizen as a paid worker. One knock-on effect of this is the creation of inferior rights for many of those outside the PLM. The right to move and reside in another member state, and any attendant rights to social welfare, is often contingent on a number of conditions set out in EU legislation. Within European social policy it is often secondary legislative measures (as referred to in Article 18; see *Box 9.3*), such as Regulations and Directives, that define the access and scope of social rights available to member state nationals in respect of their status as European citizens. To date, migrant workers (and latterly dependent members of their families) enjoy superior rights in comparison to those who are economically inactive. The 'endemic' preoccupation with paid work that is central to the legal and financial framework of the EU not only negatively discriminates against older retired people (for detailed discussions, see Dwyer, 2000b, 2001; Ackers and Dwyer, 2002, 2004), but it also fails to recognise the valid contribution of many women (and certain men) who engage in unpaid familial care work. Married women who engage in such domestic work currently derive their rights as EU citizens directly from their spouse. This is problematic for those who are not legally married or who subsequently divorce. While legal definitions of European citizenship remain centred on paid work alone the welfare rights of many EU migrant women will remain marginalised (Ackers, 1998; Levitas, 1998).

Migration and the hierarchy of social entitlement

Both migration of third country nationals (TCNs) into the EU and the migration of EU citizens across national borders within the EU are increasingly a feature of contemporary European life. The expansion of the EU and the incorporation of the candidate countries of Central and Eastern Europe (many of which have substantially higher levels of poverty than current Community members) led to an increase in citizens from the new member states seeking work in other host EU states. Muus (2001) outlines a 'mosaic' of past migratory movements into and across Europe, which have resulted in a diverse range of resident migrant populations. In the 1950s to 1970s certain member states which were previously colonial powers (for example, the UK, France, the Netherlands, Portugal) experienced an influx of migrants from around the globe as part of their imperial legacies. The recruitment of 'temporary' workers from Southern and Eastern Europe and North Africa to meet certain labour shortages was also a feature of migration up until the mid-1970s. More recent migratory trends in the EU, for example, asylum seekers (Duvell and Jordan, 2002), the recruitment of highly skilled workers (Morris, 2001), clandestine migration (Muus, 2001) and the migratory movements of older EU citizens within Europe (King et al, 2000; Ackers and Dwyer, 2002) also raise important questions about the availability of social rights for migrants.

In respect of migration, the legal framework that underpins residency rights and EU citizenship is important. As previously stated, it acts to enhance the rights of some migrants while simultaneously reducing or marginalising the rights of others (Ward, 1997; Hansen, 2000; Morris, 2001). According to Kleinman (2002), 'Citizenship of the Union' creates a sort of mirage of formal equality between those who are nationals of member states. He argues that essentially four categories of EU residency status, each with access to different social rights, are created by current legislative arrangements:

- EU citizens who are nationals of the member state;
- economically active inter-state EU citizens;
- economically non-active inter-state EU citizens;
- TCNs.

In relation to EU residency and migration policy, a dichotomy exists whereby the international migration of EU citizens and the social rights that accrue to them are defined by supranational regulations laid out in EU law. The rights of entry, residence and access to public welfare of TCNs are, however, generally regulated by national laws at the member state level (Muus, 2001). The use of "stratified rights in the management of migration" (Morris, 2001, p 389) remains an important element of an individual state's migration policy. EU citizenship delivers little in the way of substantive residency and welfare rights to migrants who are TCNs (Dell'Olio, 2002). Those from outside the EU who are welcomed by member states are often reliant on bilateral agreements between nation states (Schuster and Solomos, 2002). The differentiated and often highly limited rights of asylum seekers/refugees previously outlined in *Box 8.3* (Chapter Eight, this volume) illustrate how individual nation states (in this case the UK) use the denial of welfare rights to discourage certain types of migration. As Vonk notes, "it is not the existence of migration itself, but rather the desirability of migration which affects the legal position of migrants in social security" (2001, p 331).

However, many legally resident TCNs who migrate as labour migrants and then grow old in a host EU member state can and do access particular welfare rights on a par with nationals of that member state (Sales, 2002b). They are able to do this because, in many cases, access to social rights within various European nations is organised according to what Bonoli (1997, 2000) has called *Bismarckian principles*, that is, they offer benefits based on social insurance principles that take into account previous contributions made by an individual worker. Theoretically, therefore, the PLM may offer certain TCNs the opportunity to overcome some of the disadvantages that may have accumulated due to a migrant's relatively poor legal status and/ or geographical location. In practice, the evidence suggests that for many TCNs the world of paid work will not deliver comfort in old age. Many such migrants fare badly within the PLM. Muus (2001, pp 44-5) notes:

> A relatively smaller proportion of the potential labour force among non-EU citizens takes part in the labour market, while unemployment rates among this category are generally much higher than among nationals or the other EU citizens. Immigrant unemployment is especially high among the 'guest workers' of the past, and specifically among the low and unskilled of non-EU origin.

Any social rights that derive from EU citizenship status are, perhaps unsurprisingly, reserved for EU citizens rather than TCNs who are legally resident in the EU. However, as Kleinman (2002) notes, the significance of EU citizenship and the rights that it bestows vary considerably across different categories of EU citizenship. His first category, 'EU citizens who are nationals of the member state', are not migrants and generally rely on their rights as citizens of a nation state to access social rights. The second group, 'economically active inter-state EU citizens', as migrant workers, enjoy the full benefit of EU citizenship by being able to access the same rights to welfare as nationals of the member state in which they live and work under Directive 68/360 (OJ Sp Ed 1968, No L 257/13). As they grow older, and if they choose to retire in the host state, they will continue to enjoy the same rights due to their former status as mobile EU workers (and in time will presumably become a subgroup of the third category).

The position of the third category highlighted by Kleinman (2002), that of 'economically non-active inter-state EU citizens', is not as straightforward as it first appears. The classification in respect of older EU migrant citizens outlined in *Box 9.4* highlights further differentiation in socio-legal status in this generic group.

In contrast to retired migrant community workers or returning community workers, the rights of those post-retirement migrants who move abroad within the EU following retirement (and have never worked in the host state) are highly contingent and are based on a more general right of residence (see Directive 90/365 [OJ 1990, L180/28], concerned with workers who have ceased their occupational activity). As economically inactive people, their right to reside is limited by two important conditions:

> ... [that they] are covered by sickness insurance ... [and] ... have sufficient resources to avoid becoming a burden on the social assistance system of the host Member State during their period of residence. (Directive 90/364, Article 1[1])

Box 9.4: Subgroups of older 'economically non-active inter-state EU citizens'

1. *Retired migrant community workers:* people who move to another member state for work and then exercise their right to remain.
2. *Returning community workers:* those who move to another member state for work and then return home on retirement.
3. *Post-retirement migrants:* people who retire in the home state and then move to another EU host state.
4. *Joiners:* a subgroup of the third category who move in order to accompany or join their Community migrant children claiming rights as ascendant, dependent, relatives.
5. *Returning post-retirement migrants:* a subgroup of the third category who subsequently return home.

Source: Ackers and Dwyer (2002, p 5)

Resources are deemed to be sufficient if they are above the level of resources at which the host state grants the right of social assistance to its own nationals. For returning post-retirement migrants who wish to relocate back to their country of origin (and access rights to social welfare) after a period of retirement elsewhere, the situation may be further complicated by individual member states' habitual residence requirements (Dwyer, 2001; Warnes, 2002).

Citizenship of the Union: 'the concealed multiplier of occupational success?'

Many of the rights implied by EU citizenship status concern claims for collective welfare provisions. The explicit promotion at EU level of insurance-based and occupational welfare schemes (CEC, 1997), combined with the noted privileging of paid work as the basis of social contribution in EU citizenship, is likely to further exacerbate the existing inequalities between different groups of EU citizens and TCNs. Titmuss's (1958) concerns about the developing contribution of occupational and fiscal welfare to well-being and social inequality retain a particular salience to contemporary EU arrangements. Writing in the context of UK social policy following the Second World War, Titmuss argued that the state met its duty to provide for the varying needs of its citizens through three parallel systems of welfare, that is, 'social', 'fiscal' and 'occupational', each of which must be considered in any discussion of the welfare state. *Social welfare* consists of the publicly provided funds and services (social security benefits, local authority housing, the NHS, personal social services and so on) that are often the single focus of dispute when the welfare state is discussed. Additionally, Titmuss emphasises the importance of *fiscal welfare* (for example, tax allowances and relief) and also *occupational welfare*, that is, the perks derived from advantageous employment in the PLM (pensions and fringe benefits such as cars, meals, private health schemes and so on). He was concerned that occupational welfare added a new tier to the pool of social resources available to those people with already advantageous employment status. Individuals in sectors of employment that did not deliver such 'perks', or those not engaged in paid work, were forced to rely on the typically less beneficial forms of social welfare provision.

EU policy adds a new dimension to Titmuss's consideration of the advantages of occupational and fiscal welfare. Citizenship of the Union extends the ability to fully access domestic welfare systems (Titmuss's 'social welfare' sector) only to those people who achieve the status of EU migrant worker. In that sense, the 'modicum of social security' available can only be accessed by those who work (or who have previously worked) in, and contributed to, the host state. Paid work is the trigger to full social citizenship rights. Migrant EU workers also have the right to be accompanied by their family, who then derive rights by virtue of their relationship to a worker-citizen. The social entitlement of families, therefore, becomes a further extension of occupational status. In terms of accessing (in a host country) what Titmuss (1958) referred to as 'social' welfare rights, past employment contribution in the home state could not be transferred and those who had resided, but not undertaken paid work, in the host state (for example, including housewives and carers) did not derive independent personal entitlement. Community citizenship thus operates as an extension of occupational entitlement. Not only does it provide access to a second tier of benefits, it also determines access to basic social citizenship in the host state. In that sense, the 'multiplier effect' (that is, the advantages accrued by those in receipt of occupational welfare) referred to by Titmuss assumes an even greater significance (Ackers and Dwyer, 2002, 2004).

An exclusive approach?

It was previously noted that national citizenship has the capacity formally to exclude non-citizens (that is, those from beyond the borders of the nation), while simultaneously denying certain individuals who hold formal citizenship status full enjoyment of the equal rights that the status bestows. The supranational citizenship of the EU is no different. Citizenship of the Union serves to exclude on two levels. First, legally resident TCNs from beyond the borders of the EU are excluded from the collective welfare arrangements of the EU. Second, certain migrants who meet the nationality requirements of EU citizenship continue to be denied full and equal rights to residence and social welfare because they are not active in the PLM.

Rhetorically the EU is committed to reducing social exclusion across Europe, but simultaneously it continues to endorse an exclusive notion of citizenship. Formally Article 17 of the TEC (citizenship of the Union) and Article 12 of the TEC (non-discrimination on grounds of nationality) combine to declare a common status of European citizenship. However, that status is differentiated, with essentially only EU migrant workers enjoying the same social rights as host country nationals. If EU citizenship is to become a substantive reality for all member state nationals who migrate across the EU, then the institutions of the Union need to address discriminatory elements of their own legislative framework to ensure that individuals outside the PLM are not systematically denied their full rights as European citizens. Furthermore, given its commitment to free movement, and the need to encourage increased immigration in order to fill gaps in the PLM, it may be time for the EU to extend the full social benefits of European prosperity to all TCN migrants who are legally resident and settled within its borders (see Dell'Olio, 2002).

Worlds of welfare or a European social model?

Previously, the welfare systems of EU member states have been variously classified in relation to a number of criteria, by theorists engaged in comparative welfare regime analysis. A detailed discussion of welfare state typologies is not a required task here. However, a brief exploration of the continuing diversity of welfare states across the EU is warranted when addressing the emergence, or otherwise, of a common European social model. Esping–Andersen's influential study *The three worlds of welfare capitalism* (1990) was an attempt to construct a typology of welfare states based on the different ways in which they are organised in relation to market forces, social structures and political interests. Esping–Andersen recognises that, in the real world, none of the welfare states in his study could be considered a pure example of any one of his three ideal types. Nonetheless, he believes it is possible to cluster welfare states into three basic groupings: liberal, conservative/corporatist and social democratic. A fourth category, variously described as 'southern' (Ferrera, 1996) or rudimentary/ Latin rim (Leibfried, 2000), has since been added to Esping-Andersen's original classification. The key elements that distinguish Southern European welfare have been laid out by Ferrera (1996), although debate continues as to the extent that Southern European welfare states are different from their conservative/corporatist continental cousins (see Katrougalos, 1996; Rhodes, 1996; Guillén and Matsaganis, 2000). The continued expansion of the EU will add to the present diversity of regimes.

Esping-Andersen's original work has since been much criticised, contested and, indeed, subsequently developed (Arts and Gelissen, 2002), and alternative approaches to the classification of welfare states now exist (for example, Lewis, 1992; Giarchi, 1996; Ploug and Kvist, 1996; Bonoli, 1997; Gough et al, 1997; Gough, 2001). This brief discussion is offered to illustrate the fact that a diversity of welfare states exist across Europe and this is likely to continue as the EU expands. ***Box 9.5*** outlines the basic characteristics of the different clusters of European welfare regimes.

The welfare system of each member state has evolved in its own particular historical, political and cultural context, so diversity is to be expected. Given this diversity, how reasonable is it to argue that convergence between the welfare systems of member states is happening? Is it possible to identify an emergent European social model?

Towards a European welfare state?

Drawing on various Commission documents, Hantrais (2000) suggests that it is possible to outline an EU social model, in the sense that all member states are in broad agreement about the core values and objectives of future welfare policy. These include:

- democracy and individual rights to welfare;
- free collective bargaining;
- equality of opportunity for all;
- social welfare and solidarity;
- highly developed systems of social protection;
- social progress, that is, high levels of employment, raising of living standards, striking a balance between social justice and economic efficiency.

Box 9.5: The diversity of welfare regimes in the EU

Liberal welfare regimes: for example, the UK. Minimal means-tested state welfare generally targeted at the poor; private and occupational welfare for the middle classes; minimal state interference with the market. Lack of middle class–working class alliance in forging welfare state.

Conservative/corporatist regimes: for example, Germany. State-centred conservative system influenced by the church, contribution-based social insurance to the fore, which looks to preserve existing occupational and status differentials in the welfare system. Attempts to secure middle- and working-class support for the welfare system.

Social democratic regimes: for example, Sweden. Welfare based on high-quality state-run universalist services, a commitment to full employment and equal opportunity. Emerged out of solidarity between middle and working classes.

Southern welfare regimes: for example, Greece. Some similarities to the conservative/corporatist cluster in that high social insurance contributions mainly from employers provide generous benefits for individuals well placed in the PLM; important differences include high levels of familial provision and a historical lack of guaranteed minimum of social protection.

Central and Eastern European regimes: for example, Hungary. Up until recently welfare was typically highly decommodified and under the control of the central state. Many nations are grappling with welfare reform while also trying to meet the economic criteria for EU entry.

Although a general consensus around such values can be said to have emerged among member states in the 1990s, EU social policy remains subservient to economic policy (Geyer, 2000, 2003). The monetary criteria and budgetary constraints imposed as requirements for entry into European Monetary Union are more likely to promote residual type welfare systems in which private insurance plays a greater role. This has negative implications for the social rights of those who live in, or are vulnerable to, poverty. Consequently, the EU may be promoting a social model that has more in common with Esping-Andersen's (1990) 'liberal' welfare state classification than the 'social democratic' one. It is also possible that economic imperatives will continue to override any substantial future enhancement of welfare rights (Bonoli, 2000; Bonoli et al, 2000; Geyer, 2000; Chapon and Euzéby, 2002). As Hantrais notes:

> A certain amount of involuntary or spontaneous, rather than intended or planned, convergence may thus have taken place under the influence of market forces and economic imperatives that have been driving social policy. (2000, p 39)

However, the welfare systems of individual member states also appear to be remarkably resistant to radical change. Beyond the policy statements of EU institutions, and a policy agenda that appears to be centred on the containment of public expenditure and economic imperatives rather than the extension of social rights, it may be too soon to talk of the development of a common 'social Europe' (Taylor-Gooby, 1999; Bonoli, 2000). The rhetoric from Brussels is optimistic, but in reality an entrenched reluctance exists on the part of member states that are loathe to let go of the legislative and administrative powers associated with welfare provision (Warnes, 2002). The analysis of Castles (2002) highlights the real continuing differences that exist across European welfare states and further calls into question the existence of a distinct and coherent European social policy model. How then might EU social policy influence the welfare provision in individual member states? The implementation of social policy remains very much a national prerogative and, overall, the impact of EU policy in relation to welfare remains limited (Geyer, 2000). While the Lisbon Agenda has looked to introduce common data gathering on social issues and extend the influence of shared EU policy principles, the EU's social policy mosaic still remains subject to much fragmentation.

The effect of EU social policy on national welfare states

No single coherent, common European welfare state model has yet emerged. In many of the core areas of social policy (for example, redistributive social benefits), the interventions of the EU remain limited by the principle of subsidiarity. The EU's social policy role is more about establishing an institutional framework for the consideration of welfare issues at European level and setting general policy directions for member states to interpret and follow within their own specific institutional framework. Many of its pronouncements are essentially declarations of intent or sets of minimum standards with recommendations for member states to work towards, rather than legally enforced requirements. This is often referred to as 'soft' legislation. 'Hard' legislation, that is, laws which member states must implement and follow, are scarce in the social sphere.

The direct impact of EU legislation is, therefore, limited. However, the indirect effects of the EU may, in the long run, be more significant for citizens (Cram, 1998). Most recently, the EU has been keen to promote OMC within the social policy arena. This involves the 'mainstreaming' of social policy issues (that is, bringing them to the fore) at EU level and the promotion of 'benchmarking', which sets out broad standards and allows member states wide margins of compliance (Geyer, 2003).

The effect of EU social policy on the UK is best described as uneven. For example, the EU has been effective at pushing gender issues onto the UK policy agenda. EU directives on working hours, parental leave and part-time working have helped to drive the work–life balance issue up the UK government's priority list. The potential of the EU to enhance the rights of gay and lesbian UK citizens has also been noted (see Chapter Six, this volume). In other areas such as disability policy (see Chapter Seven, this volume), Europe lags behind the more advanced policies of the UK (Geyer, 2003). More generally, Cram (1998) and Geyer (2003) identify five ways in which the EU has impacted on UK social policy. First, when the EU passes 'hard' legislation, the UK is duty bound to implement it. When a conflict arises between UK and binding EU law, European law prevails. Although, as previously noted, such legislation is limited in the area of social policy, EU social legislation does confer new rights on UK citizens, for example, equal treatment of men and women in the workplace. Second, the EU is keen to encourage social dialogue and welcomes input into the policy-making process from a wide range of actors including non-governmental organisations and interest groups. Europe thus opens up another potential channel of influence for organisations that may be ignored or marginalised in their own state. Third, in a similar vein, the EU enhances the role of regional and local actors. This runs counter to the increased centralisation of power that has been a feature of UK politics in recent decades. Fourth, contact with differing European systems and ways of doing things may, in the long term, influence or change the objectives, outlook and processes of social policy in the UK. Finally, individual UK citizens have the right, as European citizens, to challenge the rulings and judgments of member state governments and their agencies in the ECJ.

EU citizenship: towards a more expansive vision?

Previous discussions have noted that EU citizenship currently has only limited capacity to deliver substantive welfare rights for many EU citizens. Nonetheless, the social rights conferred on migrant Community workers offer tangible benefits to a particular privileged 'worker' class of EU citizens resident in host states. The existence of such rights counters assertions by some (Weiler, 1998; Kleinman, 2002) that EU citizenship is largely a symbolic rather than a substantive status. The legal framework of EU citizenship is not set in stone, but is open to redefinition through agreed reworking of European Treaties by member states, and also as a result of rulings given by the ECJ. In the past, the ECJ has taken a broad definition of 'paid work' and on a number of occasions found in favour of migrant citizens making claims for welfare in a host state on the basis of their status as part-time or intermittent workers. The Court has, however, been reluctant to recognise informal, familial care or voluntary work as a basis on which to claim rights equal to those of paid workers (Ackers, 1998; Ackers and Dwyer, 2002). Fries and Shaw (1998) argue that the ECJ judgment in Case C-85/96 (*Martinez Sala v Freistaat Bayern*, judgment on 12 May 1998) may indicate a general right to social welfare for all EU migrants, whether or not they are economically active. It remains to be seen, however, if this judgment marks a significant step towards the development of a more expansive notion of European citizenship that grants equal social rights to all EU citizens (Ackers, 1998).

More recently, specific cases in relation to healthcare (for example, see Kohll Case C-1120/95 and Decker Case C-158/96) appear to have prompted a further expansion of citizens' rights at EU level. In December 2002, an EU Council of employment and health ministers agreed, in principle, that individuals had the right to seek treatment in another member state (at the expense of their home state) if their own health service could not provide treatment within medically justifiable time limits. National health services will have to give permission before treatment can take place, but they will not be allowed to refuse individuals whose medical condition is so serious that they cannot join a long waiting list (see Threlfall, 2001; Castle and Linton, 2002). EU citizenship may yet assume a greater significance in delivering welfare to all individual citizens in the future.

Note

[1] CORE stands for COntinuous REcording of lettings and sales. It is a system for recording information about new local authority lettings and Housing Association lettings and sales in England.

Summary

- The EU has developed an increasing interest in social policy issues in the past 25 years.
- The principle of subsidiarity ensures that the national governments of member states remain very much in charge of welfare within their national boundaries.

- The expansion of the EU in 2004 heralded a new wave of migration into the UK, The numbers of A8 nationals who chose to come to work in the UK took the government by surprise. As A8 nationals proactively exercised their new rights as EU citizens, this, in turn, triggered defensive engagement among some members of local UK host communities that drew on more bounded notions of citizenship rights and responsibilities linked to membership of a national community.
- EU citizenship, which is granted to all individuals who are nationals of a member state, is more than a hollow promise. It does deliver substantial rights to welfare but primarily to mobile EU workers and their families.
- EU citizenship remains a highly stratified status, built around an exclusive ideal of the citizen as paid worker.
- The EU has some impact on the welfare systems of member states (including the UK), but currently it would be wrong to talk in terms of a distinct, single European welfare state.
- The Lisbon Agenda has made the issue of welfare provision more visible within EU institutions but stops short of enforcing a common social policy blueprint on member states.
- A more distinct European model of welfare provision may develop in the future, but to date EU social policy is not significantly replacing or undermining the diversity of national welfare states that continue to exist across Europe.

Further reading

Hantrais' third edition (2007) offers the most up-to-date and comprehensive consideration of EU social policy debates. Likewise **Leibfried's (2005)** book chapter offers a good overview of some of the important debates about EU social policy that have been introduced here. Those looking for a more extended discussion of the interplay between EU monetary and social policy should take a look at **Martin and Ross (2004). Alcock and Craig (2001)** offer an accessible introduction to debates and issues about the comparative analysis of welfare states. A more advanced but excellent review of welfare regime theory is presented in the article by **Arts and Gelissen (2002)**.

Website resources

The EU's website can be found at **http://europa.eu.int**. It contains a wealth of information and links to various EU sites.

Global citizenship?

Having previously discussed EU citizenship, this chapter is concerned to explore the possibility that the concept of citizenship can be further extended beyond the level of the nation state, to engender a system of *global citizenship*. This debate has increasingly exercised the minds of political theorists throughout the 1990s and there continues to be disagreement as to both the plausibility and desirability of transnational and/or global citizenship. On one important issue, however, there appears to be agreement: significant economic, political and social changes occurred in the latter half of the 20th century. These changes, and the implications that they have for social citizenship in the future, are explored in the following subsections:

- the challenges facing national citizenship;
- beyond the nation state: transnational citizenship;
- towards cosmopolitanism;
- from human rights to global social rights.

Social change and the ongoing challenges to national citizenship

In Part One of this book it was noted that the development of citizenship in the modern era was linked to the nation. Membership of a nation state has been crucial for an individual to enjoy the full benefits of citizenship. It is within the confines of the nation state that the rights and responsibilities central to citizenship status have been mapped out and negotiated. In terms of social rights, citizenship was about the state, within defined national boundaries, reducing certain class-based conflicts through a limited diminution of the inequities generated by capitalism. Certain authors (Soysal, 1994; Held, 1998; Castles and Davidson, 2000b; Delanty, 2000; Turner, 2000, 2001; Tambini, 2001; Schuster and Solomos, 2002) have noted (with varying degrees of enthusiasm) that the central role of the nation state in relation to contemporary citizenship is being challenged by significant, ongoing social changes.

Tambini captures the tone of many commentators when he argues that "national citizenship emerged and national citizenship will pass" (2001, p 198). He holds that the ongoing decline of modern national citizenship is due to five linked issues. First, he believes that economic globalisation has curtailed the ability of nation states to manage capitalism and provide welfare for their citizens. The provision of social rights has long been dependent on a state managing its national economy, but as money, markets and corporations have become increasingly internationalised and global, the state is less able to exert the levels of economic control necessary to deliver substantial social provisions. Second, Tambini argues that 'cultural denationalisation' is increasingly the norm. English has become an international language and the development of information technology has enhanced global communication. Allied to this, ethnic diversity is now a key characteristic of many national populations. Consequently, the construction of a homogeneous national identity around a particular set of common practices and characteristics is problematic. Third, the 20th century saw migration on unprecedented levels. The increasing international movement of labour, forced and educational migrants across national borders is also significant, because the ethnocultural characteristics of migrants are often different from the citizens of the countries in which they settle (Castles and Davidson, 2000b). These migratory movements are further adding to cultural diversity in many nations (for relevant details and discussions, see Muus, 2001; Baucöck, 2002; Veenkamp et al, 2003). Fourth, Tambini highlights the development of transnational/global institutions. Discussions in Chapter Nine (this volume) highlighted the ways in which EU citizenship selectively grants rights beyond national borders. Tambini also argues that other supranational institutions such as the UN have developed and nurtured a growing interest in the promotion of human rights, rather than citizenship rights, as a route to welfare. Finally, Tambini notes that the intellectual and cultural challenges of communitarian, postmodern and post-imperial theorists have increasingly called into question the (false) universalist assumptions that underpin the liberal ideal of national citizenship. The central point of his argument is that the changes he notes are challenging the sovereign power of nation states and their ability to deliver citizenship. Whereas in the past the nation was central to citizenship (that is, we developed our identity and learnt what it meant to be a citizen through a shared sense of nationality), citizens are now becoming increasingly aware of the limitations of that approach:

> I learn that my health and economic security are no longer guaranteed by the nation state; and I learn that my economic welfare is linked to a global economy, or a European labour market more than to national economic growth. I learn that my national government does not, or perhaps cannot, act to improve my environment without transnational pressure, or subnational nimbyism, and, as I learn all this my sense of belonging to a nation is diminished. (Tambini, 2001, p 206)

In short, the institutions through which we negotiate our status as citizens are being transformed. Before looking at the alternatives to national citizenship that may be emerging, a brief consideration of Turner's (2000, 2001) work is useful, as it addresses welfare issues more closely.

Modern, national citizenship: going, going, gone?

Turner (2000, 2001) believes that many of the presumptions that underpinned the citizenship of the second half of the 20th century have become increasingly redundant. Societies today are more complex and differentiated than in T.H. Marshall's day, with citizens far more sceptical about the ability of the state to solve their problems. The twin forces of globalisation and postmodernity make a sense of solidarity based around a shared notion of the national common good increasingly problematic. Arguing that the growth of modern citizenship is fundamentally bound up with growth of nation states and nationalism in the 19th and 20th centuries, Turner believes that there has been an ongoing erosion of nationalistic citizenship, which is but one of the grand narratives of modernity that are challenged by the onset of the postmodern age. Citizenship tied to the nation state is a system of inclusion, distributing and allocating entitlements but, simultaneously, it is a mechanism around which to build a sense of solidarity and a particular, exclusive and national identity.

Chapter Three of this book looked at how a racialised and gendered notion of British citizenship was constructed in the last century to serve the needs of nation and empire. Turner (2000, 2001) notes that, in the past, three routes to welfare entitlement, namely, production, destruction and reproduction, were central to citizens' enjoyment of social rights. Rights derived from activity in the PLM accrued to the worker–citizen. The service and sacrifices of the soldier–citizen also formed the basis for further privileges. Reproductive citizenship bestowed further welfare entitlements on those who formed heterosexual households and, as parents, literally reproduced the citizenry. This last element was profoundly gendered, with differing roles being ascribed to male and female parents (cf Williams, 1989).

Individuals fulfilled the responsibilities incumbent on citizens in each of these arenas and, in return, were able to access certain rights. Moreover, they nurtured a specific worker-warrior-father identity as the idealised norm of the citizen. In Turner's opinion, social change has rendered this norm redundant. Today a lack of paid work for significant numbers of citizens, diverse ways of partnering and parenting (see Chapter Six), and the end of mass conscription have combined to erode the traditional bases of our identity as citizens:

> Global changes raise questions about the stability and integration of citizenship identities based on traditional modes of loyalty and commitment.... How can the state secure the loyalty of younger generations who are underemployed or unemployed, who will never serve in a national army, and who may not form families either out of personal sexual preference or financial incapacity to support children. (Turner, 2001, p 26)

For Turner, the shift from the modern to the postmodern brings with it potential risks as well as opportunities. Old nationalistic hatreds may re-emerge. The future could spawn an exclusive citizenship that fuses old neo-tribal loyalties with a cut-throat anomic market individualism. More optimistically, people may come to embrace the positive potential of the changing social landscape. They may become more indifferent to and distant from the solidarities of the past. As societies become more diverse, a lack of support for the old loyalties and identities may well prove to be a positive turn (see also Delanty, 2000). After all, on one level, the 20th century is closely associated with mass atrocities carried out in the name of the nation state, and/or the extreme Left/Right ideologies that, at times, prevailed in certain nations. Turner hopes that a cosmopolitan citizenship will come to prevail in which "uncertain loyalties and contingent identities may become virtues of a post-modern society" (2001, p 30). Whatever the outcome, according to Turner (2000, 2001), T.H. Marshall's world has disappeared and his nation-centred approach to citizenship is now obsolete. A number of authors have outlined responses to this position, and their views are considered next.

Beyond the nation state: transnational citizenship

In developing their discussion of migration and citizenship in Europe, Schuster and Solomos (2002) initially distinguish between two camps of scholars: "those who argue that national citizenship is giving way to a transnational or postnational citizenship and those who view national citizenship as resilient" (2002, p 39). These two groups are then further subdivided into those who believe the demise of the nation state to be positive, and those who see such changes in a negative light. This gives us four different groups:

- those who believe that the role of the nation state is in decline and see this as a positive development;
- those who agree with the decline of the nation state thesis, but who see this as negative;
- scholars who hold that the nation state remains the key actor when considering citizenship and rights and that this is positive;
- those who accept that the nation state retains primary position but believe this to be negative (see *Box 10.1*).

The discussions in *Box 10.1* indicate that there is much disagreement about the extent to which national citizenship is giving way to a more transnational order. Certainly the conditions in which national citizenship operates have changed. As previously noted, significant international migratory movements mean that the citizenry of many states is increasingly diverse in terms of ethnicity and culture. This increased multiculturalism has led some scholars (Young, 1990; Kymlicka, 1995) to argue that rights should no longer be reserved solely for individuals and that within modern liberal states certain rights should also be afforded to culturally defined groups (see Chapter Eleven, this volume, for a fuller discussion of this issue). Other commentators have been keen to develop a wider vision of cosmopolitan or global citizenship. They argue that the central elements of national citizenship, namely, rights/responsibilities, participation, meaningful membership and a sense of belonging, can all exist without or beyond the nation state.

Towards cosmopolitan citizenship?

Cosmopolitanism is not a new idea. The notion that an individual was a citizen of the cosmos (world) can be traced back to the stoics of ancient Greece. In medieval Europe cosmopolitanism became associated with an international elite who shared a common language of Latin and embraced the idea of high culture. Advocates of cosmopolitanism believe that a postnational, global notion of citizenship is both possible and necessary in an increasingly globalised world (Heater, 1999; Delanty, 2000). The central points of Falk's (1994) discussion of global citizenship (also reviewed in Drover, 2000), and Delanty's (2000, ch 4) consideration of cosmopolitanism, are summarised in *Table 10.1*.

Box 10.1: Four positions on national/transnational citizenship

1. Nation state in decline: a positive development

Writers such as Soysal (1994) have argued that a 'transnational' citizenship status based on "universal personhood rather than national belonging" (p 1), that is, universal human rights rather than citizenship of a nation state, has gradually emerged post-Second World War. Pointing to the recent development of supranational systems of government (such as the EU, UN), she argues that many international migrants are able to enjoy substantive rights to welfare even though they are not formally citizens of the nation in which they reside. Her central point is that, in effect, a new form of citizenship which transcends national borders has emerged. Critics argue that Soysal fails to recognise the differentiation in rights that occurs between TCNs and 'citizens of the Union', and that the claims of EU citizens are derived from their status as national citizens of a member state (see Chapter Nine, this volume). Furthermore, many minority ethnic migrants continue to suffer discrimination and disadvantage in their host states (Muus, 2001), and it may be too soon to talk about post-national membership based on universal human rights (Faulks, 2000).

2. Nation state in decline: a negative development

This group of writers (for example, Horsman and Marshall, 1994; Jacobson, 1996) agree with Soysal's view that the power of the state is in decline. International migration and the granting of rights to migrants beyond national borders is effectively diminishing the importance of citizenship of a nation state. Horsman and Marshall (1994) are particularly concerned that, as the power of the nation state declines, a new world order of unchecked global capitalism may ensue that would do little to protect or enhance the rights of poor and marginalised people around the world.

3. Nation state remains the key actor: a positive state of affairs

Scholars such as Brubaker (1992), Freeman (1995) and Morris (1997a, 1997b) argue that the welfare and migration policies of nation states remain the single most important factor in defining the rights of both citizens and migrants within national borders. The most comprehensive and secure social rights remain intrinsically linked to full citizenship status of a particular nation state, rather than to universal human rights. National citizenship may be imperfect, of limited worth to legally resident non-citizens, and problematic for outsiders, but the nation state remains the best institution to ensure the provision of welfare.

4. Nation state remains the key actor: a negative state of affairs

This final group of authors (for example, Castles, 1996; Castles and Davidson, 2000b; Schuster and Solomos, 2002) accept that the nation state retains its powerful influence in determining the rights enjoyed by citizens and migrant non-citizens entering/residing within specific national borders. However, such writers are concerned to highlight how national citizenship is often constructed around, and exacerbates, exclusive ethnocultural identities. In turn, this may have a negative impact on the rights of minority ethnic citizens already resident within a state and/or those who may subsequently seek to enter a state (see previous discussions in Chapter Eight, this volume).

Source: Developed from Schuster and Solomos (2002); see also Faulks (2000); Tambini (2001)

Although they assign different labels to the various key aspects of global/cosmopolitan citizenship, it is apparent that Falk and Delanty acknowledge similar issues and developments. Within this approach, rights remain an important element but responsibilities at all levels (individual, local, national and global) are important. The developed nations of the world must recognise their responsibilities to the developing world by ensuring that the basic needs of human beings beyond their own borders are met, a task that requires global institutions of welfare. On a more personal level, cosmopolitan citizenship enables individuals to make links between personal patterns of consumption and worldwide concerns about global resources, the future of the planet and the welfare of subsequent generations. The essence of this vision is outlined in ***Box 10.2***.

Critics (see Heater, 1999, ch 4) argue that cosmopolitan citizenship is at best a vague concept that lacks legal or political status. It encompasses an expansive sweep of differing positions that range from those who prioritise human rights to those whose main concern is the well-being of the planet. Effective global democratic institutions remain a distant dream and nation states continue to wield power in contemporary systems of global governance such as the EU and UN. Furthermore, citizenship has its basis in a sense of community that implies a shared language, culture and customs. Humanity has no common history or culture to nurture a cosmopolitan identity. Heater notes that there is no guarantee that contact with others will induce a sense of commonality or shared global citizenship status. Difference may breed contempt rather than empathy and it may be undesirable and impossible to appropriate the notion of citizenship to a global level. In sum, cosmopolitan citizenship has been heavily criticised as "undefinable in theory, non-existent in practice and ... undesirable in any case" (Heater, 1999, p 143).

Table 10.1: Aspects of global/cosmopolitan citizenship

Cosmopolitan citizenship[a]

Internationalism and legal cosmopolitanism: a theory of internationalism with nation states governed by international law in which 'citizens of the world' by virtue of their common humanity may move across national borders unmolested

Globalisation: the view that the power of the nation state is challenged by global and local (sub-national) politics. There are a number of important developments here:

1. the rise of idea of postmodernism, that is, that identities are more fluid and less fixed by class and nation than in the modern era. This is leading to a cultural pluralism within nation states

2. the development of ecological citizenship

3. the evolution of global civil society, for example, anti-globalisation movements

4. a post-statist supranational approach to citizenship (for example, Held, 1995)

Transnationalism: the existence of cosmopolitan communities, ie, highly mobile citizens such as labour migrants, displaced migrants. Academics interested in transnationalism are often more concerned with the identities and rights of displaced citizens rather than new world governance

Global citizenship[b]

Aspirational citizenship: a desire for peace, order and good government across the globe that is centred on ensuring the well-being of all humankind

Transnational citizenship: typically the world of internationally mobile, high status, global workers involved in international business and commerce

Environmental citizenship: sometimes referred to as ecological or green citizenship, it moves welfare debates forward to consider issues such as deforestation, pollution and global warming. Concerns about sustaining natural resources over time are combined with more traditional social policy considerations of (global) poverty, inequity and redistribution

Regionalist citizenship: usually based on common ethnic or economic ties. This kind of citizenship extends the reach of citizenship beyond the nation state but within defined limits. The best example is EU citizenship, which stretches the potential of citizenship to include the territories of all member states but offers nothing to those beyond such boundaries

Citizenship of activism: refers to those citizens who actively engage in organisations within civil society to promote human rights agreements and associated agendas on a global level, for example, the anti-global capital movement

Post-nationalism: supra- (eg, EU) and sub-national (devolved) forms of government that erode the dominance of the nation state. The development of a vibrant international civil society with specific interests, identities and cultures transcending national boundaries, for example, New Social Movements, pressure groups and so on

Sources: [a] Delanty (2000); [b] Falk (1994)

One writer who has attempted to present a coherent theory of 'cosmopolitan governance' for contemporary conditions is Held (1995, 1998). He argues that we live in a world of interconnected "overlapping communities of fate" (1998, p 24), and that in response to globalisation it is necessary to institutionalise the values of social democracy at all levels, including the global, so that:

> People can enjoy membership in the diverse communities which significantly affect them and, accordingly, access to a variety of forms of political participation. Citizenship would be extended, in principle, to membership in all cross-cutting political communities from the local to the global. (1995, p 272)

A central element of his approach is the establishment and development of a new political system at the global level. Proposing a system of global social democracy, Held (1995) outlines an international charter of fundamental rights and obligations as the legal basis of a cosmopolitan world order; all political actors including nation states would be bound by it. The ultimate goal of cosmopolitanism is to ensure that the global economy can be tamed, so that the effective autonomy of individual citizens can be ensured.

In outlining a Marxist critique, Smith (2003) believes that several central elements of Held's (1995) theory relating to welfare are flawed. First, he argues that the long-term cosmopolitan objective of an adequate and guaranteed basic income for all adults (see the discussion in Chapter Eleven, this volume) is an optimistic dream. If it were to be set at an acceptable level, incentives to engage in paid work would be undermined. Also, given the current economic inequalities that exist between nations, Smith states that, presumably, a basic income would have to be set at differing levels around the globe. This would act to reinforce rather than alleviate inequalities between nations and individuals. Furthermore, setting a guaranteed baseline income does not in itself tackle economic inequalities. Second, Smith thinks that Held (1995) is naive in proposing 'access avenues' (that is, rights for workers and local communities to influence decisions on financial and industrial matters) as a means of influencing policy more locally. Smith (2003) argues that this may merely exacerbate social divisions within the working class. Those who are best placed within the labour market would use their position to their sectional advantage (see also Mann, 1992). In the unlikely event that management would allow workers access to the decision-making process, he argues that managers are more likely to favour investors rather than workers. Access avenues would do nothing to override the basic capital–labour conflict; participation does not necessarily deliver empowerment (see Chapter Four). Third, Held talks of a new economic

Box 10.2: Cosmopolitan citizenship

[There is ...] an emerging cosmopolitan thesis concerning citizenship beyond the state. The key aspect of this I shall argue, is that citizenship and nationality have today become separated and the state is no longer the exclusive reference point of sovereignty. This is the negative definition of cosmopolitanism. Cosmopolitan citizenship in the positive sense refers to new possibilities for participation and rights both within and beyond the state. In yet more concrete terms, for cosmopolitan citizenship the fundamental criterion is no longer birth, as in the case of most national citizenship, but residence.... Cosmopolitanism could thus be seen in the emergence of post-national forms of inclusion and in what might be called the enhanced interconnectivity of cultures.... (p 53)

Citizenship has ceased to be a unitary framework reflecting the geopolitics and geoculture of nation states; its components have become separated from each other having become taken up in other discourses. Rights have become embodied in discourses that extend beyond the legal reach of the nation state; responsibility has shifted from a discourse of personal obligation focused on the state to a discourse of co-responsibility for nature and for future generations; participation is less focused on the national community than on others' spaces, which have opened up as a result of subnational mobilisation linked to globalisation; and identity has become pluralised to the extent that citizenship must now contend with reconciling the pursuit of equality and with the recognition of difference. (p 132)

Source: Delanty (2000)

agency that would direct investment towards different disadvantaged areas of the world, utilising preferential interest rates to provide low-cost credit to 'developing' nations/regions. Smith believes that this will have little effect in delivering substantial levels of economic and social welfare to poorer regions, as it would simply complement rather than replace the hegemonic system of global capital. He concludes that:

> ... a new international financial architecture ... and attempts to institute social democracy on a global scale will not reverse this state of affairs. Without a radical break from the social forms of global capitalism, the dreams of cosmopolitan-democratic theorists are doomed to disappointment. (Smith, 2003, pp 29-32)

In effect, he elevates the Marxist criticisms of national social democratic citizenship outlined in Chapters Three and Four (this volume) to the global level (cf Ferge, 1979; Offe, 1982; Bottomore, 1992).

From human rights to global social rights?

It has already been noted that one of the key claims of cosmopolitan theorists is that transnational human rights are of increasing importance while, simultaneously, the benefits attached to national citizenship are in decline. In the context of social citizenship in a changing world, a key question concerns the usefulness of human rights in securing, for citizens, rights to substantive social provisions and benefits. In the latter half of the 20th century a legal expression of human rights to welfare can be found in the UN Declaration of Human Rights and the UN International Covenant on Economic, Social and Cultural Rights (see *Box 10.3*). More recently the EU has also outlined its own European Convention on Human Rights and in the UK one consequence of this has been the 1998 Human Rights Act. At the very least, it is reasonable to argue that human rights based on what Dean (2001) calls a 'doctrinal principle' (see Chapter One, this volume) are now an established part of the ways in which rights are enunciated. It may also be accurate to suggest that rights are sometimes extended to certain people (for example, migrants) on the basis of legal residence or employment and/or 'universal personhood' (Soysal, 1994; Delanty, 2000; Baucöck, 2002). Nonetheless, the question remains, do human rights deliver?

Heater (1999) notes that a set of legal (civil) rights do now exist on a global scale existing in parallel to the rights that accrue from citizens' membership of a particular nation state. However, he believes that the present reality is that such declarations, laudable as they may be, are more statements of intent rather than enforceable rights. Similarly, it is possible to see the emergence of a more active elaboration of global political citizenship. As noted in *Table 10.1*, citizens are participating in a vibrant global civil society. Humanitarian and environmental pressure groups (such as Greenpeace and Amnesty International) are part of the fabric of contemporary social life. The various agencies of the UN are also at work around the globe striving, in often dangerous conditions, to deliver emergency support and establish democratic institutions. Within the legal and academic spheres, international human rights lawyers and political theorists such as Held (1995) are engaged in mapping out new legal and democratic institutions at a global level. Dean (2002a) is, however, less optimistic about the ability of international declarations of human rights to foster and enhance meaningful social citizenship. He notes that the damaging dichotomy between negative (civil and political) and positive (social) rights, as outlined in Chapter One, is evident in the workings of the UN and the EU. Social rights appear once again to be the poor cousins in the family of rights. Dean also observes that within the human rights discourse, rights to welfare and social protection are increasingly seen as being conditional on attendant responsibilities. At an international level this seems to translate into the poorer nations of the 'developing' world accepting their responsibility to embrace the 'opportunities' that globalisation brings, rather than wealthier nations recognising that they have a responsibility to protect the world's poorer citizens from the insecurities that globalised capital will inevitably generate (Dean, 2004).

For the foreseeable future the nation state will remain the most significant domain for citizens to access substantive social rights. This appears to be accepted by even cosmopolitanism's most fervent advocates. For example, Delanty (2000) spends a great deal of time arguing that citizenship is being reconfigured and that the tie between nationality and rights has only recently been broken. He then somewhat contrarily asserts:

> National governance is still one of the most important levels of governance. For instance, with respect to social rights there is no equivalent model on either the sub-national nor the transnational. The welfare state remains an important dimension of social citizenship. (2000, p 135)

The sovereignty of the nation state has been challenged by globalisation. National governments operate in changed circumstances and have to be aware of international corporations and globalised markets, but they are still the major players in relation to welfare (Castles and Davidson, 2000a, 2000b). Similarly, at a European level the principle of subsidiarity ensures that national member states maintain the upper hand. It may be some time before supranational or global/cosmopolitan institutions usurp the central role of nation states in delivering social citizenship.

Box 10.3: Welfare rights recognised in UN declarations

UN Declaration of Human Rights (1948)

Article 22: everyone, as a member of society, has the right to social security and is entitled to realisation, through national effort and international cooperation and in accordance with the organisation and resources of each state, of the economic, social and cultural rights indispensable for his [sic] dignity and the free development of his personality.

Article 25(1): everyone has the right to a standard of living adequate for the health and well-being of himself and his family, including food, clothing, housing and medical care and necessary social services, and the right to security in the event of unemployment, sickness, disability, widowhood, old age or other lack of livelihood in circumstances beyond his control.

Article 26(1): everyone has the right to education. Education shall be free, at least in the elementary and fundamental stages. Elementary education shall be compulsory. Technical and professional education shall be made generally available and higher education shall be equally accessible to all on the basis of merit.

UN International Covenant on Economic, Social and Cultural Rights (1966)

Article 6: ... the right to work.

Article 9: ... the right of everyone to social security, including social insurance.

Article 11: ... the right of everyone to an adequate standard of living for himself and his family, including adequate food, clothing and housing, and to continuous improvement of living conditions.

Article 12: ... the right of everyone to the enjoyment of the highest attainable standard of physical and mental health.

Article 13: ... the right of everyone to education.

Source: Extracted from www.un.org

Summary

- The second half of the 20th century has been a period of significant economic, political and social change.
- These changes, globalisation, increased international migration, the development of transnational institutions and so on, have implications for 'modern' nation state-centred notions of citizenship that emerged in the late 19th and mid-20th century.
- Certain authors believe that the era of national citizenship is giving way to a period in which transnational citizenship is becoming the norm; others are more sceptical about such claims and view national citizenship as resilient.
- Those who support the idea of global or cosmopolitan theories of citizenship believe that the sovereignty of the nation state in relation to citizenship is being systematically and fundamentally undermined. Cosmopolitan theorists believe that it is both possible, and indeed preferable, for a meaningful sense of citizenship to be nurtured without, or beyond, the nation state.
- The era of global citizenship may yet emerge. However, particularly in relation to social citizenship, the nation state retains a pre-eminent role.

Further reading

The articles by **Tambini (2001)** and **Schuster and Solomos (2002)** both provide good reviews of debates about the erosion of national citizenship and the emergence of new supranational/global citizenship. The edited collection by **Yeates (2008)** and the book by **Yeates and Holden (2009)** are the best place to start for readers who want to explore global social policy in more depth. Parts 2 and 3 of **Delanty's (2000)** book provide a good overview of cosmopolitanism and those who wish to pursue their enquiries further should read **Held (1995)**.

Website resources

The UN's website can be accessed at **www.un.org** and contains links to its various agencies.

eleven

Conclusions

This concluding chapter begins by offering some thoughts on two important questions that have emerged from discussions in previous chapters. First, how might contemporary citizenship deal with difference? Second, is there a need for a multilayered understanding of citizenship? The chapter then moves on to outline the shift from what Walters (1997) has called a *welfare society* to an *active society*, and traces the implications that this has for social rights in the future. These issues are explored in the following subsections:

- dealing with difference;
- multiple sites of social citizenship;
- towards a new welfare settlement;
- dependency, agency and social citizenship.

Dealing with difference

The homogeneous society that T.H. Marshall (1949/92) assumed as the backdrop for his theory of citizenship has been much criticised (see Chapter Three, this volume). Today any viable theory of citizenship needs to consider and reflect the diversity of cultures and lifestyles that are increasingly part of society. Chapters Five to Eight of this book have considered issues of difference (in relation to class, gender, ethnicity and disability) and their significance for citizenship status, and more particularly welfare rights. A number of responses to the dilemmas that various aspects of difference present to the universalism that is central to any conception of citizenship are possible. This section outlines three approaches, namely, citizens' income, group rights and differentiated universalism.

Citizens' income: decoupling paid work and welfare

In Chapter Six it was noted that, although social citizenship was about providing benefits and services, it simultaneously privileged certain types of contribution, most notably and routinely paid work. This linking of work and welfare has proved to be problematic for poor citizens outside the PLM and also for many women who are engaged in the provision of informal, familial care. In effect, equal social citizenship rights have not been afforded to all relevant individuals on the basis of their universal citizenship status. Instead many rights to reasonable benefits have been reserved for workers rather than citizens. A number of commentators (Held, 1995; Bauman, 1998) have argued that social citizenship will only become universal if, and when, the dichotomy between paid workers and other citizens who are not active in the PLM is resolved by the introduction of an unconditional citizens' (or basic) income. Citizens' income is a universal, unconditional income paid by the state to every citizen as a right of citizenship. Arguments for and against the idea of citizens' income are outlined in *Table 11.1*.

Supporters of citizens' income (for a good discussion, see Twine, 1994, ch 14) argue that the right to a universal benefit without resort to means testing or the requirement of previous contribution should become a hallmark of citizenship. However, for some this is a step too far as everybody, 'freeloaders' included, would be able to claim their citizens' income. In response to such criticisms, proposals for a participation income, paid to all individuals who contribute to wider communal well-being in some positive way (for example, paid work, informal care works, voluntary/charitable activity and so on), have been mooted. This second option preserves some notion of social rights being linked to responsibilities, while recognising that people make many valid contributions to society outside the realm of the PLM. At a basic level, the introduction of a citizens' income or a participation income would remove or reduce the differences that exist between citizens who are in paid work and those who are not.

Group rights

Both Young (1990) and Kymlicka (1995) have been keen to argue that the individual rights central to citizenship should be complemented by group rights afforded to oppressed or disadvantaged minority groups. Young (1990) outlines a critique of what she sees as the false universality at the heart of the liberal notion of citizenship. She argues that minority groups that deviate from the dominant norm (that is, heterosexual, masculine and white) favoured by liberalism are often subject to marginalisation and oppression. Echoing the communitarian critiques discussed in Chapter

Table 11.1: Arguments for and against citizens' income

Arguments in favour	Arguments against
It breaks the link between work and social rights.	It breaks the link between rights and responsibilities that is a central aspect of citizenship.
The introduction of a decommodified universal social right that is not linked to the PLM would lend particular meaning and strength to popular notions of citizenship.	It would be too expensive to implement.
	It is not a politically viable option. People would not vote for a political party that attempted to introduce a citizens' income as it goes against commonly held views about claim and contribution.
It would simplify the tax and benefit system.	

Two, Young believes that we develop our capabilities and identities from our particular location within certain constitutive communities or groups, many of which are oppressed. Noting five aspects of oppression, namely exploitation, marginalisation, powerlessness, cultural imperialism and violence, she states that groups (for example, women or ethnic groups) who experience one or more of these aspects are subject to oppression from the majority culture. Oppressed groups, she believes, should have special rights of representation and veto in relation to policies that affect them. This would allow for the development of a 'differentiated citizenship' that reflects the needs and concerns of the diverse social groups that exist within current societies and would challenge the false, hegemonic equality of liberal citizenship that presently subordinates minority group interests in many democracies.

Faulks (2000) accepts that the false universality of liberalism can hide and deny difference, and that the voices and needs of certain groups can be ignored, but he believes that Young's approach is problematic for several reasons. First, how should a particular society decide which groups have a valid claim to oppression and thus special additional group rights? Second, how do we define membership of that group when internal differences within a particular 'group' may be of more significance? Third, as individuals have multiple aspects to their identities, which ones are to be privileged as a basis for special group rights? These points are neatly summarised by Harrison (with Davis, 2001), who, when discussing difference in relation to housing, points out that there is 'difference within difference' and that:

> People make their own histories as individual actors, negotiating their identities against particular settings, and experiencing

> housing in different ways. They may occupy more than one
> position and may deploy more than one identity (as has long
> been the case). For example, an individual might simultaneously
> be chair of a local residents' group, a member of an extended and
> powerful kinship network, a participant in a disabled people's
> organisation and an active trade unionist at work. Each role
> might have different implications in terms of personal identity,
> status, obligations, sense of solidarity or claims on public policy.
> (Harrison with Davis, 2001, p 7)

Group rights could themselves lead to more oppression and an overemphasis
on difference may undermine the universality that citizenship entails
(Faulks, 2000).

It has already been noted that many nations today have culturally diverse
populations. Kymlicka (1995) outlines a theory of group-specific rights in
the context of multicultural societies. He outlines three specific types of
rights that would be available to minority ethnic groups, as appropriate,
within a nation state (see *Box 11.1*).

Kymlicka draws a distinction between polyethnic states, in which
diversity is as a result of increased migration, and multination states, where
cultural diversity arises from a process whereby "previously self-governing
territorially concentrated cultures" (1995, p 6) have become incorporated
into a larger state. An example of this latter category would be the Celtic
nations of Scotland, Wales and part of Ireland, which have become the
constituents of the United Kingdom over time. As the extended quotation
in *Box 11.1* makes clear, his approach is about ensuring that cultures and
practices of minority ethnic groups are protected, provided that they do
not deny the rights of other individuals or groups. In essence, minority
rights will be honoured and protected as long as ethnic groups agree to an
overarching value of respect for other individuals and groups within the
national community. This is an approach that has parallels to that proposed
by Lister (1997), who has called for the development of 'differentiated
universalism' as the basis for contemporary citizenship. It is to this idea
that we now turn.

Differentiated universalism

Lister (1997) believes that a reformulated conception of citizenship can
accommodate diversity and difference. Rights can be particularised to
take into account the situation of particular groups at specific times. Social
citizenship can become proactive in the sense that welfare institutions

can work to counter the disadvantaged position of certain individuals in a variety of ways (for example, anti–discrimination legislation, affirmative action programmes and so on). Citizenship rights would then become anchored in a dynamic and differentiated politics of need (see also a similar argument made by Harrison, 1995). This would provide the basis for a new

Box 11.1: Multicultural citizenship

A comprehensive theory of justice in a multicultural state will include both universal rights, assigned to individuals regardless of group membership, and certain group differentiated rights or 'special status' for minority cultures. (p 6)

Three types of minority rights:

* Self-government rights (the delegation of powers to national minorities, often through some form of federalism).
* Polyethnic rights (financial support and legal protection for certain practices associated with particular ethnic or religious groups).
* Special representation rights (guaranteed seats for ethnic or national groups within the central institutions of the larger state). (p 6)

I have tried to show throughout this book that political life has an inescapably national dimension, whether it is in the drawing of boundaries and distributing of powers, or in decisions about the language of schooling, courts and bureaucracies, or in the choice of public holidays.

We need to be aware of this, and the way it can alienate and disadvantage others, and take steps to prevent any resulting injustices. These steps might include polyethnic and representation rights to accommodate ethnic and other disadvantaged groups within each national group, and self-government rights to enable autonomy for national minorities alongside a majority nation. Without such measures, talk of 'treating peoples as individuals' is itself just a cover for ethnic and national injustice.

It is equally important to stress the limits on such rights. In particular, I have argued that they must respect two constraints: minority rights should not allow one group to dominate other groups; and they should not enable a group to oppress its own members. In other words, liberals should seek to ensure that there is equality between groups and freedom and equality within groups. (p 194)

Source: Kymlicka (1995)

citizenship, based on agreed, overarching principles such as universalism and equality, but also one that is flexible enough to recognise the different rights, needs and contributions of various groups at any given time in society; "a sophisticated universalism that while committed to equality, is able to be sensitive to diversity" (Thompson and Hoggett, 1996, p 21). In many ways this vision of reconfigured social citizenship mirrors the approach and concerns of Titmuss, noted in Chapter Four (see **Box 4.1**), who was concerned to develop "a particular infrastructure of universalist services ... around which can be developed socially acceptable selective services aiming to discriminate positively, with the minimum of stigma in favour of those whose needs are greatest" (Titmuss, 1958, p 122). Debates about which particular citizens' needs should be given priority and how they should be selectively met can only take place once agreement about shared core universal values and the equal worth of every single citizen has occurred. As Bauman (2002) acknowledges, "the right to be different cannot be fulfilled unless the equality of individuals as citizens is institutionally entrenched and practised" (2002, p 326). The primary task of contemporary social citizenship should be to ensure that *access to quality welfare services and benefits* (which meet a diverse range of needs) becomes the universal experience of every citizen, regardless of their particular socio-economic standing, abilities, gender or ethnic affiliations.

Multiple sites of social citizenship

In previous discussions of European and global citizenship (Chapters Nine and Ten, this volume), two main points were noted. First, that globalisation was having some impact on the ways in which people experience citizenship and access social rights. Second, that within current global and European supranational institutions, nation states remain the key actors, especially in relation to citizenship's social element. For example, EU citizenship is derived directly from an individual's status as a citizen of a member state. The EU, therefore, has no control over who becomes a 'citizen of the Union'; such powers remain with nation states (Reich, 2001; Dell'Olio, 2002; Preuss et al, 2003). At a global level a similar state of affairs exists. Globalisation, or the emergence of global institutions, may not automatically promote increased civic human consciousness and a concern for the welfare of all humanity. It may well enable a higher level of oppression and exploitation of the vulnerable. Within the UN the national interests of powerful and prosperous elite nation states can, and often do, override global needs and/or the needs of developing nations (Heater, 1999). Globalisation is increasingly a part of social reality, but its enduring legacy may yet be to engender a process of polarisation between the developed nations of the world and poorer developing countries (Faulks, 2000). As Bauman (2002) notes, globalisation may do more to constrain rather than enhance citizenship, particularly the citizenship of the most vulnerable.

One of the defining characteristics of citizenship, as outlined by T.H. Marshall in the mid-20th century, was the shift from the realm of the *local to the national*. Equal rights were to be afforded to each citizen in respect of their membership of a *national* community. It may be that, given the social conditions that pertain at the beginning of the 21st century, once again there is a need to reframe our understanding of citizenship and make the switch this time from *national to global* citizenship. However, an important distinction between the national social citizenship envisaged by Marshall and the global/cosmopolitan citizenship discussed in Chapter Ten exists. Crucial to T.H. Marshall's approach was the fact that citizenship rights were *institutionally situated*. For example, in the UK national social rights were given reality and substance with the founding of the welfare state in 1948. Cosmopolitan/global citizenship, centred around a human rights agenda, may offer the possibility of extending welfare rights in the future, but for the time being, particularly in terms of access to sustained welfare benefits and provisions, human rights remain abstract declarations of limited substantive value. Advocates of globalism such as Held (1995) are calling for the establishment and development of supranational bodies, so that they may be realised in the future. Until such institutions exist, global social rights will remain largely ethereal.

Discussions in Chapters Nine and Ten (this volume) clearly indicate that the exclusivity of the nation state in relation to citizenship is being challenged. A number of commentators have talked variously about the contemporary emergence of decentred multilevel citizenship, with citizens becoming engaged with actors and institutions at a range of levels (local, national and supranational), as they negotiate their rights and responsibilities (Held, 1995; Heater, 1999; Delanty, 2000). Writing in the context of EU citizenship and social rights, Faist's (2001) discussion of 'nested membership' (see **Box 11.2**) highlights how contemporary social citizenship is developed and played out in a multitude of settings.

The continuing importance of the nation state in delivering welfare is stressed but, as Faist points out, local, national and supranational (the EU) communities are all important sites in which people exercise their citizenship status in the modern world. Certainly, local control of public welfare has its advocates among those at the heart of New Labour in the UK. As the government looked to its third term, the former Prime Minister, Tony Blair talked of "far more devolution of power and responsibility to the front line" (Blair, 2002, p 23), and enabling and enhancing local leadership in health, education and housing services. Blears (2003) likewise enthusiastically endorsed the view that local communities should assume greater control of their welfare institutions. According to Drover (2000) and Turner (2000), the global arena would also become a site of increasing significance in defining the quality of life and level of well-being of citizens across the world. It may well be that, as citizenship develops in the 21st century, arenas above and below the nation state will assume more importance in meeting welfare needs.

> ## Box 11.2: Nested membership
>
> The concept of *nested membership* is most appropriate to conceptualise both the federative and multilevel character of the EU governance network and the citizens' rights that exist on the different levels of governance – regional, state and supra-state. This multi-tiered membership system consists of a mixture of rights guaranteed, by regional, state, interstate and genuinely European institutions. The safeguarding of people's rights functions on several levels, which are set within each other. (p 39)
>
> The concept of nested membership says that membership of the EU has multiple sites and there is an interactive system of politics, policies and social rights between the sub-state, state, interstate and supra-state levels ... what has evolved in the EU is an extraordinarily intricate network of overlapping social rights in which Member States play a central but by no means exclusive role. (p 46)
>
> *Source:* Faist (2001)

Towards a new welfare settlement

Built around three rights elements (civil, political and social), Marshall's theory (1949/92) of citizenship implied an equality of status universally enjoyed by all those deemed to be citizens. It was the addition of a third, social rights element that made the citizenship status of the social democratic PWWS both distinctive and substantive, when compared to that which had gone before. In recent years a number of profound economic, political and social changes (see the discussions in Chapter Ten) have resulted in what Taylor-Gooby (2002, p 601) has called "real changes of approach" in the organisation of contemporary welfare states. There has been much talk of the new 'third way' politics (see Chapter Four, this volume), most notably but not exclusively in the UK and US. According to a chief exponent (Giddens, 1994, 1998), the correct role for governments to assume in relation to welfare was to encourage an 'entrepreneurial culture' that rewarded 'responsible risk takers'. The new 'social investment state' would meet its commitments to social justice and equality via the redistribution of 'possibilities' (primarily the opportunity to work and the right to education), rather than wealth. Giddens was also unequivocal in making a reciprocal relationship between rights and responsibilities central to his approach. This 'new' politics could be seen as a fundamental challenge to the "post-war idea of the welfare state based on the principle of universal entitlement derived from citizenship" (Cox, 1998, p 3).

While many governments optimistically endorse a system of welfare that prioritises *responsible* individual agency as a panacea for dependency, Walters (1997) is more sceptical about the direction of welfare reform driven by New Labour. He argues that the 'welfare society' of the PWWS that promised, theoretically at least, a common citizenship status guaranteeing a universal minimum of welfare rights, was superseded by the 'active society' in which increasingly individuals could only access social rights if they were willing to accept specified responsibilities, most notably work in the PLM (cf Williams, 1999). Walters did not assert a naive view that all was well in the past. He was aware of the 'false universalism' (Williams, 1992) of the PWWS, and the fact that a person's participation and position in the highly stratified PLM had long been of central importance in defining the quality and extent of an individual's access to public provision. His key point was that a crucial shift had occurred. Although imperfect, the state defined people in the 'welfare society' of the past according to various categories, with certain 'inactive' groups exempted from PLM participation, either because they were making what were recognised as socially valid contributions elsewhere (for example, women engaged in informal/familial care work), or because they had previously contributed (for example, retired senior citizens). Such assumptions were increasingly being challenged. Whereas welfare society is:

> ... imagined [as] a collective enterprise in which workers and non-workers make their respective contributions ... many of these assumptions about the specifically *social* obligations and consequent rights of the citizen no longer apply in the active society.... The active society makes us all workers. (Walters, 1997, pp 223-4; original emphasis)

Policies that seek to promote or improve unconditional entitlement to public welfare benefits are seen as entrenching welfare dependency. If necessary, reluctant individuals should be forced into activity by the application of benefit sanctions. Only those who 'take charge' of their own lives are deemed to be responsible 'active citizens' (Wetherly, 2001). This is certainly an agenda that New Labour has been keen to endorse in the UK, and such ideas enjoy more extensive support. Increasingly they have informed policy across Europe (Lødemel and Trickey, 2000; van Oorschot, 2000; van Berkel and Moller, 2002), in the US (O'Connor, 1998; Prideaux, 2001; Deacon, 2002), Australia and elsewhere (Goodin, 2002).

From social rights to conditional entitlements

The consequences of such reforms for social citizenship should not be dismissed lightly. Pierson (1996, 2001) has argued that mature welfare states are resilient institutions that are often resistant to retrenchment. The new politics of welfare is different from the earlier politics of expansion. Retrenchment is generally unpopular and politicians who attempt to cut back public welfare are in the business of blame avoidance rather than credit claiming. They also often face entrenched opposition from voters and interest groups. Pierson states that measuring retrenchment is a difficult task. One significant indicator of a structural shift in welfare states is "dramatic changes in benefit and eligibility rules that signal a qualitative reform of a particular program" (1996, p 157). The welfare reforms discussed in this book illustrate that such a *qualitative* shift is ongoing in the way that social citizenship is conceived and operates. The idea of social rights is being superseded by one of *conditional entitlement*. This change is not limited to Britain. For example, Deacon (2002) notes that ending the right to welfare was central to US welfare reform in the 1990s. It is possible to dismiss the shift to active welfare policies and reforms that make access to collective welfare rights increasingly conditional on individual responsibilities (see, for example, *Box 5.3*) as minor manoeuvres and of little long-term consequence. However, as Cox notes, such 'tinkering' often has far-reaching consequences:

> Though tinkering is often viewed as a substitute for real reform it can lead to important change especially when its cumulative impact is taken into consideration. Years of austerity measures, numerous small manipulations in programme eligibility, decentralisation of administrative responsibility, a shift from passive to active unemployment measures, all of these are important changes. (1998, p 2)

It would appear that many Western governments are distancing themselves from the notion of welfare rights and increasingly embracing, in both principle and practice, the idea that public welfare provisions are conditional entitlements. This diminishes the limited equality that the citizenship of the PWWS promised. The diminution of such rights will have the greatest negative effect on those most in need. The shift towards 'active/third way' welfare states is an attempt by Western governments to renegotiate the welfare deal between citizen and the state. This represents a significant qualitative shift away from the public welfare envisaged in the PWWS, built around notions of need and entitlement. On one level, the changes outlined in this discussion can be seen as incremental, but such changes are significant (Pierson, 1996; Cox, 1998; Taylor-Gooby, 2002).

According to Pierson, "the contemporary politics of the welfare state is the politics of blame avoidance" (1996, p 179). A new welfare orthodoxy that stresses reduced access to public welfare provision, a strong link between rights and responsibilities, and an increasingly moral agenda, is now dominant. This approach to citizenship fits the requirements of the political architects of welfare retrenchment well. The exclusion of certain individuals from public welfare arrangements becomes less problematic for the provider of welfare. 'Irresponsible' citizens who do not meet certain state-endorsed standards can have their (conditional) right to collective support withdrawn or reduced, while simultaneously apportioning any blame for the subsequent exclusion to the individuals concerned (Dwyer, 1998, 2000a). In short, a more conditional and constrained notion of social citizenship is currently being mapped out. It is important to ensure that the unconditional right to welfare does not become part of yesterday's vision.

Dependency, agency and social citizenship

Reference has already been made to Titmuss's (1958) famous essay on the social division of welfare in relation to EU citizenship (see Chapter Nine, this volume). In the context of this concluding chapter and a consideration of the current reform of social citizenship, the insights of Titmuss and others who have subsequently developed the social division of welfare thesis (Sinfield, 1978; Rose, 1981; Mann, 1992, 1998a, 2001) are relevant. Titmuss (1958) argues that the state has a duty to meet the varying welfare needs of its citizens. This it attempts to do, not with a single method, but through three parallel systems of welfare: 'social', 'fiscal' and 'occupational', each of which must be considered in any discussion of the welfare state. *Social welfare* consists of the publicly provided funds and services (social security benefits, local authority housing, the NHS, personal social services and so on) that are often the single focus of dispute when the welfare state is discussed. In addition, Titmuss emphasises the importance of *fiscal welfare* and *occupational welfare* (see p 184, this volume). By redefining welfare in a wider context, Titmuss illustrates that differing welfare provisions, fully sanctioned by the state, are delivered to different groups within British society and that the middle classes gain substantially from public welfare in the wider sense.

By focusing their attention almost exclusively on Titmuss's 'social' component, it has been easy for certain politicians and commentators to set a narrow agenda when debating welfare (Mann, 1998a). This agenda, which concentrates on both the pressing need to reduce the social security budget and the necessity to control and remoralise members of a welfare-dependent and deviant 'underclass', is a central feature of the ongoing active/third way theorising that is currently influential on the reordering of social citizenship. Organisational changes in the delivery of public welfare, and the emergence of the selective application of a principle of conditionality, have undermined any previous notion of common citizenship that the social division of welfare thesis implied. Against this backdrop, it becomes easier for those who already enjoy substantial, but relatively concealed, benefits from social (the public healthcare and education sectors), occupational and fiscal welfare to denounce those with the most visible claims (that is, those who rely on social welfare benefits) as passive welfare dependants:

> Inequality in the visibility of benefits is an important and integral part of the social division of welfare. The hierarchy of benefits moreover is clearly considerable, providing very different amounts, under a wide range of conditions that may reinforce or strip the recipients of their status. (Sinfield, 1978, pp 136-7)

Third way welfare policies fail adequately to theorise welfare dependency and individual responsibility. The dependency of the majority enjoying the benefits of occupational and fiscal welfare, "which they have done nothing to earn" (Goodin, 2000, p 13), is basically ignored. The dependency of a minority reliant on meagre social welfare benefits is used to castigate claimants as irresponsible and undeserving of support, presumably because they will not help themselves by engaging in the PLM. Such approaches that legitimise certain claims to welfare by prioritising crude ideas of claim and contribution, and moralistic ideas of individual agency and responsibility, are deeply flawed.

Vincent (1991) reminds us that rich and poor are actively engaged in managing their risks, but that wealthy citizens are more effective in ensuring they get what they want due to the advantages that they have accrued in the past. The promotion of themes such as opportunity and choice, which are central to ongoing reforms of social citizenship, reaffirms more generally the advantage of more affluent citizens, who use their economic and social capital to relocate to areas with the best schools, childcare and healthcare facilities. It is unlikely that those involved will be denounced as irresponsible, despite the fact that their active agency, their exercising of choice, compounds the marginalisation of the "worst off citizens left in districts with the worst public services, as well as highest rates of crime, drug use, violence and other social problems" (Jordan, 2001, p 529). Against this backdrop of increased marginalisation and the 'enforcement ethos' of various 'New Deals', poor citizens at the sharp end of public welfare are active themselves in using a variety of methods, including claiming social security while working, to ensure that their needs are met (Jordan, 2001). The key question is: who are the responsible, reflexive citizens and who are the calculating, irresponsible, self-interested welfare dependants?

In reality, who gets what from the welfare state, and when and how they get it, has little to do with personal responsibility and desert. If necessary, people will mobilise various 'deservingness criteria' (van Oorschot, 2000) to make or validate a claim for public welfare services/benefits, even if they have previously spent a lot of time and energy trying to minimise their contributions to collective welfare in the past (White, 2000). It is often the most skilful operators, rather than those with the most pressing needs, who engage most successfully within the maze of rights, rules and administrative discretion (Adler, 1997) that make up contemporary welfare states. As Taylor-Gooby (2000, 2001) notes, 'risk' is differentially experienced by different social groups in contemporary society. Active/third way welfare works to the advantage of more privileged citizens and to the detriment of vulnerable groups. Social/economic divisions still matter in relation to welfare risks and an individual's ability to manage them.

It is important to assert a more sophisticated understanding of agency and welfare dependency than the one currently in vogue. As theorists concerned with the social division of welfare point out, such narrow conceptions of social rights/responsibilities and dependency are flawed. A simplistic dichotomy between two ideal types of citizen, namely the independent, responsible active (full-time) paid worker and the irresponsible, passive, welfare dependant who does not engage with the PLM, is at the heart of many current welfare reforms and much dominant theorising of social citizenship. It fails to recognise a more complex social reality in two ways. First, it takes no account of the extent to which a functioning market economy and formal public welfare system depend on gendered, informal welfare for their continued successful operation. Second, it ignores the extent to which many so-called dependants assume such burdens of informal, familial care yet remain unrecognised and undervalued (Rose, 1981; Lister, 1990, 1997). It is imperative that any new welfare settlement affords those undertaking such care work social rights on a par with those engaged in paid work.

Active/third way theories that dominate contemporary welfare reforms are built around the principle of highly conditional social welfare rights and limited notions of socially valuable contribution and agency. They will lead us towards exclusive and coercive systems of social citizenship in the future. It is important to recognise the limited potential of such approaches for meeting the needs of marginalised social groups (see Dean, 2000a; Taylor-Gooby, 2000). How, then, do we move forward positively in relation to social citizenship? Clearly, it would be equally wrong to view the PWWS as a golden age to be recaptured. Social change (see Chapter Ten) and the shortcomings and the tendencies of past notions of citizenship to exclude those who failed to live up to a gendered, able-bodied, ethnocentric norm (see Chapters Six, Seven and Eight) make such an aim undesirable and inappropriate. Today, welfare dependency is narrowly defined by many as a *stigmatising signal of individual failure* (Batsleer and Humphries, 2000). This view needs to be countered. Simplistic debates that contrast dependence and independence are flawed; we are all socially interdependent. Our very sense of self, who we are, is constructed over time through our links and relationships with other human beings. We all exercise choice and agency in relation to welfare against the backdrop of the complex and changing welfare institutions. These may provide both opportunities to, and constraints on, particular groups at different times (Twine, 1994; Harrison, 2001).

Greater levels of economic redistribution in favour of poor citizens must be a central feature of future welfare policy, because, as Twine notes, "redistributing resources also redistributes freedom and choice" (1994, p 12). The promotion of policies that prioritise the notion of *interdependence* also need to be to the fore, not least as a counter to the fallacy of the celebrated, independent self-reliant citizen. As Williams notes, "we need to recognise that we are all necessarily dependent on others, but at the same time challenge the institutions, structures and social relations which render some groups unnecessarily dependent" (1999, p 667) (see also Parry, 1991; Barnes, 2000). This may be hard for some citizens to accept, not least because it means that we are faced with the reality that our progress, or elevated social status, is often achieved with the help of, or at the expense of, others. It may well be time to prioritise values such as need and interdependence when theorising welfare. Inclusive and substantive social citizenship at local, national and global levels will only become a future reality when, and if, we all readily acknowledge that the best starting point for meeting the diversity of needs that exist in modern societies is a recognition of *our common humanity* (Harris, 2002).

References

Acheson, D. (1998) *Independent inquiry into inequalities in health*, London: The Stationery Office, reissued as Gordon, D., Shaw, M., Dorling, D. and Davey Smith, G. (eds) (1999) *Inequalities in health*, Bristol: The Policy Press.

Ackers, H.L. (1998) *Shifting spaces: Women, citizenship and migration within the EU*, Bristol: The Policy Press.

Ackers, H.L. and Dwyer, P. (2002) *Senior citizenship? Retirement, migration and welfare in the European Union*, Bristol: The Policy Press.

Ackers, H.L. and Dwyer, P. (2004) 'Fixed law, fluid lives', *Ageing and Society*, vol 24, no 3, pp 451-72.

Adler, M. (1997) *Welfare rights, rules and discretion: All for one or one for all*, New Waverley Paper SP 12, Edinburgh: Department of Social Policy, University of Edinburgh.

Ahmad, W. and Craig, G. (2003) 'Race and social welfare', in P. Alcock, A. Erskine and M. May (eds) *The student's companion to social policy* (2nd edn), London: Blackwell/Social Policy Association, pp 113-20.

Ahmad, W.I. and Husband, C. (1993) 'Religious identity, citizenship and welfare: the case of Muslims in Britain', *American Journal of Islamic Social Science*, vol 10, no 2, pp 217-33.

Ahmed, K. (2003) 'Transsexuals win right to marry', *The Observer*, 6 July, p 1.

Alcock, P. (1989) 'Why citizenship and welfare rights offer new hope for new welfare in Britain', *Critical Social Policy*, vol 19, no 2, pp 32-43.

Alcock, P. (1996) 'The new right', in P. Alcock, *Social policy in Britain: Themes and issues*, Basingstoke: Macmillan, pp 126-30.

Alcock, P. (1997) *Understanding poverty* (2nd edn), Basingstoke: Macmillan.

Alcock, P. (2006) *Understanding poverty* (3rd edn), Basingstoke: Palgrave Macmillan.

Alcock, P. and Craig, G. (eds) (2001) *International social policy*, Basingstoke: Palgrave.

Alcock, P. and Oakley, A. (2001) 'Introduction', in P. Alcock, H. Glennerster, A. Oakley and A. Sinfield (eds) *Welfare and wellbeing: Richard Titmuss's contribution to social policy*, Bristol: The Policy Press, pp 1-9.

Alcock, P., Erskine, A. and May, M. (eds) (2003) *The student's companion to social policy* (2nd edn), London: Blackwell/Social Policy Association.

Alcock, P., May, M. and Rowlingson, K. (2008) *The student's companion to social policy* (3rd edn), London: Blackwell/SPA.

ALI (Adult Learning Inspectorate) (2002) *Qualifications 2002/26: Annual report of the Chief Inspector*, Coventry: ALI.

Amas, N. (2008) *Housing, new migration and community relations: A review of the evidence base*, London: Information Centre about Asylum and Refugees.

Anderson, B. (1983) *Imagined communities: Reflections on the origins and spread of nationalism*, London: Verso.

Aristotle (1948) *Politics* (translated and edited by E. Barker), Oxford: Clarendon Press.

Arts, W. and Gelissen, J. (2002) 'Three worlds of welfare capitalism or more? A state of the art report', *Journal of European Social Policy*, vol 12, no 2, pp 137-58.

Avineri, S. and de Shalit, A. (eds) (1995) *Communitarianism and individualism*, Oxford: Oxford University Press.

Barbalet, J.M. (1988) *Citizenship*, Milton Keynes: Open University Press.

Barnes, C. (1991) *Disabled people in Britain and discrimination: A case for anti-discrimination legislation*, London: Hurst/BCODP.

Barnes, C. (1992) 'Institutional discrimination against disabled people and the campaign for anti-discrimination legislation', *Critical Social Policy*, vol 12, no 1, pp 5-22.

Barnes, C. (2000) 'A working social model? Disability, work and disability politics in the 21st century', *Critical Social Policy, Special Issue: Disability and the Restructuring of Welfare: Employment, Benefits and the Law*, vol 20, no 3, pp 441-58.

Barnes, C. and Mercer, G. (eds) (1997) *Exploring the divide: Illness and disability*, Leeds: The Disability Press.

Barnes, C. and Mercer, G. (2003) *Disability*, Cambridge: Polity Press.

Barnes, C. and Oliver, M. (1995) 'Disability rights: rhetoric and reality in the UK', *Disability and Society*, vol 10, no 1, pp 111-16.

Barnes, C., Mercer, G. and Shakespeare, T. (1999) *Exploring disability: A sociological introduction*, Cambridge: Polity Press.

Barton, L. (1993) 'The struggle for citizenship: the case of disabled people', *Disability, Handicap and Society*, vol 8, no 3, pp 235-48.

Batsleer, J. and Humphries, B. (2000) 'Welfare, exclusion and political agency', in J. Batsleer and B. Humphries (eds) *Welfare, exclusion and political agency*, London: Routledge, pp 1-21.

Baucöck, R. (2002) *How migration transforms citizenship: International, multinational and transnational perspectives*, IWE Working Paper Series No 24, Vienna: Institutionellen Wandel und Europäische Integration.

Bauman, Z. (1998) *Work, consumerism and the new poor*, Buckingham: Open University Press.

Bauman, Z. (2002) 'Postscript: cultural variety or variety of cultures?', *Critical Studies*, vol 20, pp 317-30.

Bell, D. (1995) *Communitarianism and its critics*, Oxford: Clarendon Press.

Bellamy, R. and Greenaway, J. (1995) 'The new right conception of citizenship and the citizen's charter', *Government and Opposition*, vol 30, no 4, pp 467-91.

Beresford, P. (2000) 'Service users' knowledges and social work theory: conflict or collaboration?', *British Journal of Social Work*, no 30, pp 489-503.

Beresford, P. (2001) 'Critical commentaries: service users', *British Journal of Social Work*, vol 31, pp 629-30.

Beresford, P. (2002) 'User involvement in research and evaluation: liberation or regulation', *Social Policy and Society*, vol 1, part 2, pp 95-106.

Beresford, P. and Turner, M. (1997) *It's our welfare: Report of the citizens' commission on the future of the welfare state*, London: NISW.

Beresford, P., Green, D., Lister, R. and Woodard, K. (1999) *Poverty first hand: Poor people speak for themselves*, London: CPAG.

Berthoud, R. (2000) 'Ethnic employment penalties in Britain', *Journal of Ethnic and Migration Studies*, vol 26, no 3, pp 389-416.

Blair, T. (1995) *Let us face the future: The 1945 anniversary lecture*, London: The Fabian Society.

Blair, T. (1996) *New Britain: My vision of a young country*, London: Fourth Estate.

Blair, T. (1998) *The Third Way: New politics for a new century*, The Fabian Society Pamphlet No 588, London: The Fabian Society.

Blair, T. (1999) Beveridge lecture, 18 March, London: Labour Party, reproduced in full in R. Walker (ed) *Ending child poverty: Popular welfare for the 21st century?*, Bristol: The Policy Press, pp 7-20.

Blair, T. (2000) Speech to Women's Institute's triennial meeting, 7 June (available at www.pm.gov.uk/news.asp?NewsId=979&SectionId=32).

Blair, T. (2002) *The courage of our convictions: Why welfare reform of the public services is the route to social justice*, Fabian Ideas 603, London: The Fabian Society.

Blakemore, K. (2003) *Social policy: An introduction* (2nd edn), Buckingham: Open University Press.

Blears, H. (2003) *Communities in control: Public services and local socialism*, Fabian Ideas 607, London: The Fabian Society.

Bloch, A. (2000) 'Refugee settlement in Britain: the impact of policy on participation', *Journal of Ethnic and Migration Studies*, vol 26, no 1, pp 75-88.

Bloch, A. and Schuster, L. (2002) 'Asylum and welfare: contemporary debates', *Critical Social Policy*, vol 22, no 3, pp 393-413.

Blond, P. (2008) 'Red Tory', in J. Cruddas and J. Rutherford (eds) *Is the future Conservative?*, London: Soundings, Compass/Renewal, Lawrence and Wishart, pp 79-90.

Blunkett, D. (1998) 'New year, new deal new hope', DfEE Press Release, 3 January, London: Department for Education and Employment.

Blunkett, D. (2001) 'Measures announced to improve immigration control', Press Release 214/01, London: Immigration and Nationality Directorate, Home Office.

Bonoli, G. (1997) 'Classifying welfare states: a two dimension approach', *Journal of Social Policy*, vol 26, no 3, pp 351-72.

Bonoli, G. (2000) *The politics of pension reform: Institutions and policy change in western Europe*, Cambridge: Cambridge University Press.

Bonoli, G., George, V. and Taylor-Gooby, P. (2000) *European welfare futures: Towards a theory of retrenchment*, Cambridge: Polity Press.

Bottomore, T. (1992) 'Citizenship and social class forty years on', in T.H. Marshall and T. Bottomore (eds) *Citizenship and social class*, London: Pluto Press, pp 55-93.

Brah, A. (1992) 'Difference, diversity and differentiation', in J. Donald and A. Rattansi (eds) *'Race', culture and difference*, London: Sage Publications/ Open University Press, pp 126-45.

Brindle, D. (1999) 'Court order defaulters face 40% cut in benefits', *The Guardian,* 18 November.

Brindle, D. (2002) 'Souring the milk: critics hit out at registration rules for welfare food scheme', *The Guardian: Society*, 13 November (wysiwyg://35/ http://society.guardian.c...tyguardian/story/0,7843,838491,00.html).

Brown, G. (2006) Speech by the Chancellor of the Exchequer, to the Donald Dewar Memorial Lecture, 12 October, Press Release 74/06, London: HM Treasury (www.hm-treasury.gov.uk/newsroom_and_ speeches/press/2006/press_74_06.cfm).

Brubaker, W.R. (1992) *Citizenship and nationhood in France and Germany*, Cambridge, MA: Harvard University Press.

Burns, D. (2000) 'Practices of citizenship: interlinking community, work and family in a national single parent organisation', *Community, Work and Family*, vol 3, no 3, pp 261-77.

Byrne, D.S. (1999) *Social exclusion*, Buckingham: Open University Press.

CAB (Citizens' Advice Bureau) (2002) *Distant voices: Asylum support remains in chaos*, London: CAB.

Cabinet Office (2005) *Improving the life chances of disabled people*, London: Cabinet Office Strategy Unit.

Cameron, D. (2009) 'Putting Britain back on her feet', Party leader's speech to the Conservative Party Conference, Manchester 8 October (www. conservatives.com/.../Speeches/2009/.../David_Cameron_Putting_).

Cantle, T. (2001) *Community cohesion: A report of the independent review team*, London: Home Office.

Carlen, P. (ed) (2002) *Women and punishment: The struggle for justice*, Cullompton: Willan Publishing.

Carr, S. (2005) 'Participation, power, conflict and change: theorising dynamics of service user participation in the social care system of England and Wales', *Critical Social Policy*, vol 25, pp 164-79.

Carter, B., Harris, C. and Joshi, H. (1987) *The 1951–55 Conservative government and the racialisation of British immigration policy*, Warwick: Centre for Research into Ethnic Relations, University of Warwick.

Carvel, J. (2001) 'Violent patients may be refused care', *The Guardian*, 28 December, p 9.

Castle, S. and Linton, L. (2002) 'EU opens borders for health treatment', *The Independent*, 4 December, p 1.

Castles, F.G. (2002) 'The European social policy model: progress since the early 1980s', *European Journal of Social Security*, vol 3/4, pp 299-313.

Castles, S. (1996) 'Democracy and multiculturalism in Western Europe', *Journal of Area Studies*, vol 8, pp 51-76.

Castles, S. and Davidson, A. (2000a) *Citizenship and migration: Globalisation and the politics of belonging*, Basingstoke: Macmillan.

Castles, S. and Davidson, A. (2000b) *The citizen who does not belong: Citizenship in a global age*, Basingstoke: Macmillan.

CEC (Commission of the European Community) (1997) *Social Europe: The outlook on supplementary pensions in the context of demographic, economic and social change*, Supplement 7/96, Luxembourg: Office for Official Publications of the European Community.

Cesarani, D. (1996) 'The changing character of citizenship and nationality in Britain', in D. Cesarani and M. Fullbrook (eds) *Citizenship, nationality and migration in Europe*, London: Routledge, pp 57-73.

CESI (Centre for Social and Economic Inclusion) (2002) 'New Deal sanctions', *Training and Employment Network Weekly Briefing*, no 194, 17 June, London: CSEI (http://cesi.org.uk/_newsite2002/newdeal/weeklybriefing/brief194.htm).

Chapon, S. and Euzéby, C. (2002) 'Towards a convergence of European social models?', *International Social Security Review*, vol 55, no 2, pp 37-56.

Cheong, P.H., Edwards, R., Goulbourne, H. and Solomos, J. (2007) 'Immigration, social cohesion and social capital: a critical review', *Critical Social Policy*, vol 27, no 1, pp 24-49.

Clarke, J. (1996) 'The problem of the state after the welfare state', *Social Policy Review 8*, London: Social Policy Association, pp 13-39.

Clarke, J. (1998) 'Consumerism', in G. Hughes (ed) *Imagining welfare futures*, London: Routledge, pp 55-102.

Clarke, J. (2005) 'New Labour's citizens: activated, empowered, responsibilized, abandoned?', *Critical Social Policy*, vol 25, no 4, pp 447–63.

Clarke, J. and Langan, M. (1998) 'Review', in M. Langan (ed) *Welfare, needs, rights and risks*, London: Routledge/Open University Press, pp 259–72.

CLG (Communities and Local Government) (2008) *Managing the impacts of migration: A cross-government approach*, London: CLG.

Coats, D. (2008) *Migration myths: Employment, wages and labour market performance*, London: The Work Foundation.

Cohen, S. (2002a) 'Dining with the devil: the 1999 Immigration and Asylum Act and the voluntary sector', in S. Cohen, B. Humphries and E. Mynott (eds) *From immigration controls to welfare controls*, London: Routledge, pp 141–56.

Cohen, S. (2002b) 'The local state of immigration controls', *Critical Social Policy*, vol 22, no 3, pp 518–43.

Cohen, S., Humphries, B. and Mynott, E. (eds) (2002) *From immigration controls to welfare controls*, London: Routledge.

Commission on Integration and Cohesion (2007) *Our shared future*, London: Crown Copyright.

Connell, R.W. (1995) *Masculinities*, Cambridge: Polity Press.

Conservative Party (2008a) *Work for welfare: REAL welfare reform to help make British poverty history*, Policy Green Paper no 3, London: Conservative Party.

Conservative Party (2008b) *REPAIR: Plan for social reform*, London: Conservative Party.

Conservative Party (2008c) *A stronger society: Voluntary action in the 21st century*, Responsibility Agenda, Policy Green Paper no 5, London: Conservative Party.

Conservative Party (2009) *Get Britain working: Conservative proposals to tackle unemployment and welfare reform*, London: Conservative Party.

Cook, J., Dwyer, P. and Waite, L. (2008) *New migrant communities in Leeds*, Leeds: Leeds City Council.

Cook, J., Dwyer, P. and Waite, L. (2010: forthcoming) 'The experiences of Accession 8 migrants in England: motivations, work and agency', *International Migration*.

Coote, A. (ed) (1992) *The welfare of citizens: Developing social rights*, London: Institute for Public Policy Research.

Corden, A. and Nice, K. (2007) 'Qualitative longitudinal analysis for policy: incapacity benefits recipients taking part in Pathways to Work', *Social Policy and Society*, vol 6, no 4, pp 557–69.

Cowden, S. and Singh, G. (2007) 'The "user": friend foe or fetish?: a critical exploration of user involvement in health and social care', *Critical Social Policy*, vol 27, no 1, pp 5–23.

Cox, R.H. (1998) 'The consequences of welfare reform: how conceptions of social rights are changing', *Journal of Social Policy*, vol 27, no 1, pp 1-16.

CPAG (Child Poverty Action Group) (2002a) 'Government rethink on sanctions?', *Campaigns Newsletter*, no 24, December, p 1, London: CPAG.

CPAG (2002b) *Migration and social security handbook*, London: CPAG.

CPAG (2007) 'The Welfare Reform Act 2007', *Welfare Rights Bulletin 198*, London: CPAG.

Craig, G. (2001) 'Race and new Labour', in G. Fimister (ed) *An end in sight? Tackling child poverty in the UK*, London: CPAG, pp 92-100.

Cram, L. (1998) 'UK social policy in European Union context', in N. Ellison and C. Pierson (eds) *Developments in British social policy*, Basingstoke: Macmillan, pp 260-75.

Crick, B. (2003) *The new and the old. The report of the 'Life in the United Kingdom' Advisory Group*, London: Home Office.

Croft, S. and Beresford, P. (1989) 'User involvement, citizenship and social policy', *Critical Social Policy*, vol 15, no 2/3, pp 5-17.

Crompton, R. (2002) 'Employment, flexible working and the family', *British Journal of Sociology*, vol 53, no 4, pp 537-58.

Cruddas, J. and Rutherford, J. (eds) (2008a) *Is the future Conservative?*, London: Soundings, Compass/Renewal, Lawrence and Wishart.

Cruddas, J. and Rutherford, J. (2008b) 'Is the future Conservative?', in J. Cruddas and J. Rutherford (eds) *Is the future Conservative?*, London: Soundings, Compass/Renewal, Lawrence and Wishart, pp 9-22.

Currie, S. (2008) *Migration work and citizenship in the enlarged European Union*, Farnham: Ashgate.

Darling, A. (1998) 'Modernising the welfare state for the next millennium', DSS Press Release, London: Department of Social Security.

Davey, V., Fernandez, J.L., Knapp, M., Vick, N., Jolly, D., Swift, P., Tobin, R., Kendall, J., Ferrie, J., Pearson, C., Mercer, G. and Priestley, M. (2007) *Direct Payments Survey: A National Survey of Direct Payments policy and practice*, London: Personal Social Services Research Unit, London School of Economics and Political Science.

Deacon, A. (1993) 'Titmuss 20 years on', *Journal of Social Policy*, vol 22, no 2, pp 235-42.

Deacon, A. (1994) 'Justifying workfare: the historical context of the workfare debates', in M. White (ed) *Unemployment and public policy in a changing labour market*, London: Public Services Institute, pp 53-63.

Deacon, A. (ed) (1997a) *From welfare to work: Lessons from America*, London: Institute of Economic Affairs Health and Welfare Unit.

Deacon, A. (1997b) 'Benefit sanctions for the jobless: "tough love" or rough treatment?', *Economic Report*, vol 11, no 7, Southbank House, London: Employment Policy Institute.

Deacon, A. (1998) 'The Green Paper on welfare reform: a case of enlightened self interest?', *Political Quarterly*, vol 69, no 3, pp 306-11.

Deacon, A. (2002) *Perspectives on welfare: Ideas, ideologies and policy debates*, Buckingham: Open University Press.

Deacon, A. and Bradshaw, J. (1983) *Reserved for the poor: The means test in British social policy*, Oxford: Blackwell.

Dean, H. (1999) 'Citizenship', in M. Powell (ed) *New Labour new welfare state? The 'third way' in British social policy*, Bristol: The Policy Press, pp 213-34.

Dean, H. (2000) 'Managing risk by controlling behaviour: social security administration and the erosion of citizenship', in P. Taylor-Gooby (ed) *Risk, trust and welfare*, Basingstoke: Palgrave/Macmillan Press Ltd, pp 51-70.

Dean, H. (2001) 'Welfare rights and the "workfare" state', *Benefits*, no 30, pp 1-4.

Dean, H. (2002a) *Welfare rights and social policy*, Harlow: Pearson Education Limited.

Dean, H. (2002b) 'Business versus families: whose side is New Labour on?', *Social Policy and Society*, vol 1, no 1, pp 3-10.

Dean, H. (ed) (2004) *The ethics of welfare: Human rights, dependency and responsibility*, Bristol: The Policy Press.

Dean, H. (2007) 'Poor parents? The realities of work–life balance in a low income neighbourhood', *Benefits*, vol 15, no 3, pp 271-82.

Dean, H. and Melrose, M. (1996) 'Unravelling citizenship', *Critical Social Policy*, vol 16, no 3, pp 3-31.

Dean, H. and Melrose, M. (1998) 'Perceptions of poverty, wealth and citizenship', *Benefits*, no 21, p 27.

Dean, H. and Melrose, M. (1999) *Poverty, riches and social citizenship*, Basingstoke: Macmillan.

Delanty, G. (2000) *Citizenship in a global age: Society, culture and politics*, Buckingham: Open University Press.

Dell'Olio, F. (2002) 'Supranational undertakings and the determination of social rights', *Journal of European Public Policy*, vol 9, no 2, pp 292-310.

Dench, S., Hurstfield, J., Hill, D. and Akroyd, K. (2006) *Employers' use of migrant labour: Main report*, Home Office Online Report 04/06, produced by the Research Development and Statistics Directorate, London: Home Office.

Dench, S., Aston, J., Evans, C., Meager, N., Williams, M. and Willison, R. (2002) *Key indicators of women's position in Britain*, London: Women and Equality Unit/Department of Trade and Industry.

DH (Department of Health) (2000) 'Introduction of the Sure Start Maternity Grant', Letter from the Chief Medical Officer and the Chief Nursing Officer, 14 March, London: DH.

DH (2001) 'Treatment denied to violent patients', Press Release, 1 November, London: DH.

DH (2002a) *Withholding treatment from violent and abusive patients: Resource guide*, London: DH (www.nhs.uk/zerotolerance/wh_treatment/index. htm).

DH (2002b) *Healthy start: Proposals for reform of the welfare food scheme*, London: DH.

DH (2005) *Independence, well-being and choice: Our vision for the future of social care for adults in England*, Cm 6499, London: DH.

Dillon, J. (2003) 'Is Britain ready to pronounce this couple wife and wife?', *The Independent on Sunday*, 29 June, p 3.

Disson, J. (2001) *Asylum seekers and housing*, CHAS Policy Briefing, London: Catholic Housing Aid Society.

Dobrowolsky, A. and Lister, R. (2008) 'Social investment: the discourse and the dimensions of change', in M. Powell (ed) *Modernising the welfare state: The Blair legacy*, Bristol: The Policy Press, pp 125-42.

Doyal, L. and Gough, I. (1991) *A theory of human need*, Basingstoke: Macmillan.

Drake, R.F. (2000) 'Disabled people, new Labour, benefits and work', *Critical Social Policy, Special Issue: Disability and the Restructuring of Welfare: Employment, Benefits and the Law*, vol 20, no 3, pp 421-39.

Drake, R.F. (2001) *The principles of social policy*, New York, NY: Palgrave.

Driver, S. and Martell, L. (1997) 'New Labour's communitarianisms', *Critical Social Policy*, vol 7, no 3, pp 27-44.

Driver, S. and Martell, L. (1998) *New Labour: Politics after Thatcherism*, Cambridge: Polity Press.

Drover, G. (2000) 'Redefining social citizenship in a global era', *Canadian Social Work Review*, vol 17, pp 29-49.

DSS (Department of Social Security) (1998a) *New ambitions for our country: A new contract for welfare*, Green Paper, Cm 3805, London: DSS.

DSS (1998b) 'A new contract for welfare', Statement to Parliament on the Green Paper by the Minister for Welfare Reform, 26 March, London: DSS.

DSS (1999) *Opportunity for all: Tackling poverty and social exclusion. Indicators of success: Definitions, data and baseline indicators*, London: DSS.

DSS (2001) *Recruiting benefit claimants: A survey of employers in ONE pilot areas*, Research Report no 139, London: DSS.

DTI (Department of Trade and Industry) (2002) 'More people want flexible hours than cash, company cars or gym', Press Release, P/2002/814, London: DTI.

Duncan Smith, I. (2007) *Breakthrough Britain: Ending the costs of social breakdown. Chairman's overview*, London: The Centre for Social Justice.

Duvell, F. and Jordan, B. (2002) 'Immigration asylum and welfare: the European context', *Critical Social Policy*, vol 22, no 3, pp 498-517.

DWP (Department for Work and Pensions) (2002a) *Jobseeker's Allowance: Quarterly statistical enquiry, May 2002*, London: DWP.

DWP (2002b) *Annual report by the Secretary of State for Work and Pensions on the Social Fund 2001/2*, Cm 5492, London: DWP.

DWP (2002c) *Social Fund: Sure Start Maternity Grants. Request for information*, Report provided in response to enquiry from P. Dwyer, London: Information and Analysis Directorate and DWP.

DWP (2008a) *Transforming Britain's labour market: Ten years of the New Deal*, London: DWP.

DWP (2008b) *No one written off: Reforming welfare to reward responsibility*, Cm 7363, London: DWP.

DWP (2008c) *Raising expectations and increasing support: Reforming welfare for the future*, Cm 7506, London: DWP.

DWP (2009) 'More families will be lifted out of poverty as landmark Welfare Reform Act gets Royal Assent', Press Release, 13 November, London: DWP.

Dwyer, P. (1998) 'Conditional citizens? Welfare rights and responsibilities in the late 1990s', *Critical Social Policy*, vol 18, no 4, pp 519-43.

Dwyer, P. (2000a) *Welfare rights and responsibilities: Contesting social citizenship*, Bristol: The Policy Press.

Dwyer, P. (2000b) 'Movements to some purpose? An exploration of international retirement migration in the European Union', *Education and Ageing*, vol 15, no 3, pp 352-77.

Dwyer, P. (2001) 'Retired EU migrants, healthcare rights and European social citizenship', *Journal of Social Welfare and Family Law*, vol 23, no 3, pp 311-27.

Dwyer, P. (2002) 'Making sense of social citizenship: some user views on welfare rights and responsibilities', *Critical Social Policy*, vol 22, no 2, pp 273-99.

Dwyer, P. (2004a) 'Agency, dependency, and welfare: beyond issues of claim and contribution', in H. Dean (ed) *The ethics of welfare: Human rights, dependency and responsibility*, Bristol: The Policy Press, pp 106-22.

Dwyer, P. (2004b) 'Creeping conditionality in the UK: from welfare rights to conditional entitlements', *Canadian Journal of Sociology*, vol 29, no 2, pp 265-87.

Dwyer, P. (2005) 'Governance, forced migration and welfare', *Social Policy and Administration*, vol 39, no 6, pp 622-39.

Dwyer, P. (2008) 'The conditional welfare state', in M. Powell (ed) *Modernising the welfare state: The Blair legacy*, Bristol, The Policy Press, pp 199-218.

Dwyer, P. and Brown, D. (2005) 'Meeting basic needs? The survival strategies of forced migrants', *Social Policy and Society*, vol 4, no 4, pp 369-81.

Dwyer, P. and Brown, D. (2008) 'Accommodating "others"? Housing dispersed, forced migrants in the UK', *Journal of Social Welfare and Family Law*, vol 30, no 3, pp 203-18.

Dwyer, P. and Ellison, N. (2007) '"We nicked stuff from all over the place". Exploring the origins and character of active labour market policies in the UK', Paper to the annual Social Policy Association Conference, University of Birmingham, July.

Dwyer, P. and Papadimitriou, D. (2006) 'The social security rights of older international migrants in the European Union', *Journal of Ethnic and Migration Studies*, vol 32, no 8, pp 1301-19.

Dyer, C. (2002a) 'Poor face legal aid crisis as solicitors pull out', *The Guardian*, 30 December, p 6.

Dyer, C. (2002b) 'Tenancy ruling marks gay rights watershed', *The Guardian*, 6 November, p 6.

Eagle, A., Duff, L., Tah, C. and Smith, N. (2002) *Asylum seekers' experience of the voucher scheme in the UK: Field work report*, London: Home Office.

Ellison, N. (2000) 'Proactive and defensive engagement: social citizenship in a changing public sphere', *Sociological Research Online*, vol 5, no 3.

Ellison, N. and Pierson, C. (eds) (2003) *Developments in British social policy 2*, Basingstoke: Macmillan.

Esping-Andersen, G. (1990) *The three worlds of welfare capitalism*, Cambridge: Polity Press.

Etzioni, A. (1995) *The spirit of community: Rights and responsibilities and the communitarian agenda*, London: Harper and Collins.

Etzioni, A. (1997) *The new golden rule*, London: Profile Books.

Etzioni, A. (ed) (1998) *The essential communitarian reader*, Oxford: Rowman and Littlefield.

Etzioni, A. (2000) *The third way to a good society*, London: Demos.

Europa (2009) *Charter of Fundamental Rights: Summaries of EU legislation* (http://europa.eu/legislation_summaries/human_rights/fundamental_rights_within_european_union/l33501_en.htm).

Faist, T. (2001) 'Social citizenship in the European Union: nested membership', *Journal of Common Market Studies*, vol 39, no 1, pp 37-58.

Falk, R. (1994) 'The making of global citizenship', in B. van Steenbergen (ed) *The condition of citizenship*, London: Sage Publications, pp 127-40.

Faulks, K. (1998) *Citizenship in modern Britain*, Edinburgh: Edinburgh University Press.

Faulks, K. (2000) *Citizenship*, London: Routledge.

Favell, A. (2008) 'The new face of East–West migration in Europe', *Journal of Ethnic and Migration Studies*, vol 34, no 5, pp 701-16.

Ferge, Z. (1979) *A society in the making: Hungarian social and societal policy 1945–75*, Harmondsworth: Penguin.

Ferrera, M. (1996) 'The "southern model" of welfare in social Europe', *Journal of European Social Policy*, vol 6, no 1, pp 17-37.

Fido, J. (1977) 'The COS and social casework in London', in A. Donajgrodzki (ed) *Social control in 19th century Britain*, London: Croom Helm, pp 207-30.

Field, F. (2002) 'First take their benefits, then their children', *The Sunday Telegraph*, 18 May, p 15.

Fimister, G. (ed) (2001) *An end in sight? Tackling child poverty in the UK*, London: CPAG.

Finkelstein, V. (1980) *Attitudes and disabled people*, New York, NY: World Rehabilitation Fund.

Finkelstein, V. (1993) 'The commonality of disability', in J. Swain, V. Finkelstein, S. French and M. Oliver (eds) *Disabling barriers – Enabling environments*, London: Sage Publications/Open University Press, pp 9-16.

Finch, N. (2001) 'The support and dispersal of asylum seekers', in *Asylum seekers: A guide to recent legislation*, London: Immigration Law Practitioners' Association, pp 17-25.

Finch, N. (2002) 'New Labour's value laden social policy', Paper to the Social Policy Association Annual Conference, University of Teesside, Middlesbrough, 16-18 July.

Finn, D. (1998) 'Welfare to work: a new deal for the unemployed', *Benefits*, no 21, pp 32-3.

Fitzpatrick, T. (2001) *Welfare theory: An introduction*, Basingstoke: Palgrave.

Flint, J. (2002) 'Return of the governors: citizenship and the governance of neighbourhood disorder in the UK', *Citizenship Studies*, vol 6, no 3, pp 245-64.

Fraser, D. (2009) *The evolution of the British welfare state* (4th edn), Basingstoke: Palgrave Macmillan.

Fraser, N. (1997) *Justice interruptus: Critical reflections on the 'postsocialist' condition*, London: Routledge.

Fraser, N. (2000a) 'Rethinking recognition', *New Left Review*, vol 3, pp 107-20.

Fraser, N. (2000b) 'After the family wage: a postindustrial thought experiment', in B. Hobson (ed) *Gender and citizenship in transition*, Basingstoke: Macmillan, pp 1-32.

Fraser, D. (2003) *The evolution of the British welfare state* (3rd edn), Basingstoke, Macmillan.

Freeden, M. (1990) *Rights*, Milton Keynes: Open University Press.

Freeman, G.P. (1995) 'Modes of immigration politics in liberal democratic states', *International Migration Review*, vol XXIX, no 4, pp 881-902.

Freud, D. (2007) *Reducing dependency, increasing opportunity: Options for the future of welfare to work. An independent report to the Department for Work and Pensions*, London, Department for Work and Pensions.

Friedman, M. (1962) *Capitalism and freedom*, Chicago, IL: University of Chicago Press.

Fries, S. and Shaw, J. (1998) 'Citizenship of the union: first steps in the European Court of Justice', *European Public Law*, vol 4, issue 4, pp 533–59.

Fullinwider, R.K. (1988) 'Citizenship and welfare', in A. Gutmann (ed) *Democracy and the welfare state*, Guildford, NY: Princeton University Press, pp 261–78.

George, V. and Miller, S. (1996) *Social policy towards 2000*, London: Routledge.

George, V. and Wilding, P. (1994) *Welfare and ideology*, London: Harvester Wheatsheaf.

Geyer, R.R. (2000) *Exploring European social policy*, Cambridge: Polity Press.

Geyer, R.R. (2003) 'The European Union and British social policy', in N. Ellison and C. Pierson (eds) *Developments in British social policy 2*, Basingstoke: Macmillan, pp 286–300.

Giarchi, G.G. (1996) *Caring for older Europeans: Comparative studies in 29 countries*, Aldershot: Arena/Ashgate Publishing Limited.

Giddens, A. (1989) *Sociology*, Cambridge: Polity Press.

Giddens, A. (1994) *Beyond left and right: The future of radical politics*, Cambridge: Polity Press.

Giddens, A. (1998) *The third way: The renewal of social democracy*, Cambridge: Polity Press.

Gilbert, N. (2002) *Transformation of the welfare state: The silent surrender of public responsibility*, Oxford: Oxford University Press.

Ginn, J., Street, D. and Arber, S. (eds) (2001) *Women, work and pensions: International issues and prospects*, Buckingham: Open University Press.

GLA (Greater London Authority) (2004) *Destitution by design: Withdrawal of support from in-country asylum applicants: An impact assessment for London*, London: GLA.

Glendinning, C. (2008) 'Increasing choice and control for older disabled people: a critical review of new developments in England', *Social Policy and Administration*, vol 42, no 5, pp 451–69.

Goodin, R.E. (2000) 'Principles of welfare reform: the OECD experience', Paper to the 'Welfare Reform' Conference, Melbourne Institute, November.

Goodin, R.E. (2002) 'Structures of mutual obligation', *Journal of Social Policy*, vol 31, no 4, pp 579–96.

Gooding, C. (2000) 'Disability Discrimination Act: from statute to practice', *Critical Social Policy, Special Issue: Disability and the Restructuring of Welfare: Employment, Benefits and the Law*, vol 20, no 3, pp 533–50.

Gordon, P. (1989) *Citizenship for some? Race and government policy 1979–89*, London: Runnymede Trust.

Gough, I. (1998) 'What are human needs?', in J. Franklin (ed) *Social policy and social justice*, London: Institute for Public Policy Research/Polity Press, pp 50-6.

Gough, I. (2001) 'Social assistance regimes: a cluster analysis', *Journal of European Social Policy*, vol 11, no 2, pp 165-70.

Gough, I., Eardley, T., Bradshaw, J., Ditch, J. and Whiteford, P. (1997) 'Social assistance in OECD countries', *Journal of European Social Policy*, vol 7, no 1, pp 17-43.

Gray, A. (2001) 'Making work pay – devising the best strategy for lone parents in Britain', *Journal of Social Policy*, vol 30, no 2, pp 189-207.

Gregg, P. (2008) *Realising potential: A vision for personalised conditionality and support*, An independent report to the Department for Work and Pensions, London: Department for Work and Pensions.

Griggs, J. and Bennett, F. (2009) *Rights and responsibilities in the social security system*, London: Social Security Advisory Committee Occasional Paper no 6 (www.ssac.org.uk/pdf/occasional/Rights_Responsibilities_Social_Security.pdf).

Grover, C. (2007) 'The Freud Report on the future of welfare to work: some critical reflections', *Critical Social Policy*, vol 27, no 4, pp 534-45.

Grover, C. and Stewart, J. (2000) 'Modernising social security? Labour and its welfare to work strategy', *Social Policy and Administration*, vol 34, no 3, pp 235-52.

Grover, C. and Stewart, J. (2002) *The work connection: The role of social security in British economic regulation*, Basingstoke: Palgrave.

Guillén, A.M. and Matsaganis, M. (2000) 'Testing the "social dumping" hypothesis in Southern Europe: welfare policies in Greece and Spain during the last 20 years', *Journal of European Social Policy*, vol 10, no 2, pp 120-45.

Gutmann, A. (1995) 'Communitarian critics of liberalism', in S. Avineri and A. de Shalit (eds) *Communitarianism and individualism*, Oxford: Oxford University Press, pp 120-36.

HAC (Home Affairs Committee) (2004) *Asylum applications second report of session 2003-04, Volume 1 report together with appendix and formal minutes*, London, published by authority of the House of Commons, The Stationery Office

Hahn, H. (1986) 'Public support for rehabilitation programs: the analysis of US disability policy', *Disability, Handicap and Society*, vol 1, no 2, pp 121-37.

Hain, P. (2008) 'Fight poverty not the poor', *The Guardian*, 2 January, p 26.

Hancock, L. (2000) 'Gendered citizenship in Britain: from mother-care to worker', in A. Vandenburg (ed) *Citizenship and democracy in a global era*, Basingstoke: Macmillan, pp 156–70.

Handley, P. (2003) 'Theorising disability: beyond common sense', *Politics*, vol 32, no 2, pp 109–18.

Hansard (2002a) Question in the House of Commons from Mr Andrew Turner to Mr Denham on Behaviour Orders, *Hansard*, 14 May, col 607/8W (www.parliament.the-stationery-o...02/cmhansrd/cm02514/text/20514w27.htm).

Hansard (2002b) Question in the House of Lords from Earl Russell to the Parliamentary Under-Secretary of State, DWP, on Benefit Sanctions, *Hansard*, 8 May, col WA181 (www.parliament.the-stationery-o.../ldhansrd/pdvn/1ds02/text/20508w03.htm).

Hansen, P. (2000) 'European citizenship, or where neo-liberalism meets ethno-culturalism: analysing the European Union's citizenship discourse', *European Societies*, vol 2, no 2, pp 139–65.

Hantrais, L. (2000) *Social policy in the European Union*, Basingstoke: Macmillan Press Ltd.

Hantrais, L. (2003) 'Social policy and the European Union', in P. Alcock, A. Erskine and M. May (eds) *The student's companion to social policy* (2nd edn), London: Blackwell/Social Policy Association, pp 234–41.

Hantrais, L. (2007) *Social policy in the European Union* (3rd edn), Basingstoke: Palgrave Macmillan.

Harris, P. (2002) 'Welfare rewritten: change and interlay in social and economic accounts', *Journal of Social Policy*, vol 31, no 3, pp 377–98.

Harrison, M.L. (1995) *Housing, 'race', social policy and empowerment*, Aldershot: Avebury.

Harrison, M.L. with Davis, C. (2001) *Housing, social policy and difference: Disability, ethnicity, gender and housing*, Bristol: The Policy Press.

Hayek, F. (1944) *The road to serfdom*, London: Routledge and Kegan Paul.

Hayes, D. (2002) 'From aliens to asylum seekers: a history of immigration controls and welfare in Britain', in S. Cohen, B. Humphries and E. Mynott (eds) *From immigration controls to welfare controls*, London: Routledge, pp 30–46.

Heater, D. (1999) *What is citizenship?*, Cambridge: Polity Press.

Heenan, D. (2002) '"It won't change the world but it turned my life around": participants' views on the personal advisor scheme in the New Deal for Disabled People', *Disability and Society*, vol 17, no 4, pp 383–401.

Heenan, D. (2009) 'Mental health policy in Northern Ireland: the nature and extent of user involvement', *Social Policy and Society*, vol 8, no 4, pp 451–62.

Held, D. (1995) *Democracy and the global order: From modern state to cosmopolitan governance*, Stanford, CA: Stanford University Press.

Held, D. (1998) 'Democracy and globalization', in D. Archibugi, D. Held and M. Köhler (eds) *Re-imagining community: studies in cosmopolitan democracy*, Stanford, CA: Stanford University Press, pp 11-27.

Heron, E. (2001) 'Etzioni's spirit of communitarianism: community values and welfare realities in Blair's Britain', in R. Sykes, C. Bochel and N. Ellison (eds) *Social Policy Review 13*, Bristol: The Policy Press/Social Policy Association, pp 63-87.

Heron, E. and Dwyer, P. (1999) '"Doing the right thing": Labour's attempt to forge a new welfare deal between the individual and the state', *Social Policy and Administration*, vol 33, no 1, pp 91-104.

Hewitt, M. (1998) 'Social policy and human need', in N. Ellison and C. Pierson (eds) *Developments in British social policy*, Basingstoke: Macmillan, pp 61-77.

Hewitt, M. (1999) 'New Labour and social security', in M. Powell (ed) *New Labour new welfare state? The 'third way' in British social policy*, Bristol: The Policy Press, pp 149-70.

Hewitt, M. (2000) *Welfare and human nature: The human subject in twentieth-century social politics*, Basingstoke: Macmillan.

Hill, D.M. (1992) 'The American philosophy of welfare: citizenship and the politics of conduct', *Social Policy and Administration*, vol 26, no 2, pp 117-28.

Hill, D.M. (1994) *Citizens and cities: Urban policy in the 1990s*, London: Harvester Wheatsheaf.

Hills, J. (1998) *Income and wealth: The latest evidence*, York: Joseph Rowntree Foundation.

Hills, J., Le Grand, J. and Piachaud. D. (eds) (2002) *Understanding social exclusion*, Oxford: Oxford University Press.

Hinsliff, G. (2002) 'Parents face benefits axe over unruly children', *The Observer*, 28 April, p 1.

HMG (Her Majesty's Government) (2004) *Asylum applications: The government's reply to the second report from the Home Affairs Committee session 2003-04 HC218*, Cm 616, Norwich: The Stationery Office.

HMG (2005) *Opportunity age: Meeting the challenges of ageing in the 21st century*, London: Department for Work and Pensions.

HMT (Her Majesty's Treasury)/DTI (Department of Trade and Industry) (2003) *Balancing work and family life: Enhancing choice and support for parents*, London: The Stationery Office.

Hodge, S. (2005) 'Participation, discourse and power a case study in service user involvement', *Critical Social Policy*, vol 25, no 2, pp 164-79.

HoLSCEA (House of Lords Select Committee on Economic Affairs) (2008) *The economic impact of immigration: Volume 1 report*, London: The Stationery Office.

Home Office (2002a) 'Tackling persistent anti-social behaviour', Press Release 068/2002, London: Home Office.

Home Office (2002b) 'Taking action against anti-social behaviour', Press Release 098/2002, London: Home Office.

Home Office (2003a) *Respect and responsibility: Taking a stand against anti-social behaviour*, Cm 5778, London: The Stationery Office.

Home Office (2003b) *Asylum statistics 4th quarter 2002*, London: Home Office.

Home Office (2009) 'Government's new bill shakes up the route to citizenship', Press Release, 15 January, London: Home Office.

Horsman, M. and Marshall, A. (1994) *After the nation-state: Citizens tribalism and the new world disorder*, London: HarperCollins.

Howard, M., Garnham, A., Fimister, G. and Veit-Wilson, J. (eds) (2001) *Poverty: The facts* (4th edn), London: CPAG.

Hurd, D. (1988) 'Citizenship in Tory democracy', *The New Statesman*, 29 April.

Hutton, J. (2007) 'Improving employability for disadvantaged groups', Speech to the Welfare to Work seminar organised by Institute for Public Policy Research North, Manchester, Friday 2 March.

Hyde, M. (2000) 'From welfare to work? Social policy for disabled people of working age in the UK in the 1990s', *Disability and Society*, vol 15, no 2, pp 327-41.

IAP (Inter-Agency Partnership) (2004) *The impact of Section 55 on the Inter-Agency Partnership and the asylum seekers it supports*, London: IAP.

ICAR (Information Centre about Asylum and Refugees) (2006) 'Destitution amongst refugees and asylum seekers in the UK', ICAR Briefing, May, London: ICAR, City University.

ICoCo (Institute for Community Cohesion) (2007) *Estimating the scale and impacts of migration at the local level*, Coventry: ICoCo/Local Government Association.

Ignatieff, M. (1995) 'The myth of citizenship', in R. Beiner (ed) *Theorizing citizenship*, Albany, NY: State University of New York Press, pp 53-78.

ILPA (Immigration Law Practitioners' Association) (2001) *Asylum seekers: A guide to recent legislation*, London: ILPA.

Iredale, R. (1999) 'Public consultation and participation in policy making', in G. Keily, A. O'Donnell, P. Kennedy and S. Quin (eds) *Irish social policy in context*, Dublin: University College Dublin Press, pp 178-94.

IRR (Institute of Race Relations) (2001) *The three faces of British racism*, London: IRR.

Isin, E.F. and Wood, P.K. (1999) *Citizenship and identity*, London: Sage Publications.

Iverson, T. and Wren, A. (1998) 'Equality, employment and budgetary restraint: the trilemma of service economy', *World Politics*, vol 50, pp 507-46.

Jacobson, D. (1996) *Rights across borders: Immigration and the decline of citizenship*, London: Johns Hopkins University Press.

Jones, P. (1994) *Rights*, Basingstoke: Macmillan.

Jones, P. and Novak, T. (1999) *Poverty welfare and the disciplinary state*, London: Routledge.

Jordan, B. (2001) 'Tough love: social work, social exclusion and the Third Way', *British Journal of Social Work*, vol 31, pp 527-46.

Jurado, E. and Bruzzone, A. (2008) *Rethinking migration: Work and welfare in a mobile economy*, London: Policy Network.

Katrougalos, G.S. (1996) 'The south European welfare model: the Greek welfare state in search of an identity', *Journal of European Social Policy*, vol 6, no 1, pp 39-60.

Kearns, A.J. (1992) 'Active citizenship and urban governance', *Transactions of the Institute of British Geographers*, vol 17, no 1, pp 20-34.

Kellner, P. (1999) 'Equality of access', in R. Walker (ed) *Ending child poverty: Popular welfare for the 21st century*, Bristol: The Policy Press, pp 69-74.

Kennedy, H. (1992) 'Time for too many women', *The Independent*, 11 October.

King, D.S. (1987) *The New Right: Politics, markets and citizenship*, Basingstoke: Macmillan.

King, R., Warnes, A.M. and Williams, A.M. (2000) *Sunset lives: British retirement migration to the Mediterranean*, Oxford: Berg.

Kingston, P. (2001) 'Enrol or no dole', *Guardian Education*, 1 May, p 47.

Kleinman, M. (2002) *A European welfare state? European Union social policy in context*, Basingstoke: Palgrave.

Kymlicka, W. (1992) *Contemporary political philosophy: An introduction*, Oxford: Oxford University Press.

Kymlicka, W. (1995) *Multicultural citizenship: A liberal theory of minority rights*, Oxford: Clarendon Press.

Kymlicka, W. and Norman, W. (1994) 'Return of the citizen: a survey of recent work on citizenship theory', *Ethics*, vol 10, no 4, pp 257-89.

Labour Party (2000) 'Democracy and citizenship' (available at www.Labour.org/uk/1p/new/labour).

Labour Party (2003) 'Housing Benefit sanctions', *Weekly Brief*, no 066, 22 May, London: Labour Party Political Communications, p 2.

Langan, M. (ed) (1998) *Welfare, needs, rights and risks*, London: Routledge/Open University Press.

Law, I., Hylton, C., Karmani, A. and Deacon, A. (1994) *Racial equality and social security service delivery: A study of the perceptions and experiences of black minority ethnic people eligible for benefit in Leeds*, Working Paper 10, Department of Sociology and Social Policy, Leeds: University of Leeds/ Joseph Rowntree Foundation.

Lawson, N, (2008) 'Foreword', in J. Cruddas and J. Rutherford (eds) *Is the future Conservative?*, London: Soundings, Compass/Renewal, Lawrence and Wishart, pp 6-8.

Leibfried, S. (2000) 'Towards a European welfare state?', in C. Pierson and F.G. Castles (eds) *The welfare state: A reader*, Cambridge: Polity Press, pp 190-206.

Leibfried, S. (2005) 'Social policy: left to the judges and the markets?', in H. Wallace, W. Wallace and M. Pollack (eds) *Policymaking in the European Union* (5th edn), Oxford: Oxford University Press, pp 243-79.

Le Grand, J. (1997) 'Knights, knaves or pawns? Human behaviour and social policy', *Journal of Social Policy*, vol 26, no 2, pp 149-69.

Le Grand, J. and Bartlett, W. (eds) (1993) *Quasi-markets and social policy*, London: Macmillan.

Lemos, S. and Portes, J. (2008) *The impact of migration from the new European Union member states on native workers*, Leicester: University of Leicester/ Department for Work and Pensions.

Letwin, O. (2008) (interviewed By Alan Finlayson) 'From economic revolution to social revolution', in J. Cruddas and J. Rutherford (eds) *Is the future Conservative?*, London: Soundings, Compass/Renewal, Lawrence and Wishart, pp 71-9.

Levy, J.D. (2004) 'Activation through thick and thin: progressive approaches to labour market activation', in N. Ellison, L. Bauld and M. Powell (eds) *Social Policy Review 16*, Bristol: The Policy Press.

Levitas, R. (1996) 'The concept of social exclusion and the new Durkheimian hegemony', *Critical Social Policy*, vol 16, no 1, pp 5-20.

Levitas, R. (1998) *The inclusive society? Social exclusion and New Labour*, Basingstoke: Macmillan.

Levitas, R., Pantazis, C., Fahmy, E., Gordon, D., Lloyd, E. and Patsios, D. (2007) *The multidimensional analysis of social exclusion*, London: Communities and Local Government/Social Exclusion Task Force.

Lewis, G. (1998) 'Citizenship', in G. Hughes (ed) *Imagining welfare futures*, London: Routledge/Open University Press, pp 103-50.

Lewis, J. (1992) 'Gender and the development of welfare regimes', *Journal of European Social Policy*, vol 2, no 3, pp 159-73.

Lewis, J. (2001) 'The decline of the male breadwinner model: implications for work and care', *Social Politics*, vol 8, no 2, pp 152-69.

Lewis, J. and Campbell, B. (2007) 'Work/family balance policies in the UK since 1997: a new departure?', *Journal of Social Policy*, vol 36, no 3, pp 365–81.

Lewis, L. (2009) 'Politics of recognition: can a human rights perspective contribute to understanding users' experiences of involvement in mental health services', *Social Policy and Society*, vol 8, no 2, pp 257–74.

Lister, R. (1990) *The exclusive society: Citizenship and the poor*, London: CPAG.

Lister, R. (1997) *Citizenship feminist perspectives* (1st edn), Basingstoke: Macmillan.

Lister, R. (1998a) 'New conceptions of citizenship', in N. Ellison and C. Pierson (eds) *Developments in British social policy*, Basingstoke: Macmillan, pp 46–60.

Lister, R. (1998b) 'From equality to social exclusion: New Labour and the welfare state', *Critical Social Policy*, vol 18, no 2, pp 215–25.

Lister, R. (1999) 'What welfare provisions do women need to become full citizens?', in S. Walby (ed) *New agendas for women*, Basingstoke: Macmillan, pp 17–31.

Lister, R. (2001) '"Work for those who can, security for those who cannot": a third way in social security reform or fractured social citizenship', in R. Edwards and J. Glover (eds) *Risk and citizenship: Key issues in welfare*, London: Routledge, pp 96–110.

Lister, R. (2003a) 'Principles of welfare', in P. Alcock, A. Erskine and M. May (eds) *The student's companion to social policy* (2nd edn), London, Blackwell/ SPA, pp 260–7.

Lister, R. (2003b) 'Citizenship and gender', in K. Nash and A. Scott (eds) *The Blackwell companion to political sociology*, Oxford: Blackwell.

Lister, R. (2003c) *Citizenship: Feminist perspectives* (2nd edn), Basingstoke: Palgrave Macmillan.

Lister, R. (2004a) *Poverty,* Cambridge, Polity Press.

Lister, R. (2004b) 'A politics of recognition and respect; involving people with experience of poverty in decision making in their lives', in J. Andersen and B. Siim (eds) *The politics of inclusion and empowerment*, Basingstoke: Palgrave Macmillan

Lister, R. (2007) '(Mis)recognition, social inequality and social justice: a critical social policy perspective', in T. Lovell (ed) *(Mis)recognition social inequality and social justice: Nancy Fraser and Pierre Bourdieu*, Abingdon: Routledge.

Lister, R. (2008) 'Citizenship and access to welfare', in P. Alcock, A. Erskine and M. May (eds) *The student's companion to social policy* (3rd edn), Oxford: Blackwell/Social Policy Association, pp 260–7.

Lister, R., Smith, N., Middleton, S. and Cox, L. (2003) 'Young people talk about citizenship: empirical perspectives on theoretical and political debates', *Citizenship Studies*, vol 7, no 2, pp 233-40.

Locke, J. (1960) *Two treatises of government*, Cambridge: Cambridge University Press, edited and with an introduction by P. Laslett.

Lødemel, I. and Trickey, H. (eds) (2001) *'An offer you can't refuse': Workfare in international perspective*, Bristol: The Policy Press.

Lukes, S. (1973) *Individualism*, Oxford: Basil Blackwell.

Lukes, S. (2001) 'Housing and related benefits', in ILPA (Immigration Law Practitioners' Association) *Asylum seekers: A guide to recent legislation*, London: ILPA, pp 29-37.

Lund, B. (1999) '"Ask not what the community can do for you": obligations, New Labour and welfare reform', *Critical Social Policy*, vol 19, no 4, pp 447-62.

MacInnes, T., Kenway P. and Parekh, A. (2009) *Monitoring poverty and social exclusion 2009*, York: Joseph Rowntree Foundation.

MacIntyre, A. (1995) 'Justice as a virtue', in S. Avineri and A. de Shalit (eds) *Communitarianism and individualism*, Oxford: Oxford University Press, pp 51-6.

Macpherson, W. (1999) *The Stephen Lawrence Inquiry. Report of an inquiry by Sir William Macpherson of Cluny*, Cm 4262, London: The Stationery Office.

McLoughlin, S. (1998) 'An underclass in Purdah? Discrepant representations of identity and the experiences of young British-Asian-Muslim women', *Bulletin*, vol 80, no 3, pp 89-106.

Mann, K. (1992) *The making of an English 'underclass'*, Buckingham: Open University Press.

Mann, K. (1998a) 'Lamppost modernism: traditional and critical social policy?', *Critical Social Policy*, vol 18, no 1, pp 77-102.

Mann, K. (1998b) 'New Labour, new men and the "underclass"', *Poverty*, no 98, pp 11-14.

Mann, K. (2001) *Approaching retirement: Social divisions, welfare and exclusion*, Bristol: The Policy Press.

Mann, M. (1987) 'Ruling class strategies and citizenship', *Sociology*, vol 21, no 3, pp 339-54.

Manning, N. (1998) 'Welfare, ideology and social theory', in J. Baldock, N. Manning, S. Miller and S. Vickerstaff (eds) *Social policy*, Oxford: Oxford University Press, pp 63-90.

Marshall, A.H. (1873) 'The future of the working classes', reproduced in A.C. Pigou (ed) (1925) *Memorials of Alfred Marshall*, London: Macmillan and Company, pp 101-18.

Marshall, T.H. (1965) *Social policy*, London: Hutchinson University Library.

Marshall, T.H. (1985) *The right to welfare*, London: Heinemann Educational Books.

Marshall, T.H. (1949/92) 'Citizenship and social class', in T.H. Marshall and T. Bottomore, *Citizenship and social class*, London: Pluto Press, pp 3-51.

Marshall, T.H. and Bottomore, T. (1992) *Citizenship and social class*, London: Pluto Press.

Martin, A. and Ross, G. (2004) (eds) *Euros and Europeans: Monetary integration and the European model of society*, Cambridge: Cambridge University Press.

Mason, D. (2000) *Race and ethnicity in Britain*, Oxford: Oxford University Press.

May, M. and Brunsdon, E. (2005) *Understanding work–life balance: Policies for a family friendly Britain*, Bristol: The Policy Press.

Mead, L.M. (1982) 'Social programs and social obligations', *Public Interest*, no 69, Fall, pp 17-39.

Mead, L.M. (1986) *Beyond entitlement*, New York, NY: Free Press.

Mead, L.M. (1997a) 'From welfare to work: lessons from America', in A. Deacon (ed) *From welfare to work: Lessons from America*, London: Institute of Economic Affairs Health and Welfare Unit, pp 1-55.

Mead, L.M. (1997b) 'Citizenship and social policy: T.H. Marshall and poverty', *Social Philosophy and Social Policy*, vol 14, no 2, pp 197-230.

Mead, L.M. (ed) (1997c) *The new paternalism: Supervisory approaches to poverty*, Washington, DC: The Brookings Institute.

Meikle, J. (1994) 'Patten castigates young for apathy to country and community', *The Guardian*, 6 May.

Mill, J.S. (1859) *On liberty*, reprinted in J.S. Mill (1998) *On liberty and other essays*, edited by J. Gray, Oxford: Oxford University Press.

Millar, J. (2003) 'Social policy and family policy', in P. Alcock, A. Erskine and M. May (eds) *The student's companion to social policy* (2nd edn), London: Blackwell/Social Policy Association, pp 153-9.

Millar, J. (ed) (2009) *Understanding social security* (2nd edn), Bristol: The Policy Press.

Miller, D. (1995) 'Community and citizenship', in S. Avineri and A. de Shalit (eds) *Communitarianism and individualism*, Oxford: Oxford University Press, pp 85-100.

Modood, T. (1992) *Not easy being British: Colour, culture and citizenship*, London: R.T. Trentham.

Modood, T., Berthoud, R., Lakey, J., Nazroo, J., Smith, P., Virdee, S. and Beishon, S. (1997) *Ethnic minorities in Britain: Diversity and disadvantage*, London: Policy Studies Institute.

Morris, J. (1991) *Pride against prejudice*, London: The Women's Press.

Morris, J. (1993) *Community care or independent living?*, York: Joseph Rowntree Foundation.

Morris, J. (2003) 'Community care or independent living?', in N. Ellison and C. Pierson (eds) *Developments in British social policy 2*, Basingstoke: Macmillan, pp 211-28.

Morris, L. (1997a) 'Globalization, migration and the nation state: the path to a post-national Europe', *British Journal of Sociology*, vol 48, no 2, pp 192-209.

Morris, L. (1997b) 'A cluster of contradictions: the politics of migration in the European Union', *Sociology*, vol 31, no 2, pp 241-59.

Morris, L. (1998) 'Legitimate membership of the welfare community', in M. Langan (ed) *Welfare, needs, rights and risks*, London: Routledge/Open University Press, pp 215-58.

Morris, L. (2001) 'Stratified rights and the management of migration: national distinctiveness in Europe', *European Societies*, vol 3, part 4, pp 387-411.

Morris, L. (2002) 'Britain's asylum and immigration regime: the shifting contours of rights', *Journal of Ethnic and Migration Studies*, vol 28, no 3, pp 409-25.

Mullard, M. (2002) *Reclaiming citizenship: Discourses on the meaning of citizenship*, Working Papers in Social Sciences and Policy no 7, Hull: University of Hull.

Murray, C. (1984) *Loosing ground*, New York, NY: Basic Books.

Murray, C. (1994) *Loosing ground* (10th anniversary edn), New York, NY: Basic Books.

Murray, C. (1996a) 'The emerging British underclass', in R. Lister (ed) *Charles Murray and the underclass: The developing debate*, London: Institute of Economic Affairs Health and Welfare Unit, pp 23-56.

Murray, C. (1996b) 'Underclass: the crisis deepens', in R. Lister (ed) *Charles Murray and the underclass: The developing debate*, London: Institute of Economic Affairs Health and Welfare Unit, pp 99-138.

Murray, C. (1999) *The underclass revisited*, Washington, DC: American Institute for Public Policy Research (www.aei.org/publications/filter.all,bookID.268/book_detail.asp).

Muus, P. (2001) 'International migration and the European union, trends and consequences', *European Journal on Criminal Policy and Research*, vol 9, pp 31-49.

Mynott, E. (2000) 'Analysing the creation of apartheid for asylum seekers', *Community, Work and Family*, vol 3, no 3, pp 311-31.

Mynott, E. (2002) 'From a shambles to a new apartheid: local authorities, dispersal and the struggle to defend asylum seekers', in S. Cohen, B. Humphries and E. Mynott (eds) *From immigration controls to welfare controls*, London: Routledge, pp 106-25.

NACAB (National Association of Citizens' Advice Bureaux) (1991) *Barriers to benefit: Black claimants and social security*, London: NACAB.

NAO (National Audit Office) (2006) *The Home Office: Tackling anti-social behaviour*, Report by the Comptroller and Auditor General, London: The Stationery Office.

Needham, C. (2003) *Citizen consumers: New Labour's market place democracy*, London: The Catalyst Forum.

Nozick, R. (1995) 'Distributive justice', in S. Avineri and A. de Shalit (eds) *Communitarianism and individualism*, Oxford: Oxford University Press, pp 137-50.

O'Brien, M. and Penna, S. (1998) *Theorising welfare: Enlightenment and modern society*, London: Sage Publications.

O'Connor, J. (1998) 'US Social welfare policy: the Reagan record and legacy', *Journal of Social Policy*, vol 27, no 1, pp 37-61.

Offe, C. (1982) 'Some contradictions of the modern welfare state', *Critical Social Policy*, vol 2, no 2, pp 7-16.

Oldfield, A. (1990) *Citizenship and community, civic republicanism and the modern world*, London: Routledge.

Oliver, D. and Heater, D. (1994) *The foundations of citizenship*, London: Harvester Wheatsheaf.

Oliver, E. (2003) 'Balancing work and family life: on paper and in practice', Unpublished working paper, Leeds: Centre for the Study of Law and Policy in Europe, University of Leeds.

Oliver, M. (1983) *Social work with disabled people*, Basingstoke: Macmillan.

Oliver, M. (1990) *The politics of disablement*, Basingstoke: Macmillan.

Oliver, M. (1996) *Understanding disability from theory to practice*, Basingstoke: Macmillan.

Oliver, M. and Barnes, C. (1991) 'Discrimination, disability and welfare: from needs to rights', in I. Bynoe, M. Oliver and C. Barnes (eds) *Equal opportunities for disabled people: The case for a new law*, London: Institute for Public Policy Research, pp 7-16.

Oliver, M. and Barnes, C. (1998) *Disabled people and social policy: From exclusion to inclusion*, London: Longman.

ONS (Office for National Statistics) (1998) *Social focus on men and women*, London: ONS/The Stationery Office.

Oppenheim, C. (1999) 'Welfare reform and the labour market: a Third Way?', *Benefits*, no 25, April/May, pp 1-5.

OPSI (Office of Public Sector Information) (2009a) *Explanatory notes to Welfare Reform Act 2009*, London: OPSI (www.opsi.gov.uk/acts/acts2009/ukpga_20090024_en_1).

OPSI (2009b) *Explanatory notes to Gender Recognition Act 2004*, London: OPSI (www.opsi.gov.uk/acts/acts2004/en/ukpgaen_20040007_en_1).

OPSI (2009c) *Explanatory notes to Work and Families Act 2006*, London: OPSI (www.opsi.gov.uk/acts/acts2006/en/ukpgaen_20060018_en_1).

Osler, A. (2009) 'Testing citizenship and alliegiance: policy, politics and the education of adult migrants in the UK', *Education, Citizenship and Social Justice*, vol 4, no 1, pp 63-79.

Page, R. (1997) 'Caring for strangers: can an altruistic welfare state survive?', Paper to the 'Citizenship and welfare: fifty years of progress?' Conference, Ruskin College Oxford, December.

Parker, G. and Clarke, H. (2002) 'Making ends meet: do carers and disabled people have a common agenda?', *Policy & Politics*, vol 30, no 3, pp 347-59.

Parry, G. (1991) 'Conclusion: paths to citizenship', in U. Vogel and M. Moran (eds) *The frontiers of citizenship*, Basingstoke: Macmillan.

Pascall, G. (1997) *Social policy: A new feminist analysis*, London: Routledge.

Pateman, C. (1989) *The disorder of women*, Cambridge: Polity Press, extracts reproduced as 'The patriarchal welfare state', in C. Pierson and F.G. Castles (eds) (2000) *The welfare state: A reader*, Cambridge: Polity Press, pp 133-50.

Patrick, R. (2009) 'Disabling or enabling: the extension of work related condtionality to disabled people', Unpublished BA Social Policy dissertation, University of Leeds.

Paul, K. (1997) *Whitewashing Britain: Race and citizenship in the post-war era*, New York, NY: Cornell University Press.

Pearson, C. (2000) 'Money talks? Competing discourses in the implementation of direct payments', *Critical Social Policy, Special Issue: Disability and the Restructuring of Welfare: Employment, Benefits and the Law*, vol 20, no 3, pp 459-78.

Peck, J. (2001) 'Job alert! Shifts, spins and statistics in welfare to work policy', *Benefits*, no 30, pp 11-15.

Pennycook, M. (2008) 'State, society and New Conservatism', in J. Cruddas and J. Rutherford (eds) *Is the future Conservative?*, London: Soundings, Compass/Renewal, Lawrence and Wishart, pp 49-56.

Penrose, J. (2002) *Poverty and asylum in the UK*, London: Oxfam/Refugee Council.

Pierson, C. and Castles, F.G. (eds) (2006) *The welfare state: A reader* (2nd edn), Cambridge: Polity Press.

Pierson, P. (1996) 'The new politics of the welfare state', *World Politics*, no 49, pp 143-79.

Pierson, P. (ed) (2001) *The new politics of the welfare state*, Oxford: Oxford University Press.

Plant, R. (1978) 'Community: concept, conception and ideology', *Politics and Society*, no 8, pp 50-107.

Plant, R. (1988) *Citizenship, rights and socialism*, London: The Fabian Society.

Plant, R. (1992) 'Citizenship rights and welfare', in A. Coote (ed) *The welfare of citizens: Developing social rights*, London: Institute for Public Policy Research, pp 15-30.

Plant, R. (1998) 'So you want to be a citizen?', *New Statesman*, 6 February, pp 30-2.

Ploug, N. and Kvist, J. (1996) 'Welfare states and old-age pensions', in N. Ploug and J. Kvist, *Social security in Europe: Development or dismantlement?*, The Hague: Kluwer Law International, pp 75-89.

Plummer, K. (2006) 'Rights work: constructing lesbian, gay and sexual rights in late modern times', in L. Morris (ed) *Rights: Sociological perspectives*, Abingdon: Routledge, pp 152-67.

Pollard, D. and Ross, M. (1994) *European Community law: Texts and materials*, London: Butterworths.

Pollard, N., Latorre, M. and Sriskandarajah, D. (2008) *Floodgates or turnstiles? Post-EU enlargement migration flows to (and from) the UK*, London: Institute for Public Policy Research.

Powell, M. (ed) (1999) *New Labour new welfare state? The 'third way' in British social policy*, Bristol: The Policy Press.

Powell, M. (2000) 'New Labour and the Third Way in the British welfare state: a new and distinctive approach?', *Critical Social Policy*, vol 20, no 1, pp 39-60.

Powell, M. (2002) 'The hidden history of social citizenship', *Citizenship Studies*, vol 6, no 3, pp 229-45.

Powell, M. (ed) (2008) *Modernising the welfare state: The Blair legacy*, Bristol: The Policy Press.

Pratt, A. (1997) 'Citizenship and welfare', in M. Lavalette and A. Pratt (eds) *Social policy: A conceptual and theoretical introduction*, London: Sage Publications, pp 182-95.

Presidency Conclusions (2000) Lisbon European Council, 23/24 March (http://ue.eu.int/Newsroom/LoadDoc.asp?BID=77&DID=60917&from=&LANG=1).

Preuss, U.K., Everson, M., Koenig-Archibugi, M. and Lefrebvre, E. (2003) 'Traditions of citizenship in the European Union', *Citizenship Studies*, vol 7, no 1, pp 3-14.

Prideaux, S.J. (2001) 'New Labour, old functionalism? The underlying contradictions of welfare reform in the UK and the US', *Social Policy and Administration*, vol 35, no 1, pp 85-115.

Prideaux, S.J. (2003) 'From organisational theory to the "Third Way": continuities, and contradictions underpinning Amatai Etzioni's communitarian influence on New Labour', in L. Martell, S. Hale and W. Leggitt (eds) *The Third Way and beyond: Criticisms, futures and alternatives*, Manchester: Manchester University Press, pp 255-300.

Prideaux, S.J. (2009) 'The welfare politics of Charles Murray are alive and well in the UK', *International Journal of Social Welfare*, vol 18, pp 1-10.

Priestley, M. (1998) 'Constructions and creations: idealism, materialism and disability theory', *Disability and Society*, vol 13, no 1, pp 75-94.

Priestley, M. (2003) *Disability: A life course approach*, Cambridge: Polity Press.

Rawls, J. (1971) *A theory of justice*, London: Oxford University Press.

Rawls, J. (1995) 'Justice as fairness: political not metaphysical', in S. Avineri and A. de Shalit (eds) *Communitarianism and individualism*, Oxford: Oxford University Press, pp 189-204.

Reed, H. and Latorre, M. (2009) *The economic impacts of migration on the UK labour market*, London: Institute for Public Policy Research.

Rees, A.M. (1995a) 'The promise of social citizenship', *Policy & Politics*, vol 23, no 4, pp 313-25.

Rees, A.M. (1995b) 'The other T.H. Marshall', *Journal of Social Policy*, vol 24, no 3, pp 341-62.

Refugee Council (2002a) *Government announcement and proposals since its White Paper on asylum: A summary*, Briefing, July, London: Refugee Council.

Refugee Council (2002b) *The Nationality Immigration and Asylum Act 2002: Changes to the asylum system in the UK*, Briefing, December, London: Refugee Council.

Refugee Council (2004) *Hungry and homeless: The impact of the withdrawal of state support on asylum seekers, refugee communities and the voluntary sector*, London: Refugee Council.

Reich, N. (2001) 'Union citizenship – metaphor or source of rights', *European Law Journal*, vol 7, no 1, pp 4-23.

Revill, J. (2008) 'Cameron's U-turn on jobless plan', *The Observer*, 6 January, p 13.

Rhodes, M. (ed) (1996) *South European Society and Politics, Special Issue on Southern European Welfare States*, vol 1, no 3.

Richardson, D. (1998) 'Sexuality and citizenship', *Sociology*, vol 32, no 1, pp 83-100.

Richardson, D. (2000) *Rethinking sexuality*, London: Sage Publications.

Richardson, E.H. and Turner, B.S. (2001) 'Review article: sexual, intimate or reproductive citizenship?', *Citizenship Studies*, vol 5, no 3, pp 329-38.

Ridge, T. and Wright, S. (2008) *Understanding inequality, poverty and wealth: Policies and prospects*, Bristol: The Policy Press.

Rioux, M.H. and Bach, M. (eds) (1994) *Disability is not measles*, North York, Ontario: Roeher Institute.

Roberts, J.M. (2003) *The aesthetics of free speech: Rethinking the public sphere*, London: Palgrave.

Roberts, K. and Harris, J. (2002) *Disabled people in refugee and asylum seeking communities*, Bristol/York: The Policy Press/Joseph Rowntree Foundation.

Robinson, D. (2007) 'European Union accession state migrants in social housing in England', *People, Place and Policy Online*, vol 1, no 3, pp 98-111.

Roche, M. (1987) 'Citizenship, social theory and social change', *Theory and Society*, vol 16, pp 363-99.

Roche, M. (1992) *Rethinking citizenship: Welfare, ideology and change in modern society*, Cambridge: Polity Press.

Room, G. (ed) (1995) *Beyond the threshold: The measurement and analysis of social exclusion*, Bristol: The Policy Press.

Rose, H. (1981) 'Rereading Titmuss: the sexual division of welfare', *Journal of Social Policy*, vol 10, no 4, pp 477-502.

Roulstone, A. (2002) 'Disabling pasts, enabling futures? How does the changing nature of capitalism impact on the disabled worker and jobseeker?', *Disability and Society*, vol 17, no 6, pp 627-42.

Roulstone, A. and Morgan, H. (2009) 'Neo-liberal individualism or self directed support: are we all speaking the same language on modernising adult social care?', *Social Policy and Society*, vol 8, no 3, pp 333-46.

Rowntree, B.S. (1901) *A study of town life*, London: Macmillan, reissued in 2000, Bristol: The Policy Press.

RTF (Respect Task Force) (2006) *Respect action plan*, London: RTF, Home Office.

Rummery, K. (2006) 'Disabled citizens and social exclusion: the role of direct payments', *Policy & Politics*, vol 34, no 4, pp 633-50.

Rutter, J. and Latorre, M. (2009) *Social housing allocation and immigrant communities*, Research Report 4, Manchester: Equalities and Human Rights Commission.

Rutter, J., Latorre, M. and Sriskandarajah, D. (2008) *Beyond naturalisation: Citizenship policy in an age of super mobility*, London: Institute for Public Policy Research (www.ippr.org/publicationsandreports/publication. asp?id=594).

Runnymede Trust (1997) *Islamaphobia: A challenge to us all*, London: Runnymede Trust.

Ryan, L., Sales, R., Tilki, M. and Siara, B. (2009) 'Family strategies and transnational migration: recent Polish migrants in London', *Journal of Ethnic and Migration Studies*, vol 35, no 1, pp 61-77.

Sacks, J. (1997) *The politics of hope*, London: Jonathan Cape.

Sales, R. (2002a) 'The deserving and the undeserving? Refugees, asylum seekers and welfare in Britain', *Critical Social Policy*, vol 22, no 3, pp 456-78.

Sales, S. (2002b) 'Migration policy in Europe: contradictions and continuities', in R. Sykes, C. Bochel and N. Ellison (eds) *Social Policy Review 14*, Bristol: The Policy Press/Social Policy Association, pp 151-70.

Sandel, M. (1995) 'The procedural republic and the unencumbered self', in S. Avineri and A. de Shalit (eds) *Communitarianism and individualism*, Oxford: Oxford University Press, pp 12-28.

Schuster, L. and Solomos, J. (2002) 'Rights and wrongs across European borders: migrants, minorities and citizenship', *Citizenship Studies*, vol 6, no 1, pp 37-54.

Scott, J. (1994) *Poverty and wealth: Citizenship, deprivation and privilege*, London: Longman.

Scourfield, J. and Drakeford, M. (2002) 'New Labour and the problem of men', *Critical Social Policy*, vol 22, no 4, pp 619-40.

Selbourne, D. (1994) *The principle of duty*, London: Sinclair Stevenson.

SETF (Social Exclusion Task Force) (2007) *Reaching out: An action plan on social exclusion*, London: SETF, Cabinet Office.

SEU (Social Exclusion Unit) (2000) *Minority ethnic issues in social exclusion and neighbourhood renewal*, London: Cabinet Office.

Shaw, M., Dorling, D., Gordon, D. and Davey Smith, G. (2001) 'Health and poverty', in G. Fimister (ed) *An end in sight? Tackling child poverty in the UK*, London: CPAG, pp 63-75.

Sinfield, A. (1978) 'Analyses in the social division of welfare', *Journal of Social Policy*, vol 7, no 2, pp 129-56.

Smart, C., Mason, J. and Shipman, B. (2006) *Gay and lesbian 'marriage': An exploration of the meanings and significance of legitimising same sex relationships*, Research Report from Morgan Centre for the Study of Relationships and Personal Life, Manchester: University of Manchester (www.socialsciences. manchester.ac.uk/morgancentre/research/gay-lesbian-marriage/docs/ gay-marriage-findings.pdf).

Smith, A. (1776) (reprinted 1828) *An enquiry into the nature and causes of the wealth of nations*, Edinburgh: Adam and Charles Black.

Smith, S.R. (1999) 'Arguing against the cuts in lone parent benefits: reclaiming the desert ground in the UK', *Critical Social Policy*, vol 19, no 3, pp 313-41.

Smith, T. (2003) 'Globalisation and capitalist property relations: a critical assessment of David Held's cosmopolitan theory', *Historical Materialism*, vol 11, no 2, pp 3-35.

Soysal, Y. (1994) *Limits of citizenship: Migrants and postnational membership in Europe*, Chicago, IL: University of Chicago Press.

Spandler, H. (2004) 'Friend or foe? Towards a critical assessment of direct payments', *Critical Social Policy*, vol 24, no 2, pp 187-209.

SSAC (Social Security Advisory Committee) (1997) *Social security for disability: A case for change?*, London: SSAC/The Stationery Office.

SSAC (2002) *Fifteenth report April 2001–March 2002*, London: The Stationery Office.

Stanley, K. (2008) 'The new Conservatives and family policy', in J. Cruddas and J. Rutherford (eds) *Is the future Conservative?*, London: Soundings, Compass/Renewal, Lawrence and Wishart, pp 42-8.

Stenning, A., Champion, T., Conway, C., Coombes, M., Dawley, S., Dixon, L., Raybould, S. and Richardson, R. (2006) *Assessing the local and regional impacts of international migration*, Final Report of a research project for Communities and Local Government, formerly the Office of the Deputy Prime Minister (ODPM).

Stepney, P., Lynch, R. and Jordan, B. (1999) 'Poverty, social exclusion and New Labour', *Critical Social Policy*, vol 19, no 1, pp 109-27.

Stonewall (2003) *Civil partnership: Legal recognition for same-sex couples*, Briefing, June, London: Stonewall.

Stychin, C.F. (2001) 'Sexual citizenship in the European Union', *Citizenship Studies*, vol 5, no 3, pp 285-301.

Tam, H. (1998) *Communitarianism: A new agenda for politics and citizenship*, Basingstoke: Macmillan.

Tambini, D. (2001) 'Post-national citizenship', *Ethnic and Racial Studies*, vol 24, no 2, pp 195-217.

Tatchell, P. (2009) 'I'm backing straight civil partnerships. This segregation based on sexuality is just as reprehensible as a legal apartheid based on race', *The Guardian*, 24 November (www.guardian.co.uk/commentisfree/2009/nov/24/straight-civil-partnerships).

Taylor, C. (1995) 'Atomism', in S. Avineri and A. de Shalit (eds) *Communitarianism and individualism*, Oxford: Oxford University Press, pp 29-50.

Taylor, D. (1989) 'Citizenship and social power', *Critical Social Policy*, vol 15, no 2/3, pp 19-30.

Taylor, G. (2006), *Ideology and welfare*, Basingstoke: Palgrave Macmillan.

Taylor-Gooby, P. (1999) 'Policy change at a time of retrenchment: recent pension reform in France, Germany, Italy and the UK', *Social Policy and Administration*, vol 33, no 1, pp 1-19.

Taylor-Gooby, P. (2000) 'Risk and welfare', in P. Taylor-Gooby (ed) *Risk, trust and welfare*, Basingstoke: Palgrave/Macmillan Press Ltd, pp 1-20.

Taylor-Gooby, P. (2001) 'Risk, contingency and the Third Way: evidence from the BHPS and qualitative studies', *Social Policy and Administration*, vol 35, no 2, pp 195-211.

Taylor-Gooby, P. (2002) 'The silver age of the welfare state: perspectives on resilience', *Journal of Social Policy*, vol 31, no 4, pp 596-622.

Thatcher, M. (1988) Speech to Church of Scotland, 21 May, in J. Raban (1989) *God, man and Mrs Thatcher*, London: Chatto and Windus.

Thompson, S. and Hoggett, P. (1996) 'Universalism. Selectivism and particularism: towards a post-modern social policy', *Critical Social Policy*, vol 16, no 1, pp 21-43.

Threlfall, M. (2002) 'The European Union's social policy focus: from labour to welfare to constitutional rights', in R. Sykes, C. Bochel and N. Ellison (eds) *Social Policy Review 14*, Bristol: The Policy Press/Social Policy Association, pp 191-4.

Titmuss, R.M. (1958) 'The social division of welfare', in *Essays on the welfare state*, London: Allen and Unwin, now reprinted in P. Alcock, H. Glennerster, A. Oakley and A. Sinfield (eds) (2001) *Welfare and wellbeing: Richard Titmuss's contribution to social policy*, Bristol: The Policy Press, pp 34-55.

Titmuss, R. (1968) 'Welfare and the welfare society', reproduced in P. Alcock and A. Oakley (2001) 'Introduction', in P. Alcock, H. Glennester, A. Oakley and A. Sinfield (eds) *Welfare and wellbeing: Richard Titmuss's contribution to social policy*, Bristol, The Policy Press, pp 113-24.

Townsend, P. (1979) *Poverty in the United Kingdom: A survey of household resources and standards of living*, Harmondsworth: Penguin.

Toynbee, P. (2003) *Hard work: Life in low-pay Britain*, London: Bloomsbury.

Treolar, P. (2001) 'Compulsion creeps up', *Welfare Rights Bulletin*, no 164, October, London: CPAG (www.cpag.org.uk/cro/wrb/wrb164/compulsion.htm).

Trickey, H. and Walker, R. (2001) ' Steps to compulsion within the British labour market', in I. Lødemel and H. Trickey (eds) *'An offer you can't refuse': Workfare in international perspective*, Bristol: The Policy Press, pp 181-214.

TUC (Trades Union Congress) (2002) 'New Deal sanctions', TUC welfare reform series briefing number 47, London: TUC (www.tuc.org.uk/welfare/tuc-5430-f0.cfm).

TUC (2007) *The economics of migration: Managing the impacts*, London: TUC.

Turner, B.S. (1986) *Equality*, London: Tavistock.

Turner, B.S. (2000) 'Liberal citizenship and cosmopolitan virtue', in A. Vandenburg (ed) *Citizenship and democracy in a global era*, Basingstoke: Macmillan, pp 18-32.

Turner, B.S. (2001) 'The erosion of citizenship', *British Journal of Sociology*, vol 52, no 2, pp 189-209.

Twine, F. (1994) *Citizenship and social rights: The interdependence of self and society*, London: Sage Publications.

UKBA (United Kingdom Border Agency) (2008) *The path to citizenship: Next steps in reforming the immigration system, Government response to consultation*, London: The Home Office.

UN (United Nations) (1995) *Report of world summit for social development*, New York, NY: UN.

UPIAS (Union of the Physically Impaired Against Segregation) (1976) *Fundamental principles of disability*, London: UPIAS.

Valentine, G. and McDonald, I. (2004) *Understanding prejudice: Attitudes towards minorities*, London: Stonewall.

van Berkel, R. and Moller, I.H. (eds) (2002) *Active social policies in the EU: Inclusion through participation*, Bristol: The Policy Press.

van Gunsteren, H. (1994) 'Four conceptions of citizenship', in B. van Steenbergen (ed) *The condition of citizenship*, London: Sage Publications, pp 36-48.

van Oorschot, W. (2000) 'Who should get what and why? On deservingness and the conditionality of solidarity among the public', *Policy & Politics*, vol 28, no 1, pp 33-48.

Veenkamp, T., Bentley, T. and Buonfino, A. (2003) *People flow: Managing migration in a new European commonwealth*, London: Demos.

Vincent, J. (1991) *Poor citizens: The state and the poor in the twentieth century*, London: Longman.

Vogel, U. (1991) 'Is citizenship gender specific?', in U. Vogel and M. Moran (eds) *The frontiers of citizenship*, London: Macmillan, pp 58-83.

Vonk, G. (2001) 'Migration, social security and the law: some European dilemmas', *European Journal of Social Security*, vol 3/4, pp 315-32.

Waites, M. (1999) 'The age of consent and sexual citizenship in the United Kingdom: a history', in J. Seymour and P. Bagguley (eds) *Relating intimacies: Power and resistance*, Basingstoke: Macmillan, pp 91-117.

Walby, S. (1994) 'Is citizenship gendered?', *Sociology*, vol 28, no 3, pp 379-95.

Walby, S. (1999) 'Introduction', in S. Walby (ed) *New agendas for women*, Basingstoke: Macmillan, pp 1-16.

Walker, R. (1995) 'The dynamics of poverty and social exclusion', in G. Room (ed) *Beyond the threshold: The measurement and analysis of social exclusion*, Bristol: The Policy Press, pp 102-28.

Walker, R. (ed) (1999) *Ending child poverty: Popular welfare for the 21st century?*, Bristol: The Policy Press.

Walters, W. (1997) 'The active society: new designs for social policy', *Policy & Politics*, vol 25, no 3, pp 221-34.

Walzer, M. (1989) 'Citizenship', in T. Ball, J. Farr and R.L. Hanson (eds) *Political innovation and conceptual change*, Cambridge: Cambridge University Press, pp 211-20.

Walzer, M. (1995) 'Membership', in S. Avineri and A. de Shalit (eds) *Communitarianism and individualism*, Oxford: Oxford University Press, pp 65-84.

Ward, I. (1997) 'Law and the other Europeans', *Journal of Common Market Studies*, vol 35, p 26.

Warnes, A.M. (2002) 'The challenge of intra-union migration to social Europe', *Journal of Ethnic and Migration Studies*, vol 28, no 1, pp 135-52.

Weeks, J. (2001) 'Live and let love? Reflections on the unfinished sexual revolution of our times', in R. Edwards and J. Glover (eds) *Risk and citizenship: Key issues in welfare*, London: Routledge, pp 48-63.

Weiler, J. (1998) 'European citizenship, identity and differentity', in M. La Torre (ed) *European citizenship: An institutional challenge*, The Hague: Kluwer Law International, pp 2-19.

Werbner, P. (2000) 'Divided loyalties, empowered citizenship? Muslims in Britain', *Citizenship Studies*, vol 4, no 3, pp 307-24.

Wetherly, P. (1996) 'Basic needs and social policies', *Critical Social Policy*, vol 16, no 1, pp 45-65.

Wetherly, P. (2001) 'The reform of welfare and the way we live now: a critique of Giddens and the Third Way', *Contemporary Politics*, vol 7, no 2, pp 149-70.

White, S. (2000) 'Review article: social rights and social contract – political theory and the new welfare politics', *British Journal of Political Science*, no 30, pp 507-32.

White, S. (2007) 'Taking responsibility a fair welfare contract', in J. Bennett and G. Cooke (eds) *It's all about you: Citizen-centred welfare*, London: Institute for Public Policy Research, ch 2.

Wilding, P. (1997) 'The welfare state and the Conservatives', *Political Studies*, vol 45, no 4, pp 716-26.

Williams, F. (1989) *Social policy: A critical introduction*, Cambridge: Polity Press.

Williams, F. (1992) 'Somewhere over the rainbow: universalism and diversity in social policy', in N. Manning and R. Page (eds) *Social Policy Review 4*, London: Social Policy Association, pp 200-19.

Williams, F. (1996) 'New thinking on social policy research into inequality, poverty and social exclusion', Unpublished manuscript.

Williams, F. (1999) 'Good enough principles for welfare', *Journal of Social Policy*, vol 28, no 4, pp 667-88.

Williams, F. (2003) 'Social policy: culture and nationhood', in P. Alcock, A. Erskine and M. May (eds) *The student's companion to social policy* (2nd edn), London: Blackwell/Social Policy Association, pp 146-52.

Williams, L. (1995) 'Rights not charity', in H. McConchie and P. Zinkin (eds) *Disability programmes in the community: Disabled children in developing countries*, London: Mackeith Press, pp 214-18.

Wilson, R. (2001) *Dispersed: A study of services for asylum seekers in West Yorkshire, December 1999–March 2001*, York: Joseph Rowntree Foundation.

Wintour, P. and Smithers, R. (2002) 'New benefit crackdown: Blair backs bill to dock housing allowance for anti social behaviour', *The Guardian*, 30 April, p 1.

Woodhams, C. and Corby, S. (2003) 'Defining disability in theory and practice: a critique of the British Disability and Discrimination Act 1995', *Journal of Social Policy*, vol 32, no 2, pp 159-78.

Yeates, N. (ed) (2008) *Understanding global social policy*, Bristol: The Policy Press.

Yeates, N. and Holden, C. (2009) *The global social policy reader*, Bristol: The Policy Press.

Young, I.M. (1990) *Justice and the politics of difference*, Princeton, NJ: Princeton University Press.

Yuval-Davis, N. (1997) 'Women, citizenship and difference', *Feminist Review*, no 57, Autumn, pp 4-27.

Zetter, R. and Pearl, M. (2000) 'The minority within the minority: refugee community-based organisations in the UK and the impact of restrictionism on asylum-seekers', *Journal of Ethnic and Migration Studies*, vol 26, no 4, pp 657-97.

Index